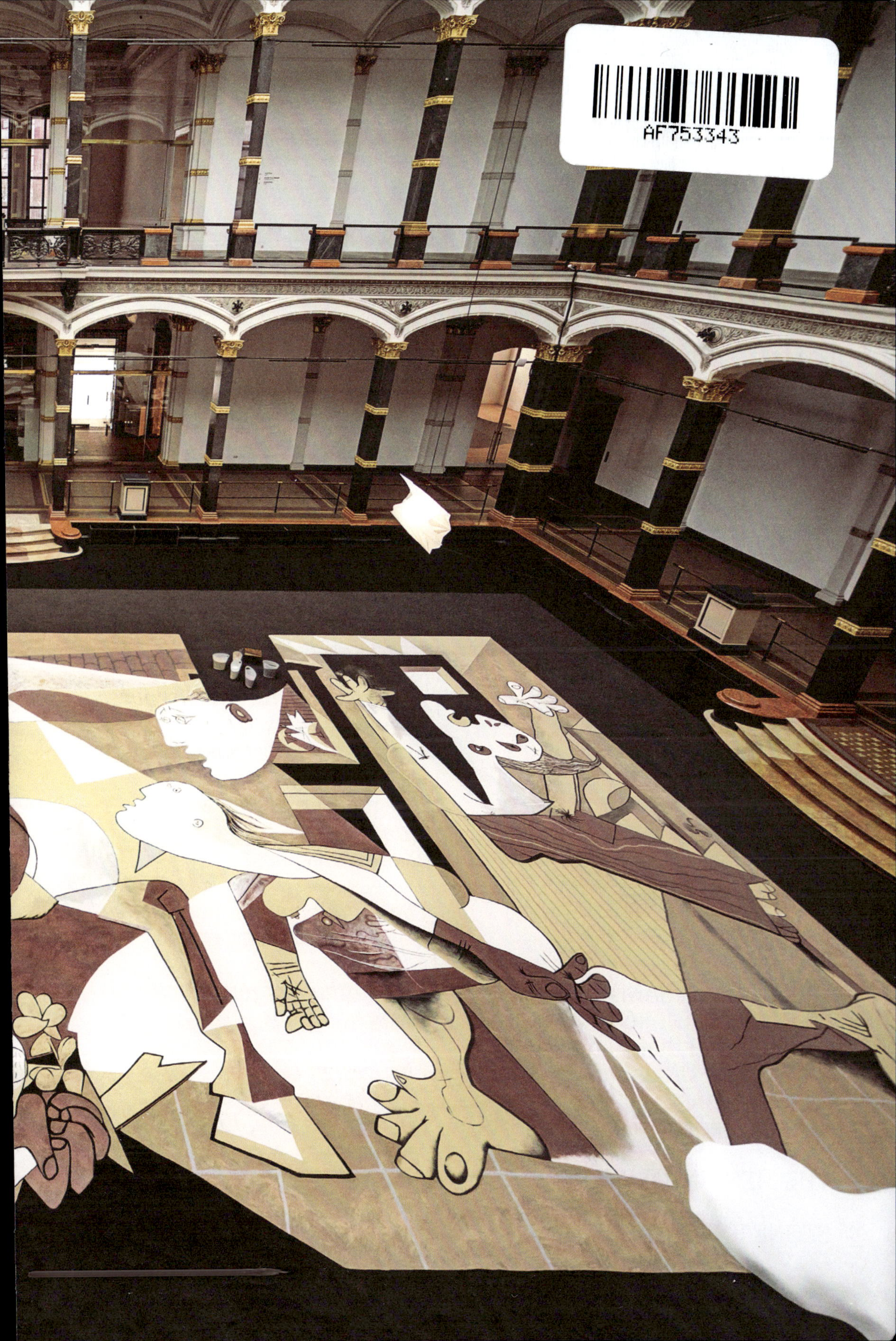

# PREFACE

THOMAS OBERENDER
Artistic Director of the Berliner Festspiele

How can we deal with the mute witnesses of our private past, such as ruptures, rips and holes in our favourite pieces of clothing, or like objects that once played an important role in our life? How to acknowledge and honour our scars – not only the scars on our body and in our direct environment, but those in our society as well? Damaged relationships with relatives, lost friends, forlorn loves, broken ties with our natural environment, with the spirits of our ancestors, with our cosmic consciousness: those are the matters that Lee Mingwei addresses in his work. He does so in the light and playful way that only the greatest artists can master. With the caring gestures of a good friend, he usually creates his works around the simplest of human actions: a conversation between two people. Whoever doubts whether art can heal should engage and connect with his participatory projects. They are masterworks of transformation. Our world needs them, more than ever.

# FOREWORD

STEPHANIE ROSENTHAL
Director of the Gropius Bau



An exhibition with works by Lee Mingwei (*1964 Taichung, Taiwan, lives and works in Paris, FR and New York, US) is a marvellous challenge for a public institution, because the mere act of realising his frequently participatory works inspires the act of rethinking the institution. Yet, he doesn't make any direct demands: “In my practice, I try my best to avoid the gesture of challenging or disrupting the existing institutional practice. Instead, I prefer to create a work that best functions within the rules of the game and maybe, just maybe, the institution might see a different way of doing things after hosting it.”[1]

His works really seduce us into redefining our role as an institution. Since early 2018, it has been an important goal for us to open up the Gropius Bau even more, on both a conceptual and an architectural level. We're interested in how we welcome our visitors, what they see first, how we can bring a lived experience of hospitality into this building. No exhibition could give us a better example of this than Lee Mingwei's show. It is a distinct pleasure to be able to present the artist's first European survey exhibition as well as the first German-language catalogue on his practice.

Lee Mingwei's exhibition *禮 Li, Gifts and Rituals* presents his works from the last three decades and explores the ability of art to act as a transformative gift, rooted in the space of intimate experience and encounters with others. It is founded on the Confucian principle of *li*, which encompasses notions of rites, rituals, gifts and rules of conduct.

Instead of the common reading of Lee Mingwei's artistic practice as part of the tradition of participatory art, the exhibition identifies the impetus behind his works as lying within traditions of giving and rituals of receiving. *禮 Li, Gifts and Rituals* shows how the combination of aesthetic and philosophical concepts of giving, embedded in Eastern and Western traditions, have influenced the artist's work. The ritual of giving is based on a particular form of attentiveness and care. This attitude can be expressed in personal relationships and also in the manner in which we handle the objects that surround us. The transformative and appreciative process of mending, for example, lies at the centre of *The Mending Project*, 2009/2020. This form of care is not only a constituent part of Lee's exhibition, it is also reflected in the architecture of the Gropius Bau: the building was heavily bombed during World War II and was subsequently restored in such a way as to ensure that both its wounds and the process of restoration remained visible and tangible. The building is witness to the belief that injury and trauma are part of its history and thus also part of all our histories. Lee Mingwei's work *Guernica in Sand*, 2006/2020, in

1 Email from Lee Mingwei to Stephanie Rosenthal, 29.1.2020.

the Gropius Bau's atrium, pays homage to Pablo Picasso's *Guernica*, 1937, and becomes, in Lee Mingwei's hands, a ritual of transformation. While we celebrate the 75th anniversary of VE Day (Victory in Europe) this year, political developments are assuming an increasingly separatist character, and so works like *Our Peaceable Kingdom*, 2020, are a vital invitation to develop new visions of peace for today.

The material and conceptual threads that bind this catalogue together reflect the ritual of giving on a number of levels. On the one hand, the numerous statements shared by eyewitnesses on their personal experience with Lee's works can be interpreted as a part of the reciprocity of the gift. On the other hand, the reader section of the catalogue brings together reprints of poems and excerpts from essays and classical literature that have repeatedly provided decisive impulses for Lee's artistic practice and indeed for the curatorial process of developing the exhibition.

In addition to my own recontextualisation of Lee's work, Irina Aristarkhova's essay provides interesting insights into the complex world of the host – a special kind of giving. Harvey Molotch, who has followed Lee's artistic development for many years, links his personal perspective on Lee's work with sociological observations, while Clare Molloy focuses her gaze squarely on Lee's new commission for the Gropius Bau, *Our Peaceable Kingdom*. The process of this work touches on the ritual of copying, which has a long tradition in both Eastern and in Western art history, whilst also bringing together the perspectives of 27 painters and their written statements on the concept of peace.

First and foremost, I would like to express my heartfelt thanks to Lee Mingwei for such an inspiring exchange of ideas and his deep commitment to all of the collaborations that underpin this exhibition. Beginning with workshops with the Gropius Bau team, his presence here has been an extraordinary experience. My thanks also goes to the artist's studio, especially to Daphne Chu, who supervised the project so energetically. I am grateful, too, to Sandy Wong Shin for her hands-on support with *Guernica in Sand*. I also want to thank the numerous lenders, without whom we would have not been able to realise the exhibition.

The nature of this project brought together so many collaborators and hosts. All the volunteer hosts and performers, both internal and external, deserve my warmest thanks because they continually brought new energy to the exhibition.

For co-curating the exhibition and her work on this catalogue, I am grateful to Clare Molloy, whose ideas provided vital impulses throughout the project. I would also like to thank our curatorial fellow Katharina Küster, whose precise eye was invaluable to the execution of the exhibition, as well as our intern Myriam Hofmaier, who deftly supported research for the project.

I owe a particular debt of gratitude to Simone Schmaus and her team for their keen eye in the production of the exhibition's architectural design. Our project managers – firstly Elena Montini and then Lisa Tietze – supervised the exhibition planning and installation processes with great efficiency and enthusiasm. Sincere thanks also to our technical director Bert Schülke and his team, who, as always, supported us so professionally during the realisation of the project, not to mention my thanks to my office, so ably managed and organised by my assistant Susanne Götze and associate curator to the director's office, Clara Meister. Their finesse and poise keeps countless plates spinning, for this, I am grateful. For their outstanding publicity work and support in producing texts for the exhibition, I owe thanks to Annie-Claire Geisinger, Natalie Schütze, Katrin Mundorf and the entire communications team. Eva Winkeler and her team are to be thanked for so successfully recruiting and then looking after our partners and supporters. I would also like to thank Charlotte Sieben, managing director of the Kulturveranstaltungen des Bundes in Berlin (KBB) GmbH, and the artistic director of the Berliner Festspiele, Thomas Oberender.

I wish to thank Harvey Molotch and Irina Aristarkhova for their essays, which are such valuable contributions to the publication. Many thanks to Louisa Elderton for her editorial overseeing of this catalogue; her extensive experience and carefully considered input were instrumental in the shaping of this book. Equally, my thanks goes to Julia Volkmar who was responsible for the graphic design of the exhibition as well as the elegant design of the catalogue. My thanks also to our publisher Michele Pizzi and his team for their support throughout the process.

The catalogue came together thanks to the generous support of Patrick Sun, Grace Mei-Ching Tseng, Winsing Arts Foundation, Angela Yi and Lorries Chang, Yi&C. Furniture & Projects Consulting Co. Ltd., as well as the active engagement of Rudy Tseng.

I equally thank the Federal Government Commissioner for Culture and the Media, Professor Monika Grütters, for the generous support of the Gropius Bau. I owe a great many thanks to the Taiwan Ministry of Culture for their generous funding of the exhibition.

# LEARNING FROM LEE MINGWEI

STEPHANIE ROSENTAHL

Lee Mingwei's work assumes a very special role for exhibition makers and institutions because he puts the conventions of exhibiting to the test in unusual and surprising ways. He introduces rituals of caring, of giving and of receiving (usually in the form of immaterial things) to public institutions. However, Lee brings much more than gift giving and hospitality into the museum: he creates situations that open up the opportunity to form new relationships, thereby initiating the transformation of our own modes of perception. It is an urgently needed approach to exhibition making.

Lee's work shows a connection to mould-breaking contemporary thinkers such as Donna Haraway and Fred Moten, who consider different forms of sociality to be equally valid modes of knowledge transfer. They share the view that interpersonal exchange and the creation of different, new relationship forms have huge relevance in our time.

The Taiwan-born artist's work has its origins in Confucian philosophy and, to a certain extent, in Buddhism. His aesthetics and philosophy have been influenced by both Western and Eastern traditions. Different cultures shaped his thinking from early on: he attended a Catholic school and for six years spent his summer holidays in a Taiwanese monastery with Chan-Buddhist monks close to Taichung. This was where he first encountered Chinese culture, in particular painting. Aged twelve he left home, together with his older sister and his cousin, continuing his education first in the Dominican Republic and later in San Francisco.
He graduated from a high school in California run by Benedictine monks, many of whom had Hungarian roots, so he received formative insights into European classical music and literature. He completed his studies on both the East and the West Coasts of the USA, receiving his Bachelor of Fine Arts in Textile Art from the California College of Arts in 1993. Then Lee received vital support from the artists Suzanne Lacy and Mark Thompson, who helped him embark on his studies at Yale University, where he graduated with a Master of Fine Arts in Sculpture in 1997.

Lee's installations and performances are frequently inspired by personal experiences and encounters, which, with slow, deliberate precision, he subsequently develops into artworks. In the Gropius Bau atrium, which is over 600 square metres, the artist uses sand in a variety of colours to create a monumental version of the installation *Guernica in Sand*, 2006/2020. In homage to Pablo Picasso's *Guernica*, 1937 (fig. 13., 121), one of the most iconic works of Western modernist art, Lee represents the motifs of trauma and grief in sand. Mingwei recalls his first encounter with the painting in the Museum of Modern Art in New York: "I was overwhelmed by its size, the abstract images of the animals and the mother and the child, as well as the obvious violence and pain emanating from the painting."[1] Picasso painted the work in reaction to the destruction of the Basque town of Guernica following the aerial bombing at Spanish Nationalist Franco's behest by the German Luftwaffe and the Italian Aviazione Legionaria. The location of the Gropius Bau, adjacent to the former headquarters of the Gestapo and opposite those of the Luftwaffe, gives the work an additional layer of semantic meaning and historical reference.



The choice of material aligns with the Tibetan Buddhist practice of sand mandala (fig. 1., 15), a precise and detailed form of sand painting, which is swept away after completion, an evocative expression of impermanence. Lee will only complete *Guernica in Sand* at the mid-way point of the exhibition. Visitors will be invited to walk barefoot over the sand painting, so that the original image is carefully "destroyed". Lee draws attention to the impermanence and inconstancy of things and to the potential for transformation that lies in the energy of destroying the figurative image. The tension between one person finishing the painting and at the same time another walking over it speaks to this potential. In a third phase of the performance, the artist and further performers will sweep the trampled sand together in a ritual of transformation. Instead of viewing the artwork as immutable as is often the case in Western art history – Lee emphasises its potential to change, thereby turning it into a hopeful allegory of our ability to use trauma as the impetus for transformation.

The notion of transforming an existing idea – in this case, a painting by the American folk artist Edward Hicks (1780-1849) – is central to *Our Peaceable Kingdom*, 2020, which is Lee's most recent work. The artist engages with two key themes: on the one hand, the concept of peace and its importance in our age, and on the other, the classical principle that the art of painting can only be learned from a master. His point of departure is a work from Hicks' series of paintings the *Peaceable Kingdom*, c. 1820-1849, of which 62 versions are extant today. In them, Hicks returned repeatedly to the motif of peace.[2] Lee invited eleven artists to copy Hicks' *Peaceable Kingdom* from c. 1833. Here, copying is not to be understood as imitation, but rather as a suggestion to develop one's own interpretation, and present an altered, individual perspective on the theme.

*The Mending Project*, 2009/2020 was created in response to the events of 11th September 2001 and is inspired by the meditative effect of mending, which Lee experienced while waiting to hear whether his partner had survived the attacks on the World Trade Center. In a ritual of repair, the artist invites visitors to bring items of clothing in need of mending and the artist himself or selected mending hosts will darn these items. They are then put on the mending table to form a constantly growing installation of sewn garments, secured to spools on the wall. Lee gestures here to the traditional Japanese art of ceramic repair known as *kintsugi*.[3] The lines of the repaired cracks remain visible and tangible, delineated in gold, "[t]his positions *kintsugi* as [a] material craft that has capacities to affect; to engage with the senses and potentialize *perceptions* of damage and repair",[4] as Guy Keulemans writes in his seminal essay on this technique. As in the tradition of *kintsugi*, the now repaired, formerly damaged item of clothing takes on a new role and is celebrated in *The Mending Project* (figs. 3-4., 16). Lee invites his participants to tell the story of their clothing to the mending hosts, frequently resulting in them sharing an important part of their lives, which he sees as being "incredibly healing".[5]

Similarly, *The Sleeping Project*, 2000/2020 was inspired by a personal encounter. Lee's fellow traveller on a sleeper train was a concentration survivor, who was travelling to Prague to receive compensation. This emotional and intimate exchange with a complete stranger prompted the artist to ask whether an art institution can provide space for emotional connections and whether this kind of conversation is only possible at night. Here, too, the act of sharing a story is key. In *The Sleeping Project*, Lee invites visitors to spend a night in the exhibition with him or one of the Gropius Bau team.

In *Sonic Blossom*, 2013/2020, Lee presents daily performances from opera singers. Through this project he goes back to his childhood, when he listened to Lieder by Schubert with his mother. When he played these back to her when she was recovering from surgery, he felt their consolatory effect. The opera singers ask exhibition goers a simple question: "May I offer you a gift of song?" Reactions are highly emotional: "I sat down and thought I knew what was going to happen. But when she started singing I was so moved, I immediately started to cry and cried throughout the whole song."[6]

*Our Labyrinth*, 2015/2020 is inspired by the rituals of sweeping sacred spaces, which Lee observed in pagodas, temples and mosques in Myanmar (fig. 2.). "There are little huts far from the temple where visitors can remove their shoes and walk barefoot. I was impressed by the path leading to the temple and noticed there were always volunteers continuously cleaning the path throughout the day. I thought this was a physical and spiritual gift from the volunteers to the visitors".[7] Stemming from this, Lee decided to ask dancers to brush rice across a black dance floor that he had cut into an inkblot-shape. Lee asked the dancers to move very slowly, to listen to the rice with their heart so that the rice can guide them through the dance. Jean-Gabriel Manolis, one of the dancers, describes his movements "as an ever renewed path led by the dialogue between the rice and the performer. It requires a peaceful state of mind so the body becomes able to express what comes from listening to the rice and to the surroundings."[8]

Characteristic features of Lee's works are their autobiographical context, concern for the well-being of visitors – frequently in the form of gifts – the establishment of intimate and personal situations, and the enabling of conversations. Based on the desire for intimate and reciprocal acknowledgement, for an ethics of care, they frequently invite visitors and participants to share feelings and memories – with their inherent poetic nature and harmonious beauty – within an institutional context where they are not usually given expression.

Lee's work touches visitors through his appeal to the personal, through the care that prevails in his work. Gift giving happens on many different levels, whether through songs, repairs or an invitation to take part. It is also present in the opportunity to share

1 Lee Mingwei, Artist Statement, 108.

2 A devoted Quaker, Hicks' paintings are inspired by Isaiah 11: 6-8 and are a meditation on the search for the redeemed soul. See essay by Clare Molloy in this catalogue, 210-214.

3 "*Kintsugi* repair is a traditional craft technique for repairing broken ceramics using *urushi*, a plant-based adhesive lacquer resin, decorated with gold or silver…A key aspect of transformative repair practices is that a material record of an object's damage and subsequent repair is overtly sensible." Guy Keulemans, "The Geo-cultural Conditions of Kintsugi" in *The Journal of Modern Craft* 9, no.1 (2016), 17. See Reader, 172.

4 Ibid.

5 Lee Mingwei in conversation with Stephanie Rosenthal, 122.

6 Ayumi Paul, Eyewitness Report, 182.

7 Lee Mingwei, Artist Statement, 189.

8 Jean-Gabriel Manolis, Eyewitness Report, 193.

9 See essay by Irina Aristarkhova in this catalogue, 54-62.

10 Édouard Glissant, *Poetics of Relation*, translated by Betsy Wing (Ann Arbor: University of Michigan Press, 1997), 11.

our stories, something that plays a decisive role in Lee's work because it allows personal connections to be built. Sharing stories can provoke empathy and emotions, as well as establishing bonds of mutual identification. Stories can be used to involve people and to activate feelings. Lee opens up the opportunity for new relationships to be formed and even presents the opportunity for change to begin.

Creating a situation that invites his visitors to share their personal stories with strangers, Lee thereby enables exchange. Lee opens up his projects to the local audience by incorporating their stories and objects in his exhibition, and in turn asks them to act as hosts for other exhibition visitors. Via three open calls Lee opened up his exhibition: for *The Mending Project*, for example, the artist looked for participants to take part in the work of darning clothing; for *Fabric of Memory*, 2006/2020, he asked for textile items associated with memories and emotional value that are displayed along with their stories; and for *The Living Room*, 2000/2020, he requested unique collections, that their "curators" would like to show to others.

Through rituals of hospitality,[9] among other things, Lee succeeds in creating a situation that conveys trust. This can result in the establishment of new relationships, which often lead to a change in our perception. As Édouard Glissant states in *Poetics of Relation*, the relationship in all its meanings – speaking, listening, being connected, the simultaneous awareness of oneself and one's surroundings – is the key to changing attitudes and to reshaping societies: "Rhizomatic thought is the principle behind what I call the Poetics of Relation, in which each and every identity is extended through a relationship with the Other."[10]

**Unframing**

The key to Lee's works is that he creates a paradoxical situation, welcoming visitors as his esteemed guests within the



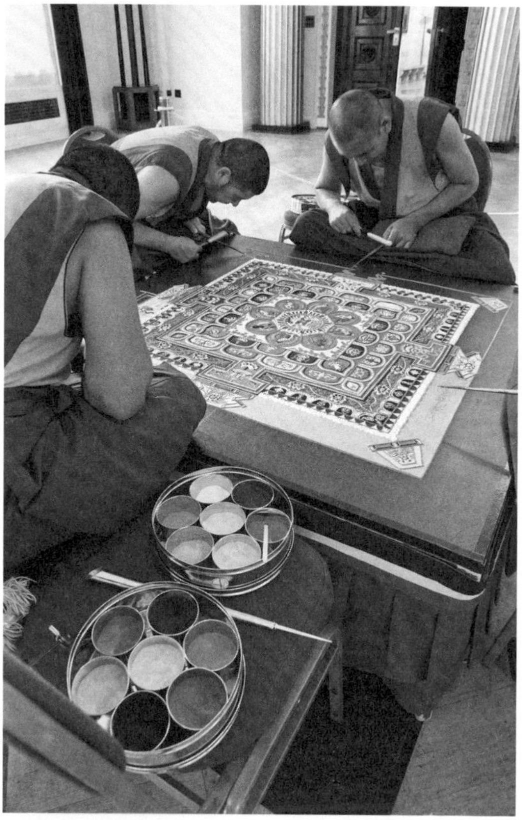

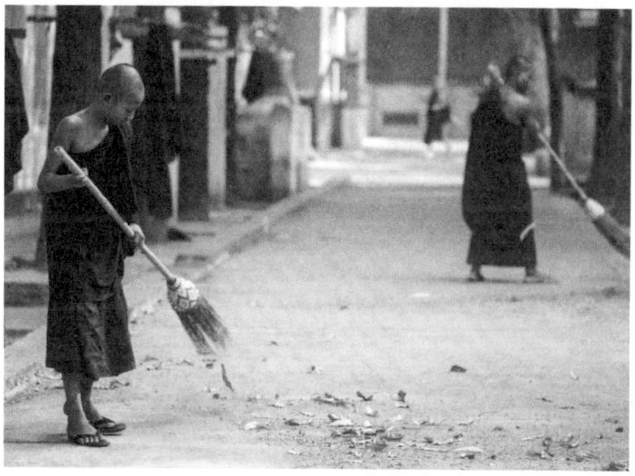

Fig. 1. Three monks work together to produce a meticulous sand mandala painting. Once the work has been completed, the sand mandala is ritualistically swept together and cleared to reflect the transitory nature of material life.

Fig. 2. Monks from Myanmar sweep leaves from a path as part of their daily practice, keeping the path continuously clean. Lee Mingwei witnessed such peaceful and thoughtful acts of sweeping when visiting various ancient temples in the countryside of Myanmar in 2014, which inspired him to integrate such movements into the work *Our Labyrinth*.

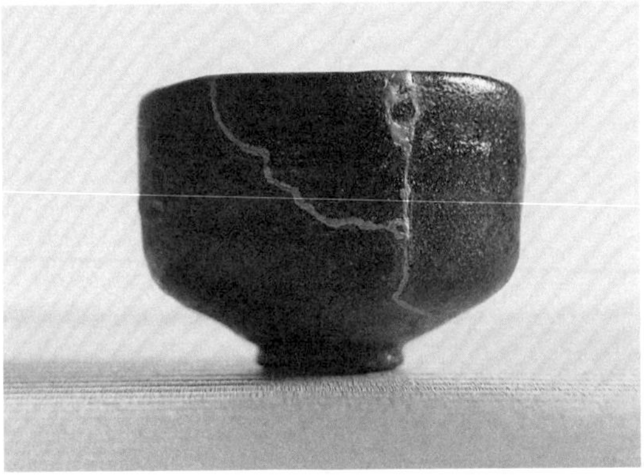

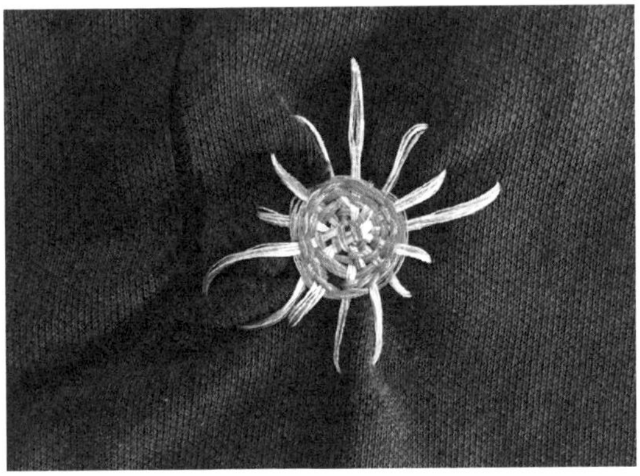

Fig. 3. The Japanese practice of *kintsugi* sees broken pottery being mended with lacquer that is then dusted or coated with a line of gold, silver or platinum. This reflects a philosophy that breakage and repair is part of the material history of an object and therefore should not be hidden or obscured.

Fig. 4. This close up of a mended piece of clothing from Lee Mingwei's *The Mending Project* depicts the delicate threads that remain attached to the garment after the mending process is finished. These connect to spools that are mounted on a nearby wall. The mending itself is clearly and purposefully visible, reflecting the material breakage and repair of the clothing as per the philosophy that underpins *kintsugi*.

space of a public institution, challenging what one might expect to encounter in an exhibition hall. Within Lee's exhibitions, rituals of hospitality are carried out, personal exchange is made possible and mutual care is shown. Leveraging the institution's character is vital for Lee's work as it provides more security than the private home of a stranger and it allows for everyday activities to be placed into a different context – a process through which, Lee believes, familiar actions are made to feel unusual. In an attempt at reducing them to their essence, he establishes a conscious awareness of simple actions and allows us to view them with fresh eyes.

These activities take place in different, unusual locations, making it possible for visitors to detach themselves from familiar aspects and focus on other, unexpected ones. Thus, after visiting *The Sleeping Project*, visitors gain a different perspective on sleep as well as on the museum. *Sonic Blossom*, in which visitors are serenaded with a song, surprises precisely because it offers us the opportunity to engage in a process of emotional reminiscence, recalling moments in which we were sung to: perhaps as a child by our parents, in kindergarten by the teacher and so on. In this way, Lee creates an environment in which visitors can experience change and gain new perspectives, along with a new sense of themselves and of their environment. By considering the words of French philosopher Félix Guattari, we might see these individual experiences as a general characteristic of the perception of art: "The work of art, for those who use it, is an activity of unframing, of rupturing sense, of baroque proliferation or extreme impoverishment, which leads to a recreation and a reinvention of the subject itself."[11]

### *Li*

Lee's work is often viewed in the context of participatory art[12] and associated with the notion of relational aesthetics.[13]

Having studied under Suzanne Lacy, among others, there can be no question that he is very conscious of the strategies of participatory art. Equally interesting is the fact that Lee's approach is also significantly influenced by a combination of aesthetic and philosophical concepts of giving that have their roots in Eastern traditions. Indeed, his entire mode of thinking and his artistic approach are deeply rooted in the aesthetic ideas of Confucius. This is evident in the many references to gift culture in Lee's works. Even one of his earliest works, which he submitted for his MFA, was a gift of traditional Japanese clothing, *hakama*, sent to three people whose artistic production he particularly valued.[14]

Although Lee repeatedly references Lewis Hyde's book *The Gift*, I prefer to see the Confucian principle of *li* (*禮*) as one of Lee Mingwei's main influences. Standard works on giving culture, such as *The Gift* by Marcel Mauss,[15] are known to him, however he says that they have played no role in the conceptual approach of his works.[16] *Li* is a key term in Confucian philosophy. It describes ritual, correct conduct or decorum, and the abstract idea of the totality of all forms of behaviour that go towards making a good person and keeping the social order intact.[17] The so-called "four-fold meaning of *li*" encompasses love, duty, law and freedom. What is important are not material objects per se, but rather that through them the rituals are maintained, as a foundation for peace and a pre-condition for social harmony. In Confucian thought, exercising *li* forms the basis for respectful and responsible conduct in society. In addition to strict ceremonial rituals, Confucian rites also comprise everyday patterns of personal behaviour. The practice of giving, which is also regulated within this, is always founded upon reciprocity.[18]

The *Liji*, or *Book of Rites*, describes how everyone "can walk the path of good if they want. And the means to success are

11 Félix Guattari, *Chaosmose*, Éditions Galilée, Paris, 1992; translated by Paul Bains and Julian Pefanis, *Chaosmosis: An Ethico-Aesthetic Paradigm* (Indianapolis: Indiana University Press, 1995), 131.

12 One of the important aspects of participatory art is the social, active component, [for discussion of this see Claire Bishop, ed. "Introduction, Viewers as Producers" in *Participation* (London: Whitechapel, 2006), 10-17, and Juliane Rebentisch "Formen der Partizipation" in *Theorien der Gegenwartskunst* (Hamburg: Junius Verlag, 2013), 58-72] and although visitors taking part play a role in Lee Mingwei's work, it feels misleading to solely read his work as part of this Western tradition of participatory art or to over emphasise the works as engaging with social politics - they are far more engaged with and indicative of traditions of gift giving and rituals of receiving, which are in their nature participatory.

13 See Mami Kataoka, "Value of Invisible Threads: Lee Mingwei and His Relations" in Ping Lin, ed., *Lee Mingwei and His Relations. The Art of Participation*, exhibition catalogue (Taipei: Taipei Fine Arts Museum, 2015), 25-41.

14 Lee and Rosenthal, 123.

15 Marcel Mauss' *The Gift*, 1925, deals with the principle of the exchange of gifts in pre-modern societies and its associated reciprocity. The ambivalence of giving lies in the tension between freedom and obligation. According to Mauss, the gift guarantees peaceful coexistence within archaic communities and thereby also guarantees the social order. This social bond forms the fundamental structural element of a society. The school of Marcel Mauss' theory has a long tradition in France. Scholars such as Claude Lévi-Strauss, Paul Ricoeur, Emmanuel Levinas, Georges Bataille, Jacques Derrida and Alain Caillé have engaged critically with Mauss' classic sociological text and found in it a starting point for their own theories of giving.

16 Lee and Rosenthal, 123.

17 The exercise of *li* has been recorded in various texts, including *Liji*, or *Book of Rites* as well as in *I-li*. Both texts outline practical rules for all areas of life.

extremely simple: a clear, comprehensive knowledge of that which is right...and, furthermore, consistent practice of what has been learned. These are the fundamentals of self-education that are available to everybody, through which that magical power of the spirit is attained to educate others."[19] In this sense, Lee also "educates". As the *Liji* records: "The problem of ethics is therefore ultimately a problem of education. The self-educated individual has a responsibility and the opportunity to educate others."[20]

**Betwixt Between – Space for Change**

Learning from Lee's works means that one of our duties as an institution could be considered to be initiating a change or at least a transition towards new ways of thinking. Such transformations, according to the ethnologist Arnold van Gennep (1873-1957), occur within the triad of transition rites. Lee's works enable us to enter the second phase, which van Gennep terms *rites de marge*.

Rites of passage, which van Gennep describes in his 1909 book *Les Rites de passage*, are rites and rituals that organise alterations in the life of an individual into an ordered process of transformation that lead from one state to another or from one world to another. These states could be entering into a new phase of life, into motherhood or marriage.[21] Van Gennep differentiates between three categories of rites, which follow on from each other: 1) *rites de séparation*: rites of separation to disengage from the old world, 2) *rites de marge*: threshold rites which signal the approach of the new world, and finally 3) *rites d'agrégation*: incorporation rites that support absorption into the new world. The innovative aspects of this model were its recognition of a repeating pattern and its emphasis on liminal rites (*rites de marge*). Also new was the figurative concept of a real, material act of passage, that a space is left, a threshold crossed and another space entered. These spaces can also be understood as "worlds". The simple act of stepping into an institution can symbolise such a transition.

For Victor Turner (1920-1983), who developed this concept of the pattern of rites of passage further, it is the middle phase, that of the threshold, that represents the most significant aspect of transition. In his essay "Betwixt and Between", he takes up van Gennep's idea that the liminal phase frequently gains a certain autonomy and that the ritual behaviours that determine it are often an inversion of normal behaviour.[22] It is the most important phase, as it is the fulcrum of the transformation. Turner transposes liminal rites onto various cultural systems. He describes clowns, shamans, prophets and even artists as permanent boundary-crossers, as liminal beings, who live in the spaces "betwixt and between"; they are neither one thing nor the other; they undergo a single, permanent and ongoing process of transformation. Thanks to their liminal existence, their partial distance and isolation, they develop an attitude of consciousness that is interpretative, reflexive and critical.

It can be argued that, with his works, Lee turns the institution into a place that is itself "betwixt and between" – in which the transition into another world can take place. He alters our perception and our behaviour within an institutional context, allows us to experience institutions differently and to think about our tasks in new ways.[23] The ideal of an exhibition hall is that it should be precisely such a betwixt-between space. A place in which care and attention are given in a way that is on the one hand an irritant, but on the other hand also prompts one to think in new ways.

As mentioned at the start of this essay, Lee's oeuvre can be viewed in the context of an important group of artistic practitioners and thinkers who have engaged with the question of how to establish new forms of relationship. Haraway writes: "Making kin seems to me the thing that we most need to be doing in a world that rips us apart from each other, in a world that has already more than seven and a half billion human beings with very unequal and unjust patterns of suffering and well-being. By kin I mean those who have an enduring mutual, obligatory, non-optional, you-can't-just-cast-that-away-when-it-gets-inconvenient, enduring relatedness that carries consequences. I have a cousin, the cousin has me; I have a dog, a dog has me."[24] The relationship to an individual exhibition visitor may in practice only be fleeting, but it makes visible and comprehensible the fact that there is, in any case, a deep kinship among humans – and not only them: "all earthlings are kin in the deepest sense"[25] – and the fact that an activity (and maybe also certain spaces) is still required to *make* encounter into kinship: not to be kin (and certainly not "akin"), but to make kin!

18 As described in *Liji*: "In the highest antiquity they (sages) prized (simply conferring) good; in the time next to this, giving and repaying the thing attended to. And what the rules of propriety value is that reciprocity. If I give a gift and nothing comes in return, that is contrary to propriety; if the thing comes to me and I give nothing in return that also is contrary to propriety." (*Liji*, 1967 [Qu i §6]) cited in: Alison Hulme, *The Changing Landscape of China's Consumerism* (Oxford: Chandos, 2014), 138.

19 Translated from the German: Richard Wilhelm, *Li Gi. Das Buch der Riten, Sitten und Gebräuche* (Cologne: Anaconda, 2007), 14.

20 Ibid.

21 Arnold van Gennep, *Rites of Passage* (Chicago: University of Chicago Press, 1960), 2-3, 10-11.

22 Ibid.

23 Antje von Graevenitz associates the *rites de passage* specifically with the arts. In "Rites of Passage in Modern Art", she demonstrates that many artists work with similar strategies in order to ensnare the viewer and so influence them all the more effectively into taking a path of transition by changing them internally. Antje von Graevenitz, "Rites of Passage in Modern Art", in Irving Lavin, ed., *World Art. Themes of unity in diversity. Acts of the XXVIth International Congress of the History of Art*, vol. 3, (University Park: Penn State University Press, 1989), 588.

24 Steve Paulson, "Making Kin: An Interview with Donna Haraway. Steve Paulson interviews Donna Haraway" in *Los Angeles Review of Books*, online, 6.12.2019, https://www.lareviewofbooks.org/article/making-kin-an-interview-withdonna-haraway/

25 Donna Haraway, *Staying with the Trouble: Making Kin in the Chuthlucene* (Durham and London: Duke University Press, 2016), 130.

# MONEY FOR ART

## 1994 / 2020

5 inkjet prints
Each 28 x 36 cm

## 2006/2020

Wooden cabinet, 100 dollar notes
70 x 30 x 14 cm

On January 1, 1994 nine sculptures were given to:

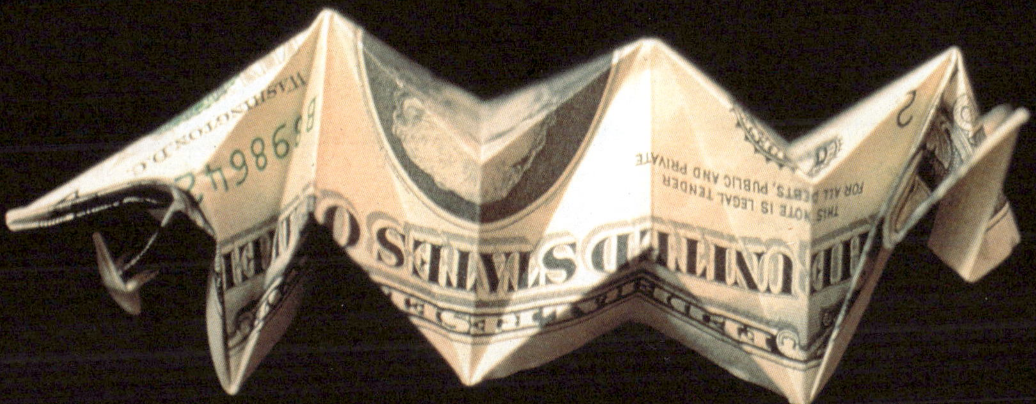

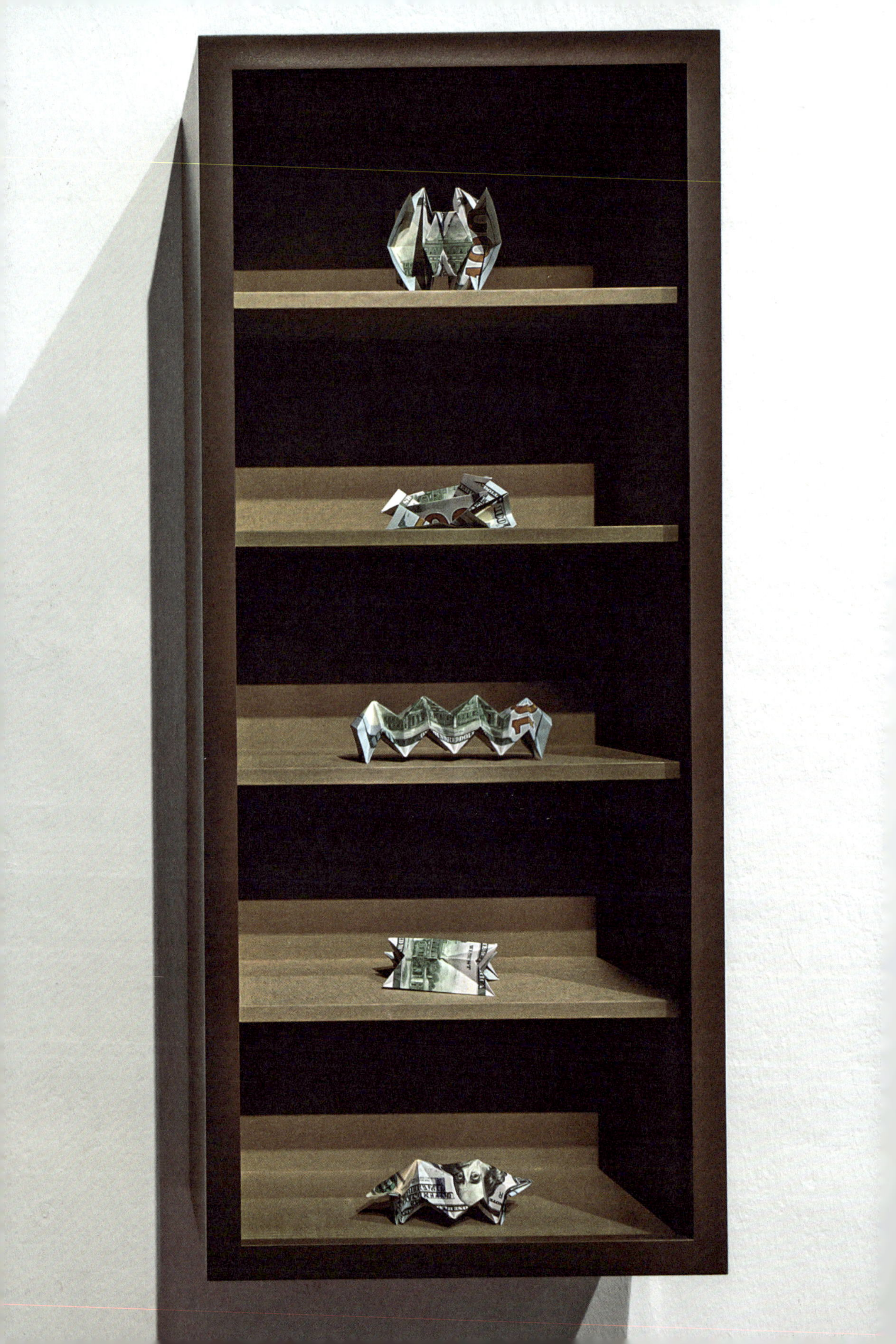

"Money and art are not the same. In this case, the question is: once the ten-dollar bill is folded by an artist, is it still worth ten dollars, slightly more or slightly less? I spent a day folding ten-dollar bills into abstract origami sculptural forms and asked people if they would be interested in owning the artwork, all of whom said yes. In exchange, I asked them to provide me their phone number so that I could call them in six months to a year to see how their relationship might have evolved with this sculpture. When I called these people, one of them had used it to buy moccasins, another had bought food, but most had kept it.

A woman called Jennifer told me she was so hungry at one moment that she had unfolded the ten-dollar bill to buy an ice cream and a banana. She continued to tell me a moving story of her great-grandmother, who had arrived in the United States as a refugee. Once a wealthy person, she had sold all of her possessions, which were mostly artworks, to gather enough money for her ticket. I remember vividly when Jennifer said, 'when push comes to shove, artworks go first'.

Another participant actually left her ATM card with me, along with its code. She was surprised that I did not take money out from it. This became the seed of interest for some of my later projects that deal with trust, intimacy and relationships between strangers. Then there was John, who was homeless at the time but now lives in a shelter. For the past years, whenever I go back to the San Francisco Bay Area, I visit him with a new ten-dollar bill origami sculpture, so he now has 14 of these. He told me he is extremely happy and honoured to participate in an art project, especially one that allows him to own a piece of art. For him, money can buy food, but art is even better because it can help to give food for his body as well as food for his emotional and spiritual self."

LEE MINGWEI

In 1993, Lee Mingwei sat in a café in the US, delicately folding nine small origami forms from ten-dollar bills. He gave these bills to interested passers-by, asking in exchange that they remain in touch with him for a year, after which time he contacted them to ask how they had used the artwork. At a gallery in 1997, he asked participants to take an origami form from a set of shelves, leaving in exchange an object and a card with their name and profession. The objects included, among others, a bottle of Prozac and a condom. At the Gropius Bau, Lee exhibited a later iteration of the work from 2006, a vitrine that contains five different origami shapes, folded from five one-hundred-dollar bills.

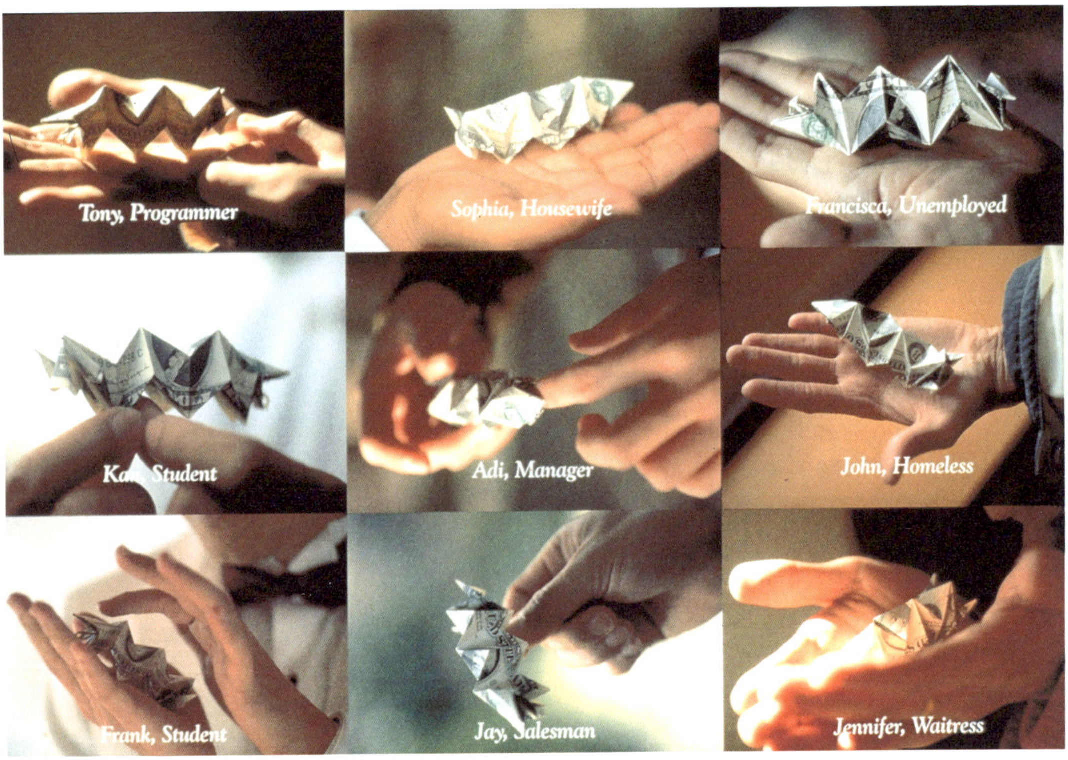
Tony, Programmer
Sophia, Housewife
Francisca, Unemployed
Ka Student
Adi, Manager
John, Homeless
Frank, Student
Jay, Salesman
Jennifer, Waitress

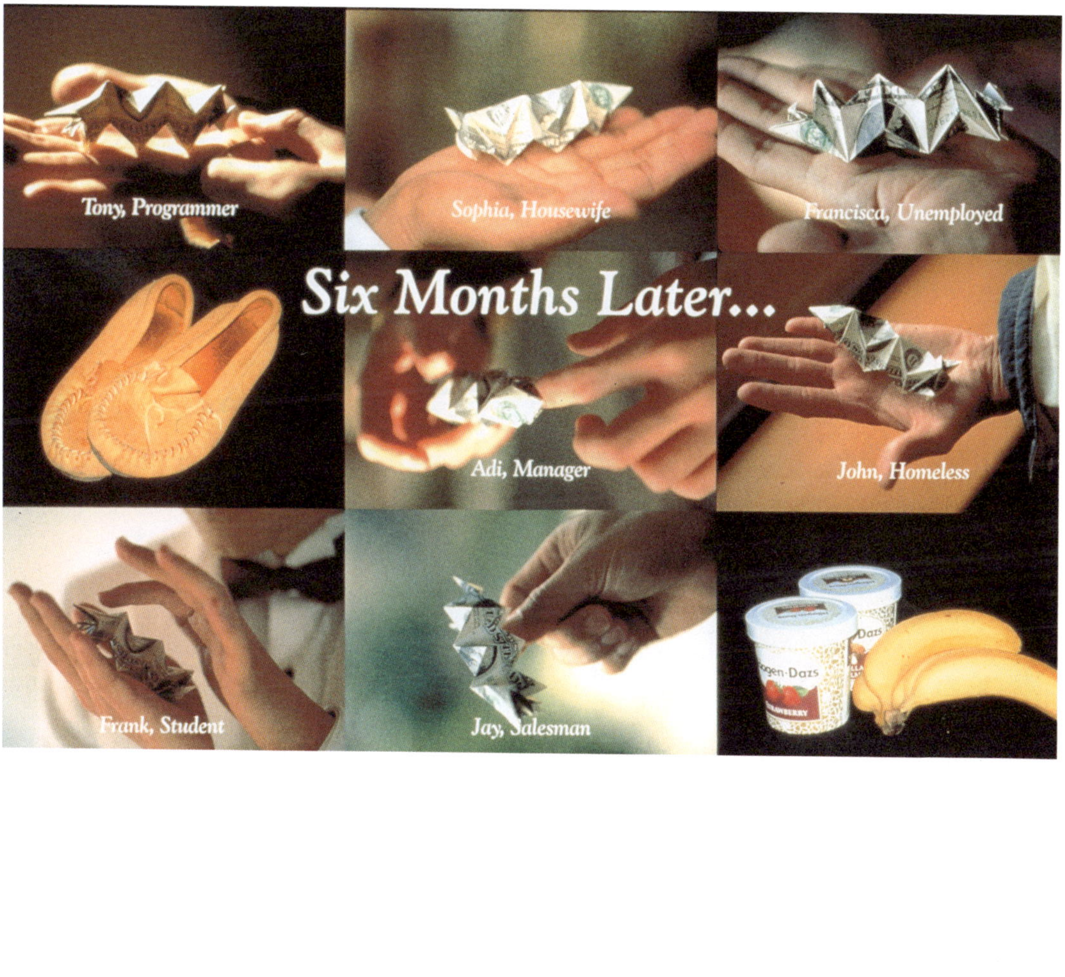
Tony, Programmer
Sophia, Housewife
Francisca, Unemployed
Six Months Later...
Adi, Manager
John, Homeless
Frank, Student
Jay, Salesman

# 100 DAYS WITH LILY

1995

5 Ilfochrome silver dye bleach prints, framed
Each 166 x 115 cm

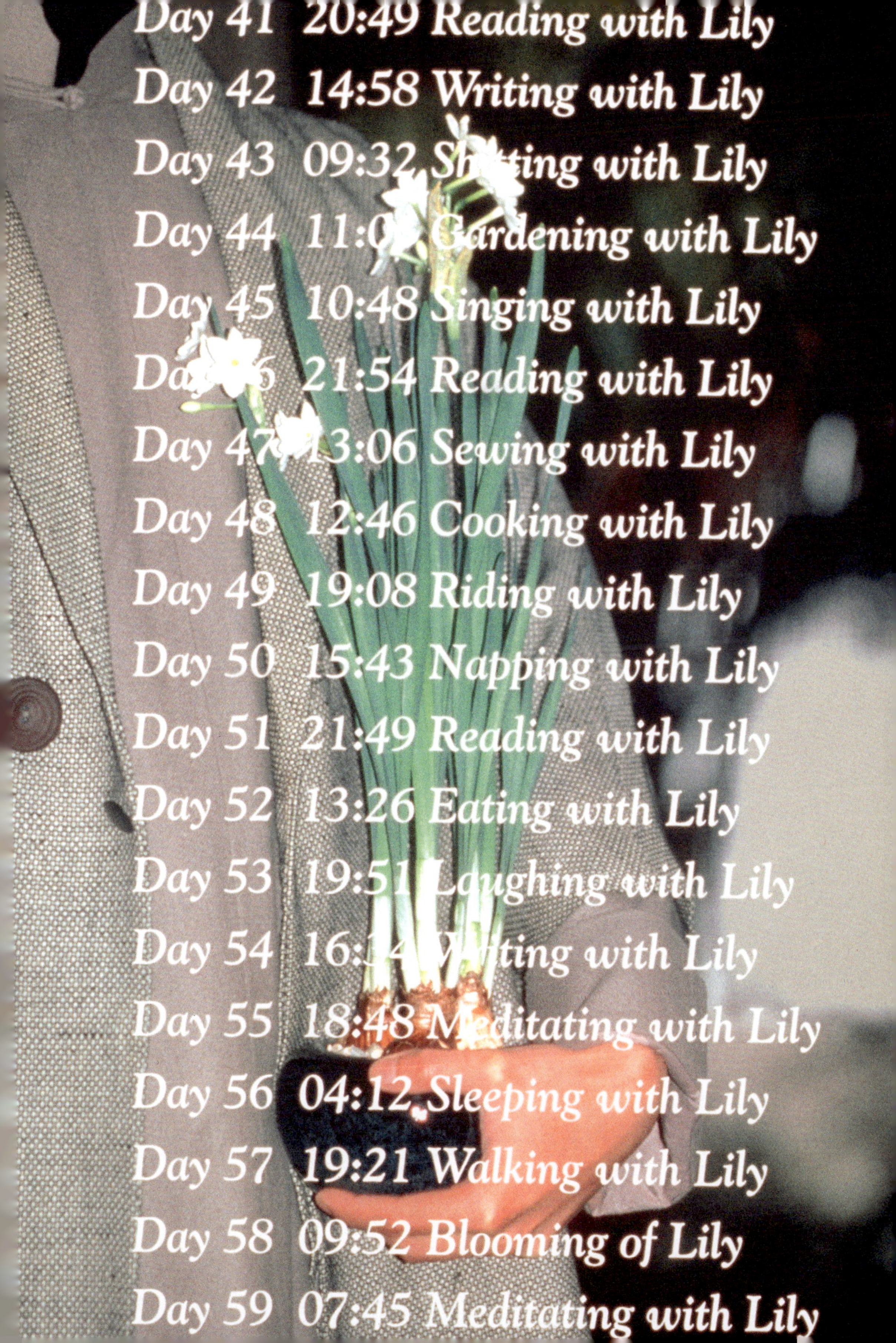

Day 41 20:49 Reading with Lily
Day 42 14:58 Writing with Lily
Day 43 09:32 Sh[illegible]ting with Lily
Day 44 11:0[illegible] Gardening with Lily
Day 45 10:48 Singing with Lily
Day 46 21:54 Reading with Lily
Day 47 13:06 Sewing with Lily
Day 48 12:46 Cooking with Lily
Day 49 19:08 Riding with Lily
Day 50 15:43 Napping with Lily
Day 51 21:49 Reading with Lily
Day 52 13:26 Eating with Lily
Day 53 19:51 Laughing with Lily
Day 54 16:34 Writing with Lily
Day 55 18:48 Meditating with Lily
Day 56 04:12 Sleeping with Lily
Day 57 19:21 Walking with Lily
Day 58 09:52 Blooming of Lily
Day 59 07:45 Meditating with Lily

"This project was inspired by my maternal grandmother and was also influenced by the performances of artists such as Joseph Beuys and Tehching Hsieh. When my grandmother passed away, I wanted to experience an intimate relationship of living with a plant. I carried it for 100 days in order to experience its stages of germination, blooming and withering. Although the plant completely withered at around day 80, I carried it for another 20 days. I then exhumed the bulb and buried it in the garden, hoping it would germinate the following year. It is one of my few photographic works and has text superimposed over the five images. The words document my daily activity, but I used minimal text to leave enough 'space' for the viewer to imagine what happens during the rest of the day. The work uses daffodils because when I went to my grandparents' home during the Chinese New Year holiday, they often had daffodils in their living room. This is what most people had during Chinese New Year. Since I couldn't say the word daffodil as a young boy, my grandmother just said the flower was called Lily."

LEE MINGWEI

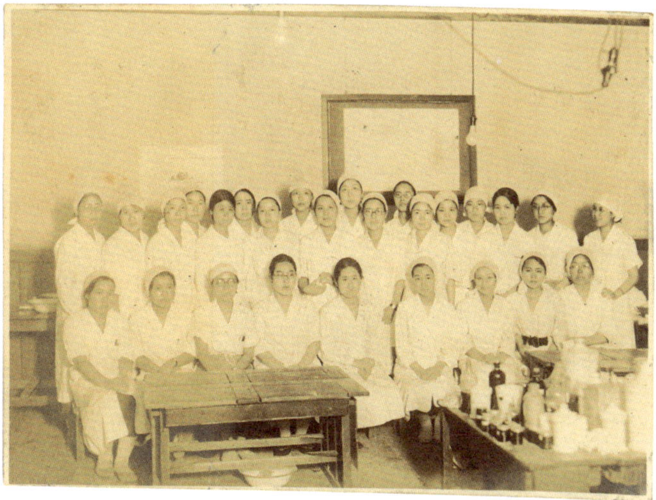

Lee Mingwei's grandmother trained as a doctor at the Tokyo Women's Medical University in Japan and graduated top of her class. In this photograph she is depicted with her fellow students – she is the eighth from the left in the back row.

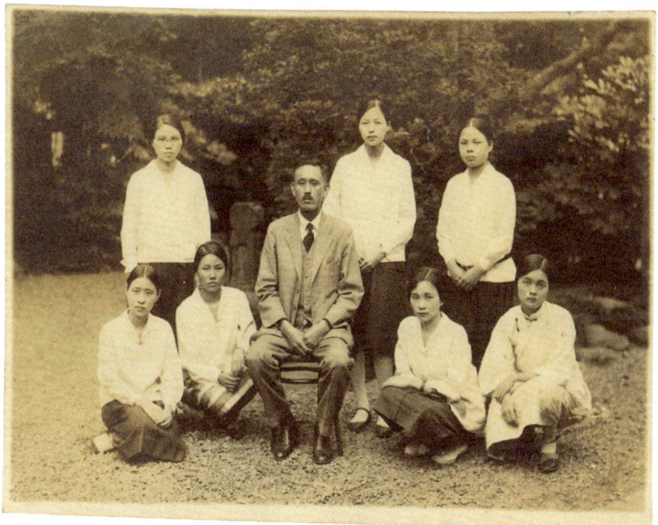

Here Lee Mingwei's grandmother is depicted with classmates – she is the second from the right in the back row.

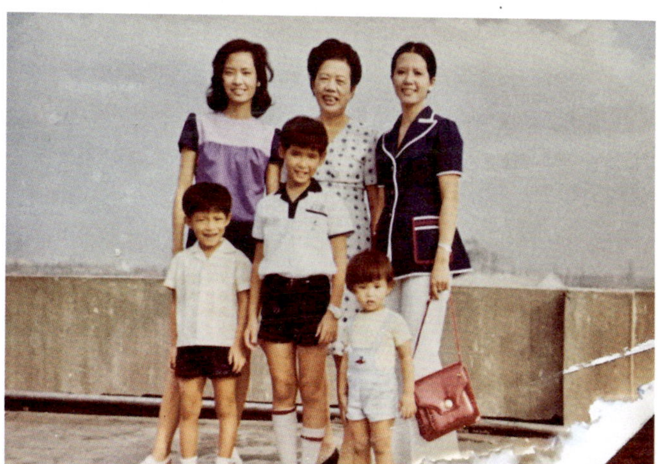

This family photograph depicts Lee Mingwei as a child – he stands bottom centre – with his mother in the back row right, with a red purse, his grandmother in the middle of the back row and his siblings.

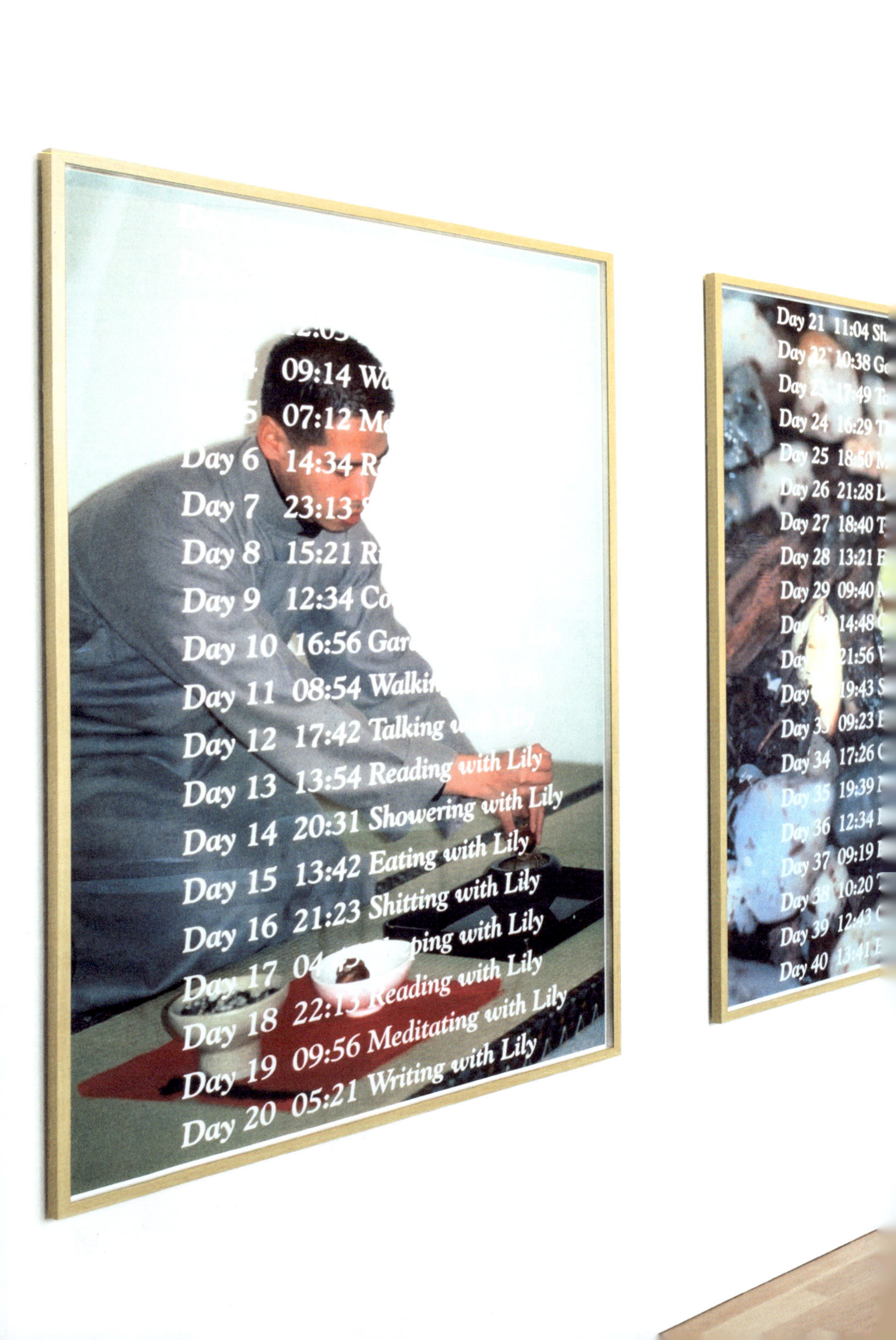
Day 6 14:34
Day 7 23:13
Day 8 15:21
Day 9 12:34
Day 10 16:56
Day 11 08:54
Day 12 17:42 Talking
Day 13 13:54 Reading with Lily
Day 14 20:31 Showering with Lily
Day 15 13:42 Eating with Lily
Day 16 21:23 Shitting with Lily
Day 17
Day 18 22:13 Reading with Lily
Day 19 09:56 Meditating with Lily
Day 20 05:21 Writing with Lily
Day 21 11:04
Day 22 10:38
Day 23 17:49
Day 24 16:29
Day 25 18:50
Day 26 21:28
Day 27 18:40
Day 28 13:21
Day 29 09:40
14:48
21:56
19:43
09:23
Day 34 17:26
Day 35 19:39
Day 36 12:34
Day 37 09:19
Day 38 10:20
Day 39 12:43
Day 40 13:41

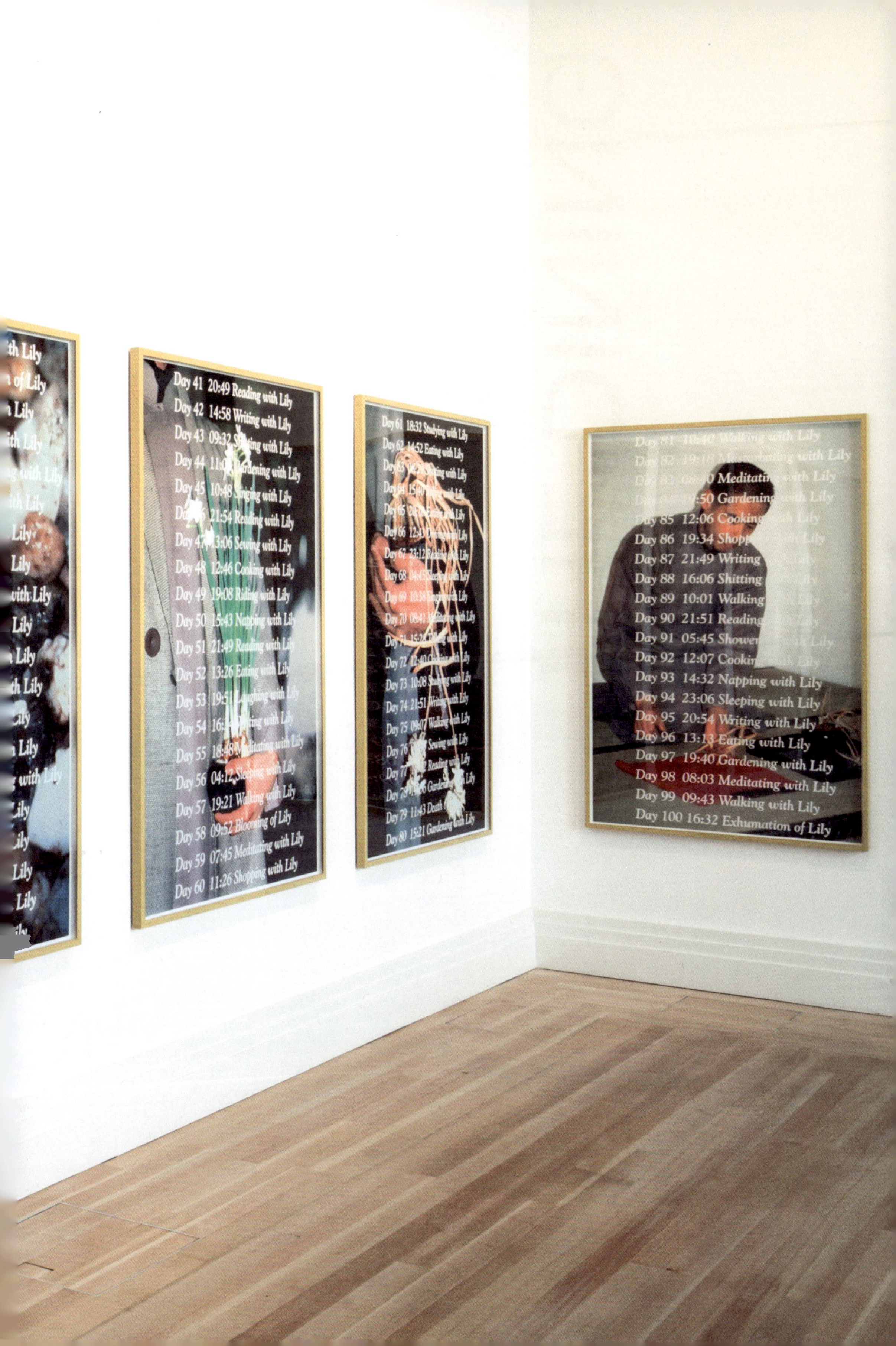
Day 41 20:49 Reading with Lily
Day 42 14:58 Writing with Lily
Day 45 10:48 Singing with Lily
Day 48 12:46 Cooking with Lily
Day 49 19:08 Riding with Lily
Day 50 15:43 Napping with Lily
Day 51 21:49 Reading with Lily
Day 52 13:26 Eating with Lily
Day 56 04:12 Sleeping with Lily
Day 57 19:21 Walking with Lily
Day 58 09:52 Blooming of Lily
Day 59 07:45 Meditating with Lily
Day 60 11:26 Shopping with Lily
Day 61 18:32 Studying with Lily
Day 62 14:52 Eating with Lily
Day 80 15:21 Gardening with Lily
Day 81 10:40 Walking with Lily
Day 93 14:32 Napping with Lily
Day 94 23:06 Sleeping with Lily
Day 95 20:54 Writing with Lily
Day 96 13:13 Eating with Lily
Day 97 19:40 Gardening with Lily
Day 98 08:03 Meditating with Lily
Day 99 09:43 Walking with Lily
Day 100 16:32 Exhumation of Lily

# THE DINING PROJECT

1997 / 2020

Wooden platform, tatami mats, black beans,
rice, single-channel video, sound
335 x 335 x 85 cm

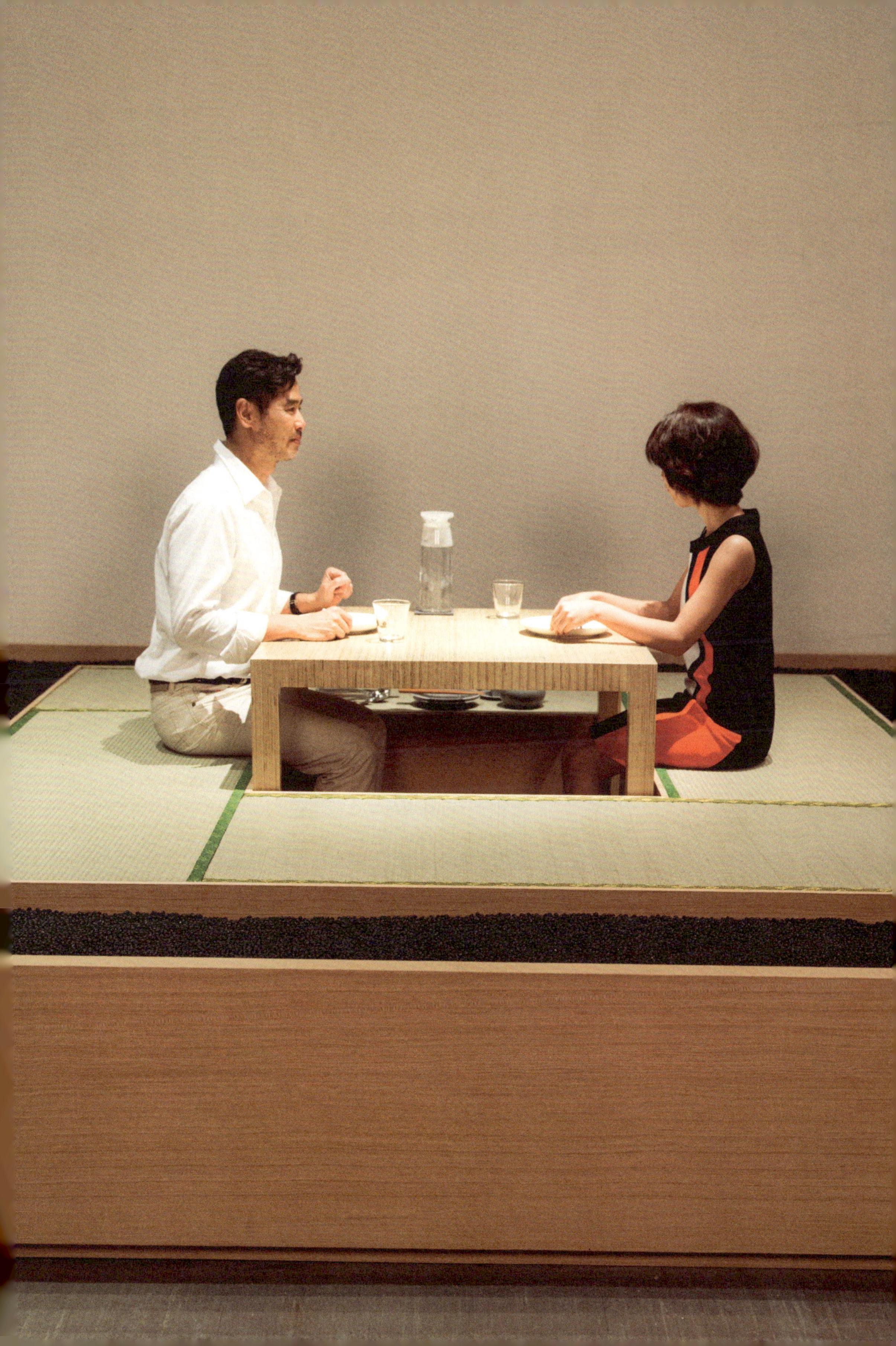

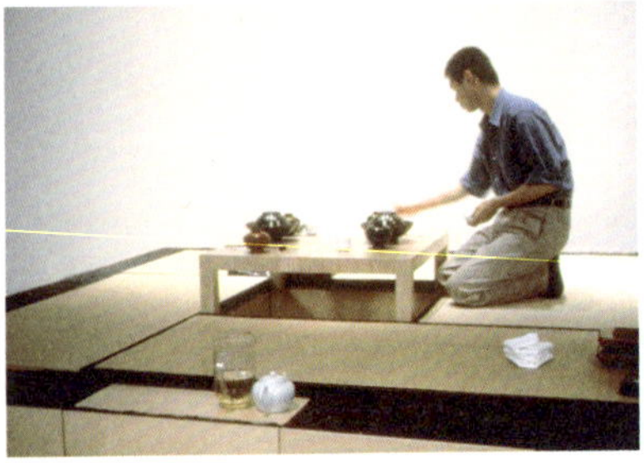

At the Gropius Bau, Lee Mingwei staged *The Dining Project* on Tuesday lunchtimes throughout the course of the exhibition. He invited members of the public, who were selected using a lottery-card system, to dine in the space on the day that the exhibition is closed to the general public, sharing a meal that had been personally prepared for them. Lee Mingwei, as well as other members of the Gropius Bau staff, were the hosts who welcomed the various participants. In the photograph above, Lee Mingwei sets the table for the work's iteration at The Whitney Museum of American Art in 1998.

"*The Dining Project* is about using food as a medium for trust and intimacy among strangers. It was one of my earliest one-on-one participatory projects. I arrived at Yale University to take my Master's programme in 1995. I mainly grew up in Taiwan and in Berkeley Hills on the West Coast of the United States, so I didn't know anyone in New Haven, Connecticut. Therefore I placed about 50 advertisements around Yale's campus, inviting people to have a meal prepared just for them, completely free of charge. All they needed to do was show up and let me know if they had any dietary restrictions. That evening, when I returned to my studio I had over 45 calls and messages waiting for me on my answering machine (this was at a time before mobile phones). The messages were from all different kinds of people: students, professors, janitors, the homeless and general people who lived around New Haven. Most of them were quite curious, so I had to explain that I was a Taiwanese-American student feeling lost and very lonely in a new environment.

There was an Asian market in New Haven and I would often go to the store after my class, spending several hours preparing the meal. My guest would arrive around seven o'clock. The food I cooked was usually simple home-cooked Asian dishes such as tofu with minced chicken and stir-fried vegetables plus brown rice. Miso soup was also part of the meal. We would then just spend the next two-to-three hours eating, talking and enjoying each other's company. At first, I thought of asking people to write their reactions to the evening on a notebook, however, fairly quickly it became obvious this was not the thing to do because it was almost like asking someone to do homework and distracted from the moment."

LEE MINGWEI

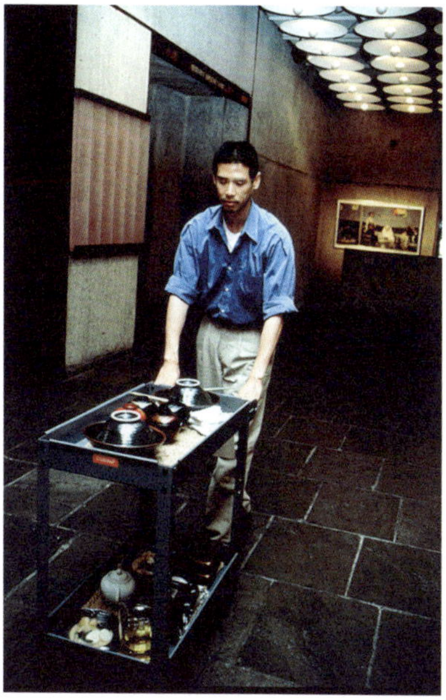

As a lonely student new to Yale University, Lee Mingwei began *The Dining Project* as a way of connecting with people, making new friends and sharing food as well as stories. At the time he was exploring durational performance and for this project he dined with a different person every second night for a year. His original poster, in which he requested the company of fellow diners, can be seen here in the image bottom right; the artist's preparation for the work's iteration at The Whitney Museum of American Art in 1998 can be seen in these other images.



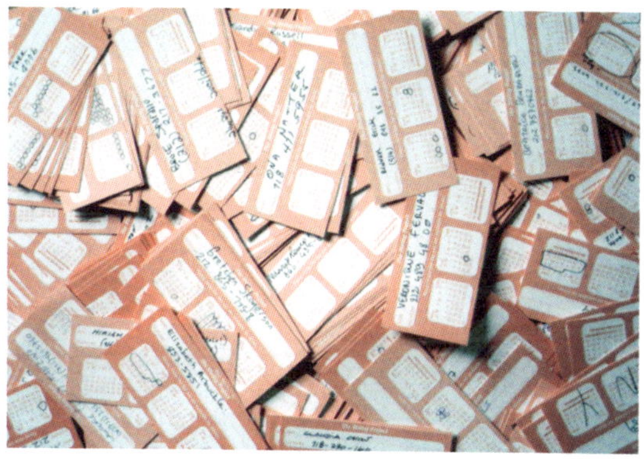

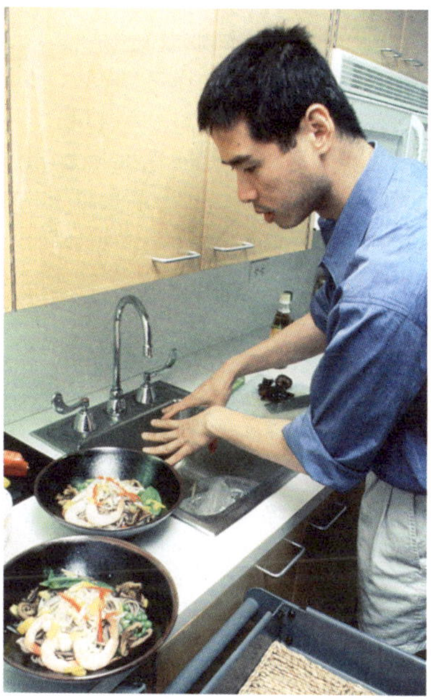

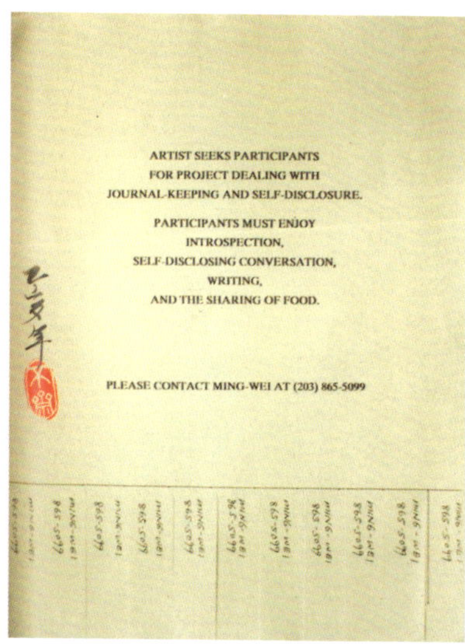

"In early 1996 a friend at Yale told me about a flyer inviting students for a dining project. If I remember correctly, my friend made the appointment. He never went, I did. It took place in the old sculpture department building. I particularly remember the dessert – bean cubes with Mandarin signs. Ming said this would be the first of several dinners. He said that after this one, he would make a notebook. He would give it to me, and I could pen my thoughts about the experience into it. The book would be exhibited with other remnants of the dinners. Alongside writing my dissertation at the time, I was also writing for German media. The idea of this extra (unpaid) writing assignment was not attractive to me. I told him. A book never materialised, but we became very close friends."

HUBERTUS BREUER

Participated in *The Dining Project* while studying at Yale University

"With Lee Mingwei as the host, we spent a little over an hour enjoying vegetable soup, spicy sautéed shrimp with beans, fish satay on lemongrass stalks and fried tempeh. We discussed moments of closeness, split-second intimacy that allows people to open up and share things they normally wouldn't. While sitting on that tatami, dipping my feet in the rice, I was on the receiving end of gift after gift; delicious food of different kinds and textures, insights into the life and work of an artist that I admire, all wrapped up as an uplifting experience. I think the real beauty of *The Dining Project* is how it acts as a sharing platform, allowing a true connection between strangers who get their names picked by chance. And just like in the movies, inexplicable magic takes place as the result of the lottery matchmaking between the host and their guest."

DIAN INA MAHENDRA

Head of Exhibitions at Museum MACAN, Jakarta, who worked on the exhibition *Lee Mingwei: Seven Stories*, 2018

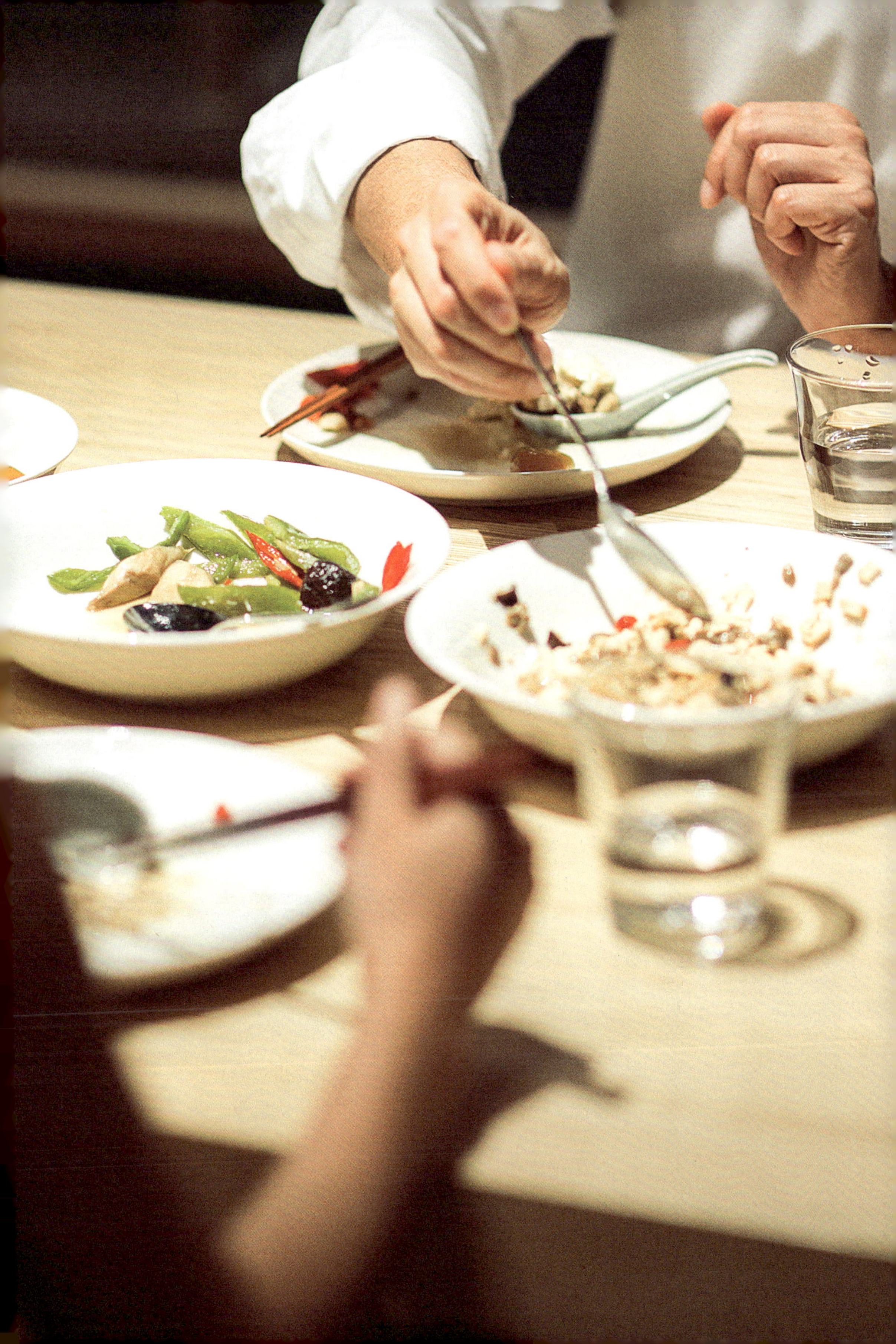

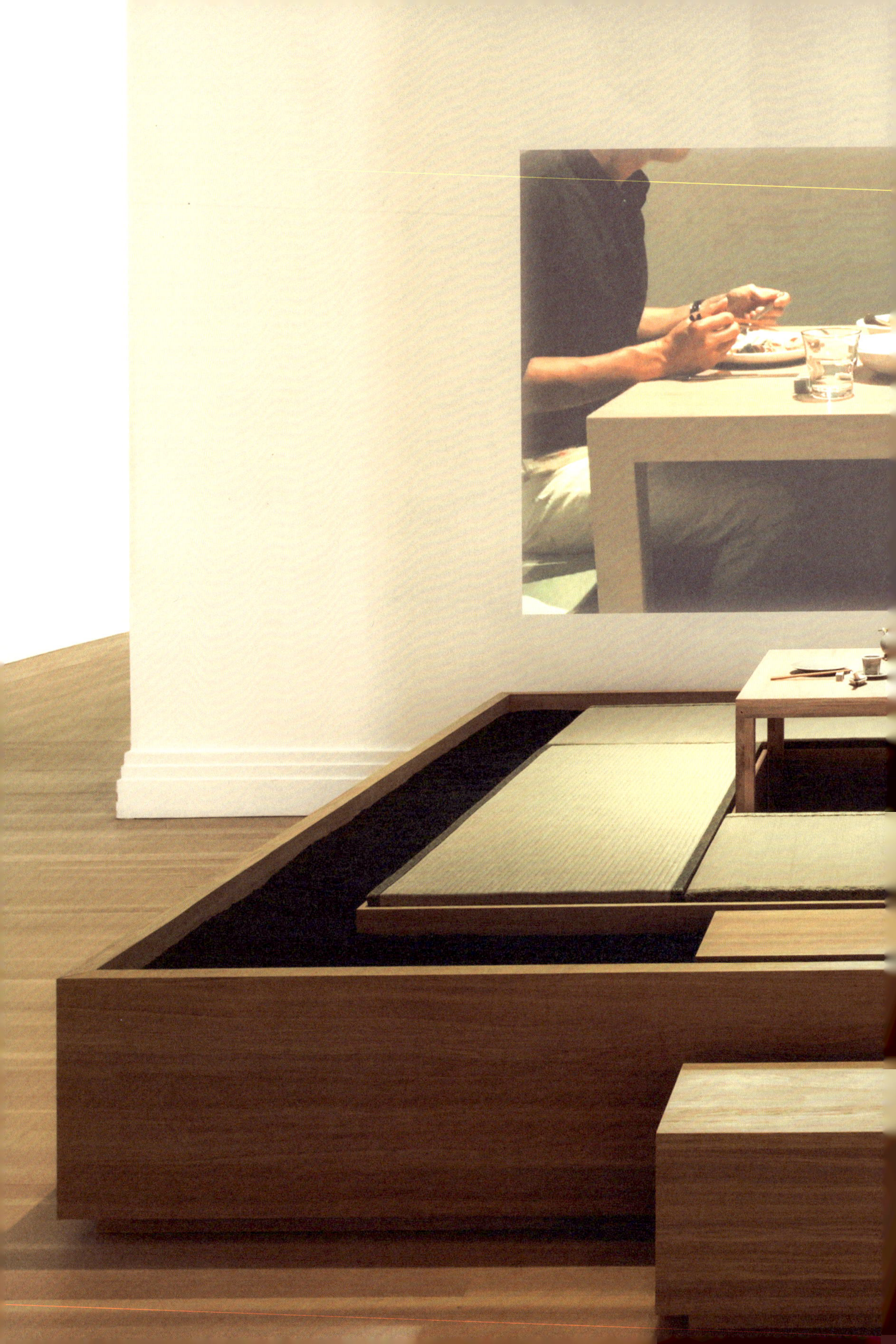

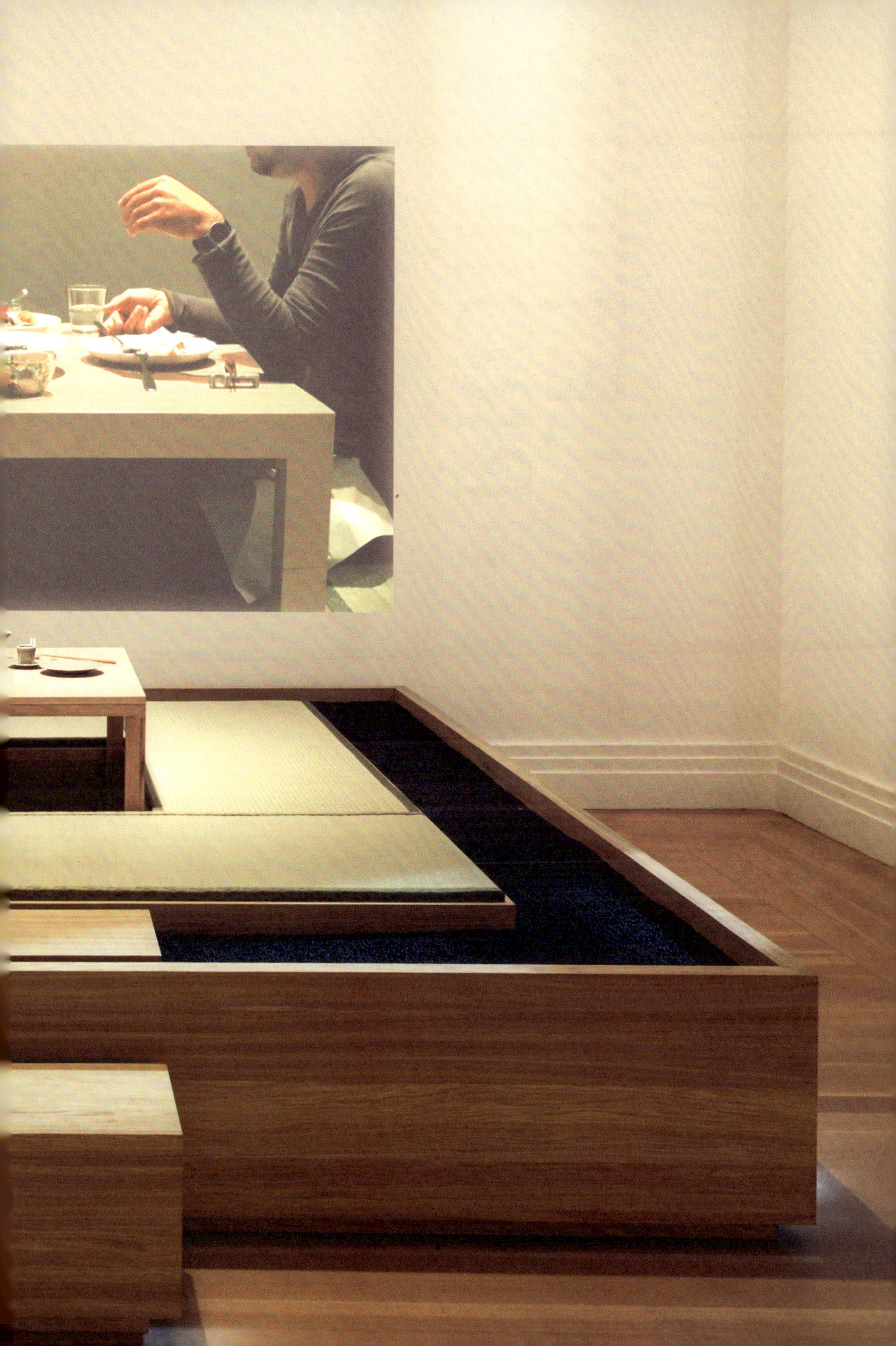

# THE LETTER WRITING PROJECT

1998 / 2020

3 wooden booths, writing paper, envelopes, pencils
Each 290 x 170 x 231 cm

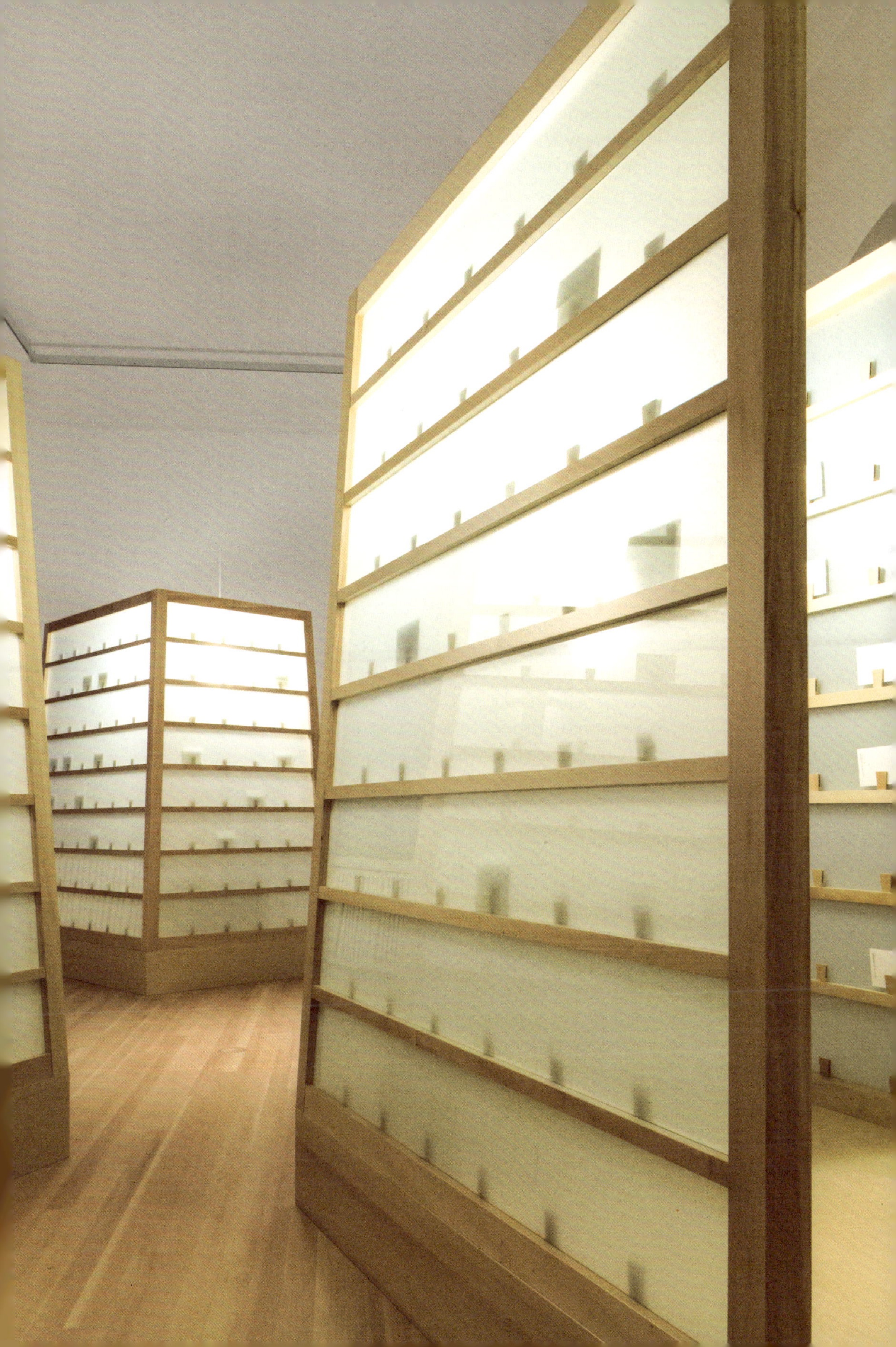

"*The Letter Writing Project* came from my emotional response to the passing of my maternal grandmother. I was in high school when this happened, while she was living with my parents in Taiwan. I had many things I wanted to say to her, but it was too late, so I spent the next 18 months writing letters to her. Some of these were long, while some of them were just drawings and random thoughts. At the end of this process, I had about 120 letters; I concluded my mourning process by burning them.

During this writing process, I would often call my mother to ask questions such as, what was she like in private, or how did she seem as a female doctor in the mountain town of Puli? Among the many untold family stories that my mum shared with me, I learned that my grandmother was relatively strict and austere with her children; it was my grandfather to whom the girls felt much closer. My family would spend every summer vacation in Puli. Once I saw a wounded indigenous patient walking into my grandmother's clinic, holding a bow and arrow in one hand and a dead mountain cat in the other. My grandmother treated his bleeding shoulder and arm with much tenderness, which I watched with fear and admiration through a small hole in the shoji screen.

When *The Letter Writing Project* comes to a natural conclusion, I would like to bring all of the letters that had no address, and therefore remain unsent, to India to burn them in a fire ceremony. All the powerful thoughts, emotions and feelings would be purified by the fire and then washed away by the water. I believe these emotions belong to the sky and the river."

LEE MINGWEI

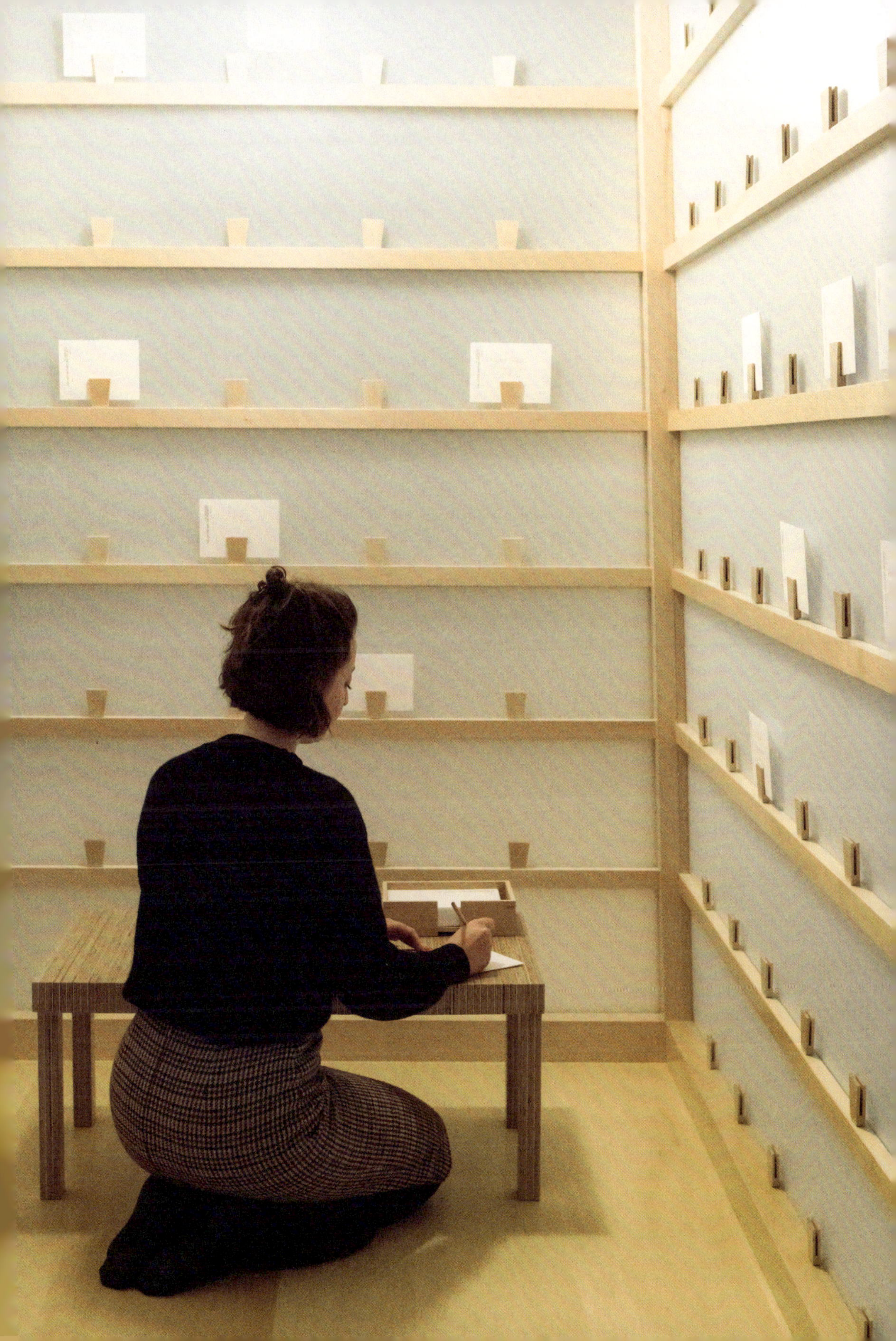

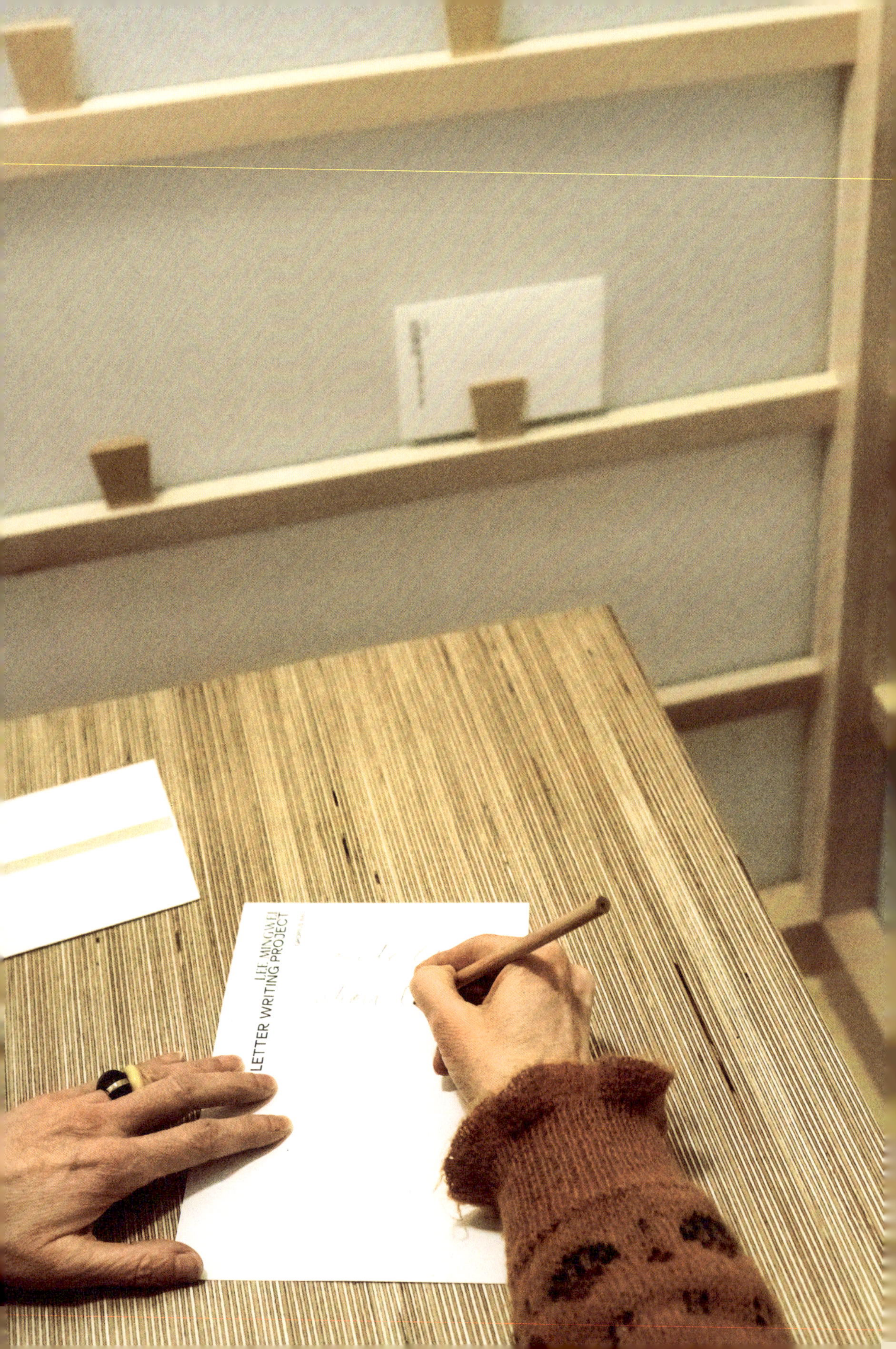
LEE MINGWEI
LETTER WRITING PROJECT

"I worked with Lee to organise *Lee Mingwei and His Relations: The Art of Participation* at Mori Art Museum, Tokyo, in 2014. During the exhibition my role was to collect the letters written by the audience and to deliver them to the post office. We were amazed by the enormous number of letters written during the exhibition – sealed, unsealed; to be sent and unsent. When we were sorting letters before bringing them to the post office, my colleague and I particularly enjoyed learning about who participated in *The Letter Writing Project* and which country or region they were from, and whether they wanted those letters to be sent within Japan or abroad. The process of my role was closer to an act of 'giving', although by going through the process of reading those unsealed letters, I also 'received' the gift of memories shared by those writers."

AYAKO YOSHIDA

Part of the project team for the exhibition *Lee Mingwei and His Relations: The Art of Participation* at the Mori Art Museum, Tokyo, 2014

# SOCIAL LIVING IN THE ART OF LEE MINGWEI

HARVEY MOLOTCH

Lee Mingwei disturbs separations – between people, cultures and between museums and publics. His medium is the social encounter, sometimes mediated with artefacts, always done with calm. He embraces the risk of the stranger. That is his art. In close-up and real-time, he engages with people he does not know – sharing a night's sleep, a dinner he cooks, the mending of a garment they bring to his table. Hardly what you'd expect in a museum, he crosses us into wild space, taking risks with real people, in real time. His audacity is to trust and enlist the trust of others. This is life on a tightrope, relying not just on nerve, but affection, gentility and respect.[1]

Given the times in which we live, this is somewhat daring. In other cultures – places of small-scale human intimacy – people know well what to expect of each other. Families are there; villages are raising everyone. Custom prevails. Now parents tell children not to talk to strangers. This warning goes deep and lingers. Who can know if the outsider will be a threat? Cautions abound – locks, alarms, gates and a wary eye. People retreat into self-styled protective shells. The great German social theorist, Georg Simmel, used the term "blasé" to capture the stance – aloof, beyond the fray, suspicious. It may appear as hauteur or disinterest. It helps mask anxiety while at the same time spreading it.

Yet, people do understand their mutual dependence on one another. If need arises, those others can help. Indeed, in ordinary life as well as in disasters, research repeatedly shows that individuals, even just bystanders, will come to one another's rescue. They jump into lakes to save children and break down doors to pull people away from fire. When there are accidents or losses, people can sense another's sadness and try to console – and at least sometimes manage it in just the right way.

The challenge for all of us is to have the pleasures and security of others while also taking precautions. We each play a double game, keeping up our guard while figuring out when to let it down. And we have to be wary not to intrude on the boundaries that others might need for their own sense of comfort. Given the potential for misreading and clumsy imposition, it is no wonder we do not always know when to go forward or when to hold back. Do we dare disturb the social distance, risk a wrongful breach of the silence between strangers? These are our private, even secret, theatre moments. It is intense out there.

Into all this comes the art of Lee Mingwei. As a frequenter of galleries, but from the vantage point of being a social scientist myself, I see him as running experiments. As his projects proceed, Lee has people encounter unlikely, almost inexplicable, circumstance. His interventions go deep to the social soul, revealing something of the human condition along the way. As witnesses of Lee's work, we are provided with what social science might term "findings". These findings add to knowledge but are also uniquely beautiful in spirit and sensibility.

The idea of beauty in a social-science experiment is radical, given the dismal nature of the precursors. Perhaps the most famous of the experiments, or at least notorious in the field of social psychology, was Stanley Milgram's 1960s "Behavioral Study of Obedience", conducted at Yale University. Milgram wanted to know how far ordinary people would go in harming innocent others – for no apparent reason other than being asked to do so. The answer: very far. While often fretting as they did it, Milgram's subjects were nevertheless willing to deliver what they thought to be hurtful (maybe even fatal) electric shocks to another person. With similar analytic intention, the social psychologist Philip Zimbardo mocked up part of a Stanford University academic building as a prison to see how far the student participants would go in adopting their assigned roles as "prisoner" or "guard" – roles that were decided by flipping a coin. Over a few days, the guards became so sadistic (and some of the prisoners so despondent) that the experiment had to be called off. In configuring their set-ups (with subjects, props and artefacts) these experimenters had created no beauty, but instead, quite the reverse. By contrast, the conditions that Lee creates give people the tools to experience kindness and wonder.

**Brightening the Lights: The Gift's Disruptive Presence**

Lee uses gifts as a methodology. Gifting is a time-honoured way of working out challenges; they bestow delight and bond people together. Many cultures have relied on systems of gift exchange, the most famous of which include the circulation of beads uniting the Trobriand Islanders (as described by the pioneering anthropologist Bronislaw Malinowski). The conspicuous mass giving among peoples of the North American Pacific coast enabled solidarity and distributed status through systems of potlatch. In current times, philanthropy is an analogous set of giving rituals. Most of our own gifting happens in more limited ways, at individualistic *rites de passage*, such as at birthdays, weddings and anniversaries. These are moments in which thoughtful items get bought and bestowed to establish, repair or ratify relations.

In his projects, Lee uses gifts – offered from him to others or from others to one another – to enact connection and open new

1 I would like to thank Glenn Wharton for comments on a prior draft.

possibilities. Among his tactics is a truly historical form of gifting – hospitality, which itself has changed form over time and place. It is indispensable when food and rest cannot otherwise be presumed, but is readily appreciated even when needs are not severe. In his *The Dining Project*, 1997/2020, Lee cooks up a visitor's meal within the museum walls, from scratch. They eat together and alone. They learn from each other, maybe copy from each other, risk offending each other. They see (and hear and perhaps even feel) how exactly the other chews, which parts of the meal do they eat in which order, how do they show satisfaction? How do they handle unscripted biological after-effects as they might arise? These risks are being handled.

Lee takes hospitality one step further with *The Sleeping Project*, 2000/2020. In a gallery space, the stranger and the artist spend the night on two separate but proximate beds. This is repeated through the course of a show with different guests. Trust is the only consistent element. Nobody knows what will happen until it does. What time will eyes close? Open? Who will talk, about what and for how long? There is no recording, no photography. Although risk is involved in this encounter, there have never been any negative incidents (there was, however, some insomnia).



In the Lee repertoire, songs are on offer. His *Sonic Blossom*, 2013/2020 (fig. 5., 49), involves a performance by a trained opera singer for a single museum visitor, which onlookers also witness. The singer, dressed in elegantly elaborate regalia, selects a gallery visitor, more or less at random, and extends an offer for a gift of song. If agreed, the recipient is invited to sit on a handsome chair designed by the artist, prominently positioned in the gallery space. Standing directly in front of the visitor, approximately four-and-a-half metres away, the singer renders a Schubert Lied. The performer looks straight into the eyes of their audience of one. And the audience of one gazes back. There is no microphone, but the beautiful voice fills the gallery. This approaches intimacy in the same vein as a lovers' embrace or a parent beaming at a child. Unlike other artworks in a museum, this gift is not catalogued, issued on a postcard, insured or even accompanied by a schedule. Instead, it concentrates on the relationship, in the moment, between two people. It reminds me of a line in a song by the Canadian songwriter Dan Hill: "And sometimes when we touch, the honesty's too much." The only solution for the recipient is to yield, to give in and to accept a gift like no other. Judging from the tears I have seen in video documentation of the work, as well as in live performance, the singer too can be em-otionally moved. This is stunning accomplishment to behold (and experience) in a museum.

The song may stay in mind (and body), as wonderful music does, long after the venue has been left behind. A speciality of Lee is to enable his gifts to go on, to travel in one way or the other. Such travel is explicit in certain works. For example, in *The Moving Garden*, 2009-present (which is not part of the exhibition at Gropius Bau), museum visitors take a beautiful flower with them as they exit the museum. They are told to present it to a stranger on their way home. The artist thus unleashes a choreography of gifting, which radiates out from the museum to indeterminate points in the surrounding city. For many it is easy; for others courage is needed. Either way, boundaries are being crossed.

**Mending the Way In: The Past as Present at Lee's Sewing**

Bonding has a literal aspect in Lee's *The Mending Project*, 2009/2020 (fig. 6., 49). As part of the work, the gallery announces that Lee would like people to bring textiles that need mending – a shirt maybe, a scarf or some other favoured item. He, or a substitute mender, sits for hours darning each offering. As the mender sits and darns alongside the owner, the two share stories about clothing, fixing, or indeed, about anything that comes to mind (just as with *The Sleeping Project* or *The Dining Project,* minds wander). As in sewing circles of old – examples include African-American quilters in the United States' Deep South and traditional embroiderers across the Baltic States – people (usually women) share stories along with the craft. Lee's work evokes such practices.

With Lee, there are some distinctive twists. When he is done with a given piece, rather than finishing it, he attaches the thread's loose end to a nearby wall where it joins all the other endings, which have come before. When the exhibition is over, each textile will be returned to its donor, but in the meantime, the loose ends unite as a colourful three-dimensional abstraction across the space between the table of folded textiles and the wall. As part of the work, the item's owner chooses the thread for the job. As a rule, it must be a different colour to the fabric itself. Lee's goal is not to restore by identical replication, but to conspicuously signal the change. These are proud patch ups. We are reminded of the Japanese tradition of *kintsugi* in which repairs, usually to pottery or lacquerware, are highlighted with gold to honour the actual material history of the object, as opposed to disguising it. As such, accidents, breakage and wear are brought out in the mending, not effaced. The tradition pays homage to the fact that life itself can be like this: it embraces disruption as an opportunity to reflect, grow and gain a new perspective. Indeed, it dismisses restorative purity; nothing is ever so perfect as to need absolute protection – not a pot, nor a garment nor a life routine. Lee underlines a philosophy that suggests jointly recognising and honouring histories as actualities.

### Endurance in Sand

In a large-scale and deliberately impermanent work, Lee replicates one of

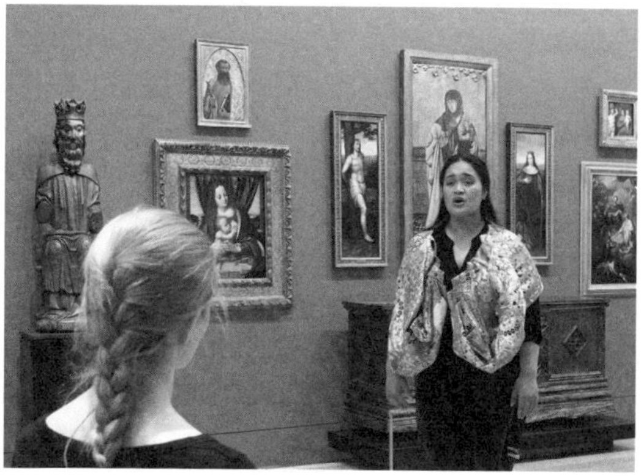

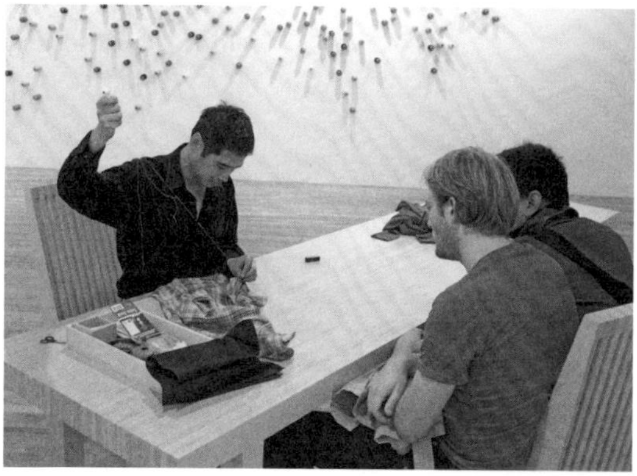

Fig. 5. Installation view of a singer reciting a Schubert Lied as part of *Sonic Blossom*'s presentation in the exhibition *Lee Mingwei and His Relations* at the Auckland Art Gallery Toi o Tāmaki, New Zealand, in 2016.

Fig. 6. Installation view of *The Mending Project* at Lombard-Freid Projects, New York, 2009.

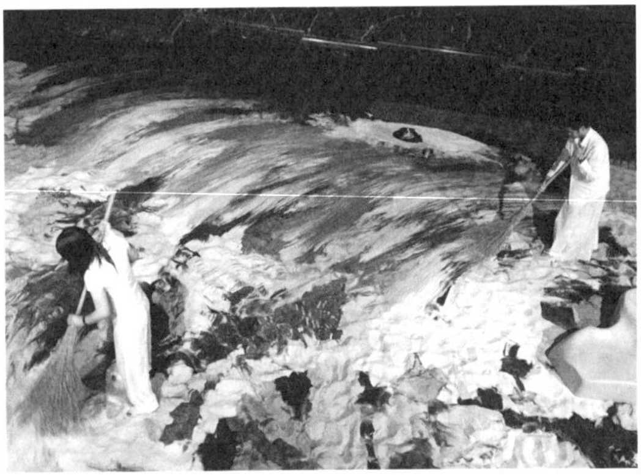

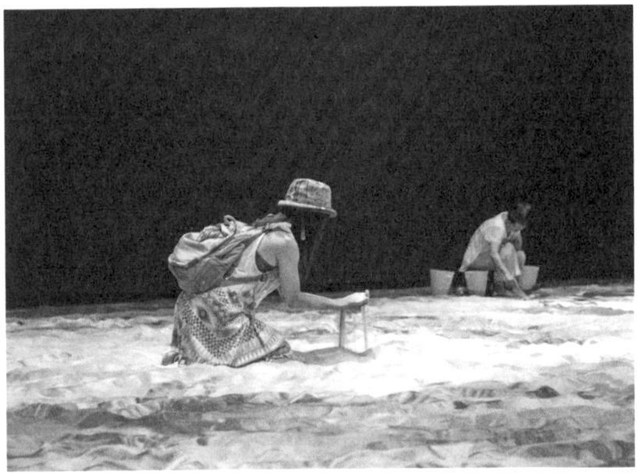

Fig. 7. After sand has been delicately placed and shaped by Lee Mingwei to reproduce Pablo Picasso's *Guernica*, selected performers brush the sand so that the work is unrecognisable and becomes a blurred abstraction. This reflects the fact that nothing in life is constant; change is the only certainty and can facilitate transformation.

Fig. 8. When *Guernica in Sand* was installed at the Taipei Fine Arts Museum in 2015 for the exhibition *Lee Mingwei and His Relations*, a member of the public crouched down to scoop up a handful of sand, letting it run through her fingers like the sands of time.



the most celebrated paintings in art history. Obviously nothing like a "true" reproduction, his *Guernica in Sand*, 2006/2020 (figs. 7-8., 50) embraces and honours Pablo Picasso's epic painting *Guernica*, 1937 (fig. 13., see 121) – by daring to undo it. Initially, he painstakingly shapes his version on the gallery floor using coloured sands. As he finally "completes" the work at one edge, he has someone start to walk across it, calmly but decisively destroying what has been accomplished. Others follow, walking through, furthering the derangement with each step taken. For me, witnessing this desecration conjures a chilling sense of the actual attacks in 1930s Spain. As a last stage, Lee's people sweep the sand into piles, yielding them into unrecognisable blurs. The sand is then returned to nature. In taking on this notion of an end, Lee confronts ultimate outcomes, including loss and death. The challenge is not to try and stop the process but to accept what has gone on, while being open to what might become better. As such, some of the fascist toxicity of Franco's regime and subsequent oppression is perhaps mitigated, suggesting alternative, more hopeful, states of being.

Lee's gestures are delivered not with might and power, but instead with Zen gentility. They are meant to induce a "chain of feeling" as they carry forward through their implementation and through the behaviours in the world of those experiencing them. He calls up his encounters not as one-offs; they are part of a flow, integral to that which came before and what will be next. As the participants meander through their further life encounters, that which changed them, if even to a small degree, changes the others.

## Risk as Aesthetics

Lee is a risk taker and a risk maker. He cannot be sure of how his envisioned connections will unfold; the intimacies are fragile. He is dealing with human beings, not inanimate objects. Even at the most well-organised museum, there might be logistical failures; some person (or artefact) could go missing. Janitors might barge into the sleeping area; food could affront religious sensibilities. A visitor could slip on the singer's gown. There is potential for emotional pain from reminders of family members facing death, missed loved ones and wayward children. In this genre of socially engaged art, elements must combine without hassle or consternation. A particular emotional and aesthetic outcome is being tenderly nurtured. As with the risks and rewards of effective improvisation in theatre, part of what needs to be right is the precise way the project connects to everyday life – glancing at a face, walking down the sidewalk, being circumspect or being at ease when a song is coming your way.

Complex ensembles of artefact and personhood perform the art into being. The works are co-produced from moment to moment, sometimes with objects as tools or mechanisms, but not as the central feature. Works like Lee's do not represent something else; the happening in real time is what the work is. Some language philosophers, followers of JL Austin in particular, might be reminded of the idea of the performative. Performatives are utterances that do not refer, like words usually do, to something outside the speaking – facts or opinions of the world. Instead, the speaking and the creating are simultaneous and part of the same action. "I do" in a marriage ceremony, for example, does not describe an event; it does it. Lee's projects consist not of things, representations or arguments, but of micro-accomplishments in series, ratified by successive acceptances of each unfolding premise as jointly produced.



## How Lee is in the Museum and How the Museum is in Lee

Museums (or *Wunderkammer*, Cabinets of Curiosities, as they were originally called) were established in the 16th Century with the aim of acquiring artefacts to express knowledge of the world through objects and oddities. Given that they were often amassed by wealthy individuals, status was an aim. Lee Mingwei's projects are not akin to that, and yet the gallery is still more than a mere setting. It is an active force. If Lee did identical things on the street, it might even be ridiculous – sweeping sand around a parking lot, for example. The institutional museum is thus intrinsic to the work. It is a public place that indeed welcomes people in but in a controlled way. It ratifies a project as something produced with care, but not as a theatrical play, opera, ballet or rally. Besides walls, restrooms and roofs (where desired), there is climate control. There is also conspicuous security, assuring some safety in accepting invitations for songs, food and a night's free lodging. Visitors can presume that events have been cleared by experts and lawyers.

Just as creatively important are the museum's bureaucratic prohibitions that, ironically perhaps, also comprise the art. Museums forbid sleeping, for example. Sleeping in the same enclosure as the artist is thereby made scintillatingly risqué. The constraints, as art-world scholar Howard Becker has argued more generally, are not in opposition to art making, but are intrinsic to it. Overcoming those rules is part of the craft; witnessing it is art appreciation. There need to be rules so that they can be confronted. That's where the avant-garde comes from. Lee's art gently pushes, investigating the boundaries, working the borders, as befits a forward-moving artist. He prods custom, expectation and proprieties.

In so doing, he is also expanding – as is often the job of artists – what is permissible for anyone making life. Breaking loose is part of the accomplishment. There is a frisson of liberation.

It is beauty to behold. Finding out that a museum can configure such sentiments excites one's sense of self. In the museum and out of it, Lee has us in unexpected manoeuvre. We may come in to see a Vermeer, but we leave with a song. Maybe it will inspire testing other boundaries – in art, in institutions and in how we live our family and civic relations. Maybe we can even go a bit farther in grappling with our individual fears and anxieties when meeting up with everyday "others" – public ones and private ones. Maybe the angst has less necessity. Even if there are strangers, we can talk to them.

# HOSPITALITY AND TIME

IRINA ARISTARKHOVA



The art of Lee Mingwei is the art of welcome. In 2009, when I asked Lee how he might describe himself as an artist, he said, "a social conceptualist whose medium is hospitality".[1] From his earlier works, such as *The Dining Project*, 1997/2020 (figs. 9-10., 56), to later works - many of which are included in his exhibition at the Gropius Bau - Lee explores the practice of hospitality. Lee has perfected the role of artist as host. Hospitality - an experience of being welcomed by others or welcoming them in private or public settings - has become a prominent topic in our times of mass dislocation and dispossession of large numbers of people as a result of both manmade and natural disasters. Hospitality provides a promise for a better future, channelling energy where we care for each other and the planet, rather than destroying them. Thus, the French philosopher Jacques Derrida, building on the discussions of hospitality by other philosophers such as Immanuel Kant and Emmanuel Levinas, has presented hospitality as one of those notions that provides an alternative vision for human relations, especially in comparison with hostility and intolerance resulting in wars and conflicts.[2]

In affinity with Derrida, Lee's artworks also enable us to understand a form of hospitality that we think we know - an invitation to dinner, sharing a conversation with a stranger or being welcomed as a tourist - in a deeper way, so that we experience it surprisingly anew. One aspect of Lee's new hospitality and on-going exploration of welcome is the artworks' nonlinear temporality. In this essay, I firstly analyse the new temporality of a scene's unfolding in Lee's work, and secondly, I connect this new temporality to questions of memory and documentation: how we remember hospitality and, as such, the role that documentation plays in our memory of welcome. Lee's work, then, would allow me to engage with Derrida's complicated theories regarding the temporality of hospitality as being able to bring together "at once timeless, archaic, modern, current, and future"[3] questions. From here, I will show how the documentation and memory of Lee's projects adds new and critical dimensions to Derrida's future-oriented (*à venir* - always "to come") theorisation of welcome.

**Nonlinear Time of Welcome: *The Dining Project***

Lee's art of hospitality also means that he is a memory maker. As a "social conceptualist" he formulates conditions that will lead to the creation of a hospitality scene: who will be welcomed, when and how. This is the "stuff", the matter that will enable our memories - as Lee's guests - made of the sensorial experiences of taste, sight, hearing, tactility and smell. As part of his making of a memory, the artist needs to construct himself as a perfect host, and indeed, to invite his visitors to become perfect guests. However, from the very beginning, Lee's relation to time is complicated, transferring this complication to us, his audience. As a perfect host, Lee needs to anticipate through his imagination, *before* he sets the scene of welcome, how his diverse guests, whom he does not know, will remember his welcome *after* they will have experienced it. If Derrida considered hospitality nonlinear because it collapses the notion of time – as a timeless and simultaneously past, present and future time, which one could say is compatible with contemporary ideas of the space-time continuum in physics – Lee's work adds another kind of nonlinearity. This is the one of subjective, intimate anticipation of making memories in others and of imagination brought about by creative empathy and intentionality of an encounter that will outlive itself by becoming memorable. This is the warped time, the future before the present, the leap into the unknown, of Lee's hospitality.

One of the pathways to trace the complex temporality of Lee's welcome is to follow the memories of those who have experienced the artist's projects, paying close attention to understanding how memories continue the unfolding of his scene of hospitality.[4] By tracing such a pathway, my case study here would be the memories of Mary, who, in 1997, experienced *The Dining Project*, one of Lee's key works devoted to the medium of hospitality. Jacques Derrida, a key philosopher to have focused on hospitality, talks of the "paralysis" of the host and also about welcome as something that is "always to come":

> Hospitality can only take place beyond hospitality, in deciding to let it come, overcoming the hospitality that paralyzes itself on the threshold which it is. It is perhaps in this sense that "we do not know (not yet, but always not yet) what hospitality is," and that hospitality awaits [*attend*] its chance, that it holds itself out to [*se tend vers*] its chance beyond what it is, namely, the paralysis on the threshold which it is. In this sense hospitality is always to come [*à venir*], but a "to come" that does not and will never present itself as such, in the present (and a future [*avenir*] that does not have a horizon, a futurity – a future without horizon).[5]

There is a certain interruption of the scene of hospitality that Derrida refers to here. It does not flow smoothly: it interrupts itself. This interruption, the disjuncture, of hospitality, happens because of the impossibility of the perfect hospitality being able to take place. Such an ideal of perfect hospitality, the one without hierarchies or any conditions for its guests, does not exist, because in reality, actual hospitality is always an approximation of an ideal: there is no unconditional, equal, hospitality. The relation of welcome is inherently unequal even as it claims to be welcoming, to be generous, to be giving, and, as a result, to be left without having to give further. The threshold here is one of the anxious host who is

1 Email from Lee Mingwei to Irina Aristarkhova, 9.3.2009.

2 A brief overview of Derrida's thinking on the concept of hospitality which is relevant to my essay and from which I quote here, is provided in his essay "Hostipitality", translated by Barry Stocker with Forbes Morlock, *Angelaki: Journal of the Theoretical Humanities* 5, no. 3 (2000): 3-18. Throughout my book *Arrested Welcome: Hospitality in Contemporary Art* (Minneapolis: University of Minnesota Press, 2020), I show that contemporary artists have a lot to contribute to pertinent discussions about hospitality, as I analyse, in addition to those of Lee Mingwei, the artworks of Ana Prvacki, Faith Wilding, Kathy High, Mithu Sen, Pippa Bacca, Silvia Moro, and Ken Aptekar.

3 Derrida, "Hostipitality", 3.

4 Eyewitness Reports included in this catalogue provide further indication of such nonlinear unfolding of hospitality that Lee's work enables.

5 Derrida, "Hostipitality", 14.

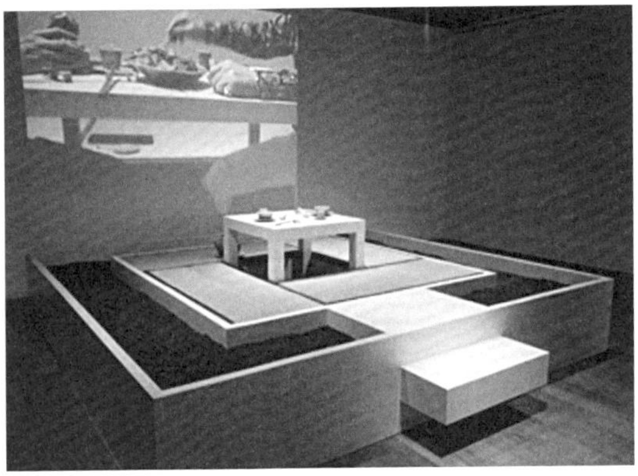

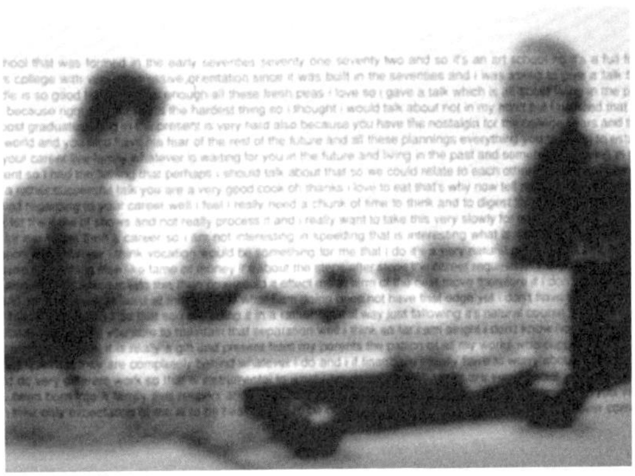

Fig. 9. When presented as part of the exhibition *Duologue* at The Museum of Contemporary Art, Taipei, in 2007, when the meal was not taking place, the wooden dining platform remained, behind which a video played, reflecting the memory of the evening's ambiance.

Fig. 10. This image of *The Dining Project* depicts Lee Mingwei and his diner, David Ross, who was Director at The Whitney Museum of American Art in 1998 when the artist had his exhibition that year. The text reproduces the conversation that the two shared during their dinner.

anticipating their guest's arrival, and of the anxious guest who does not know what to expect. There is a chance that the hospitality scene – in the future – will unfold well, or not. The uncertainty of hospitality adds to this impossibility to know in advance, where it will start and end, how long the welcome will last (forever?), and whether it will be interrupted all too early, leading to a failure of hospitality. The decision to host, or to be hosted, Derrida tells us, should not be taken lightly, because we do not really know "what hospitality is", and whether it already contains the seeds of its failure, of host/ility.

Hospitality, in this sense, is connected to the *à venir* of his theory of deconstruction, as this is such a difficult, special, notion and practice. Hospitality is neither private nor public, whether spatially or financially; it is not something that is required legally, within the realm of law and right, but as a notion and theory it bears on the notion of cosmopolitanism. In his text, "Hostipitality", Derrida starts with this idea of cosmopolitanism, as postulated by Immanuel Kant, and that has been developed in international law – that citizens of various nations could visit each other without "hostility", often permitted by a visa (a right to visitation, as among hosts and guests, based on invitations, for example, from "host" citizens). Hospitality, though not written into the law today in the precise Kantian sense, was foundational to the beginning of the international legal system, and to its notion of cosmopolitan citizenship. Thus, its liminal space is between the personal and the political.

Derrida's circling temporality of hospitality is also a testament to its performativity: there does not exist one, established, eternal, solid hospitality. It is embodied, practiced, enacted, produced and felt through gestures, senses, spaces and objects. What complicates the scene of hospitality further is the double performativity, because to take place, hospitality needs at least two beings: the one hosting and the one being hosted. Therefore, there are at least two thresholds, two hospitalities, two pasts, presents and futures of hospitality. What Derrida calls "hospitality" in the above quotation could be named as the moment between those two, the host's and the guest's experiences of welcome. This particular situation, a scene of hospitality, with its anticipatory beginning of an invitation and its acceptance, the arrival of a guest, its duration and then, its ending and memories, is complicated even further as far as art is concerned. An artist working in a contemporary setting of a museum or a gallery, such as Lee, is both hosted by those institutions, and hosting their audiences. Temporality here becomes multi-layered, as expectations of hosts and guests in private encounters do not necessarily map neatly into communal, public, settings. But this tension between private and public also creates opportunities, and Lee Mingwei has certainly pioneered many institutional "hospitalities" through his engagement with various exhibition spaces, the Gropius Bau being the latest one.

If Derrida's anxiety around hospitality is also about its uncertain futurity, Lee's work is connected to this futuristic postulation of hospitality but also departs from it. I would argue that Lee's work shows us how a projected memory is made *before* the situation itself occurs, and therefore, the future is not necessarily the problem here. The future is welcomed in the present practice of hospitality. The host prepares dinner in anticipation of leaving their guests with memories, creating a time machine of hospitality. This time machine is unpredictable because there is no "future" yet to remember. In the context of Lee's works, host and guest both remain vulnerable and unsure throughout the process; people prepare themselves for the best possible outcome, one that might not ever take place. This is a phenomenological situation, which is about the structure of experience in its individual interiority. Hospitality is based on its high ontological stakes: it is as much about our own subjectivity as it is about creating a world for the other. Issues of access, power, need and pleasure are opened up by hospitality and juggling one's own vulnerability within this context adds to the Rashomon effect of multiple realities, and hence, memories of the specific hospitality scene.



Lee began *The Dining Project* in the mid-1990s as an MFA student at Yale University. The idea of artists serving meals to expand their community had been practiced since the 1970s and, therefore, such dining allowed Lee to push at the boundaries of this foundation, developing his own unique aesthetics of hospitality into a sustained style of one-on-one welcoming situations.[6] Lee calls his artworks "participatory installations". One of the earliest participants is now a colleague of mine, who I shall call Mary.[7] Mary recollected in an interview with me that when she was in her junior year, waiting for an elevator in her dormitory, she noticed a poster on the wall inviting students to dine with an artist as part of his graduate art exhibition. Curious, Mary wrote down the number. Mary's friends feared for her safety because of the maxim "don't talk to strangers" and tried to dissuade her, but they were unsuccessful.

Was Mary too trusting? How would she know whether Lee really was an artist? She remembers cautiously entering Lee's MFA studio and immediately noticing how well he was dressed, how beautifully the food was arranged, and how nicely his room was decorated. Several images from Lee's subsequent iterations of *The Dining Project*, indeed, show the artist always impeccably and elegantly dressed when hosting such meals. Mary remembers a dinner of several courses, formally arranged with "proper" bowls and cutlery. This was the beginning of Lee's signature hospitality aesthetic. Traditionally, through hospitality, guests receive clues about their level of importance to the host: an important guest sits in the most prominent place at the table and is given the best food in the most prized vessels. These hierarchies also derive from indicators such as the complexity of the dishes served and the time needed to prepare them, and as such, the degree to which the host has considered their enjoyment of the food – their *tasting* of the elements of hospitality.

As a student, Mary had not expected Lee to welcome her with such consideration. For her, his actions complicated their social dynamic. Mary's memory was salient in relation to such moments of vulnerability and discomfort of being treated with high honour by a stranger, the artist. Hospitality, indeed, is "archaic", as Derrida calls it, because it has been used to specify hierarchies in gender, seniority, class and status, as well as cultural, religious and ethnic differences. Some guests are treated as more "special" than others in most traditions of hospitality. Although far from Lee's intention, a work like his can viscerally highlight those differentiations and expectations. Moreover, so subtly ingrained are such hierarchies that this is what memory could identify as important, no matter how hard Lee worked as an artist to create a much less complicated kind of memory: a positive sense of belonging and being welcomed. Is Lee aware of such hierarchies of hospitality? Arguably he is, and it is precisely such awareness that underpins his care, which is, essentially, a subversive act. This has been the case from this first work of welcome to using hospitality as an equalising practice toward his guests. Despite our best intentions, hospitality can make guests feel a sense of heightened awareness of self, in contrast to a sense of relaxed comfort. And a hospitality scene, such as that in *The Dining Project*, can feel overwhelming when traditional or specific roles weigh too heavily on our immediate reactions. However, Lee does not allow this "impossibility of perfect hospitality", as Derrida puts it, to paralyse him from his act of hosting.



Mary's response to Lee's hospitality was partly informed by the fact that her immediate living environment in a dormitory was, in her own words, "quite a mess". Mary compared Lee's well-appointed MFA studio at Yale, where the delicious dinner took place, with New Haven's "very few good places to eat" at the time. She proclaimed, "It was hard to imagine something [less like] the city than Mingwei's room!"[8] However, it was specifically this contrast between being an undergraduate student eating and dressing with simplicity on a daily basis, and being treated with such grace by a stranger that resulted in Mary remembering this meal with such clarity, even after many years. This emotional dimension of hospitality, as an aesthetic of creating the feeling of being welcomed as a special human being, is where the power of Lee's work is situated. Mary's memories do not need to be precise but they need to be vivid to be there, with her, so as for the welcoming effect of *The Dining Project* to continue.

The global nature of contemporary art challenges traditions of hospitality, not least between artists and audiences. Such internationalism melds various personal and cultural perspectives. This is a complicated dynamic; an artist such as Lee challenges traditional roles in hospitality in terms of how power is distributed according to gender, class, race and other markers of identity. Traditionally these have been discriminating factors impacting the exchange between hosts and guests in various settings. Lee's vision of hospitality, by contrast, is democratic. Some elements of his work therefore mine the familiar tropes of hospitality – for example his use of formal table-setting techniques – while the aim is new and radical: to create a horizontal exchange of emotion with the viewer devoid of hierarchy. Such radicalism also depends on *who* is experiencing the work, and when and where they are experiencing it.

The artist's aesthetic choices are deliberate in encouraging the participant to engage with their own embodied experience of belonging. Lee is particular about two aspects of hospitality: firstly, to treat each guest as if they are the most precious person in that moment, and secondly, to provide the best quality offerings (to be a perfect host). After graduating from Yale, Lee was asked to repeat *The Dining Project* at Lombard Freid Fine Arts in New York. In discussing how he adapted his studio-based project so that it was scaled for the gallery, he replied: "I could afford much better ingredients, and guests were chosen through the public lottery rather than through an advertisement in a dormitory. [This was used] to manage the schedule and the signing up process."[9]

This difference between a less formal space of an MFA studio, and the more formal space of a gallery or museum is important beyond the quality of food. In case of hospitality scenes, formal and crowded museum spaces might feel artificial and less prone to the intimacy of welcoming one-on-one encounters. In contemporary art criticism, many scholars consider museums to be problematic spaces for their artificiality and audiences.[10] Lee's art asks how museums and galleries can become more democratic and accessible to a wider visitor base, and indeed, how art can enable a liminal space that falls between categories.[11] The question of memory's role in hospitality adds another dimension here: the lack of privacy in large art exhibitions leads to multiple modes of documentation that is not always welcomed by those who host and are hosted.

### (Un)Documenting Welcome

On 22nd August 2017, I walked into the main exhibition venue at the 57th Venice Biennale, primarily to experience Lee's *The Mending Project*, 2009/2017. This project was visible first as an installation of colourful spools cross threaded along the wall. This created an atmosphere of colour

6 Cooking, serving and hosting audience members as guests has been practiced widely in contemporary art since the 1970s. One of the examples widely written about and relevant here is artist Rirkrit Tiravanija. Tiravanija first cooked Pad Thai in New York's Paula Allen Gallery in 1990 and since then has recreated the work in various other forms. Nicolas Bourriaud used Tiravanija's work, among others, to develop his notion of Relational Aesthetics. See Nicolas Bourriaud, *Relational Aesthetics*, translated by Simon Pleasance and Fronza Woods with the participation of Mathieu Copeland (Dijon: Les presses du reel, 2002). Additionally, the following sources provide surveys of art that deals with hosting and community participation, also described as "the art of social practice": Stephanie Smith, ed., *Feast: Radical Hospitality in Contemporary Art* (Chicago: Smart Museum, University of Chicago, 2013); Nato Thompson, ed., *Living as Form: Socially Engaged Art from 1991-2011* (New York: Creative Time Books and the MIT Press, 2012); Ted Purves, ed., *What We Want Is Free: Generosity and Exchange in Recent Art* (Albany: State University of New York Press, 2005); Sally Tallant and Paul Domela, eds., *The Unexpected Guest: Art, Writing, and Thinking on Hospitality* (London: Art/Books, 2012); Claire Doherty, ed., *Contemporary Art: From Studio to Situation* (London: Black Dog Publishing, 2004).

7 "Mary" asked me to keep her real name private.

8 Mary in an interview with the author, 19.9.2013. The quotations here are from the same interview as well as from email correspondence with the author, 21-23.6.2018.

9 Lee Mingwei in an interview with the author, 1.4.2013.

10 For divergent viewpoints on this topic see Grant H. Kester, *Conversation Pieces: Community and Communication in Modern Art* (Berkeley: University of California Press, 2004); Kester, *The One and the Many: Contemporary Collaborative Art in a Global Context* (Durham: Duke University Press, 2011); Miwon Kwon, *One Place After Another: Site-Specific Art and Locational Identity* (Cambridge: MIT Press, 2002); Renate Dohmen, *Encounters Beyond the Gallery: Relational Aesthetics and Cultural Difference* (London: IB Tauris, 2016); Claire Bishop, *Artificial Hells: Participatory Art and the Politics of Spectatorship* (New York: Verso, 2012); Tallant and Domela, *The Unexpected Guest*; Michael Corris, Jaspar Joseph-Lester and Sharon Kivland, eds., *Hospitality, Transmission Annual* (London: Artwords Press, 2010). I thank Maureen Connor for brining my attention to and gifting me the last book on this list.

11 Lewis Hyde, "Isabella's Will" in *Lee Mingwei: The Living Room* (Boston: Isabella Stewart Gardner Museum, 2000), 15-21.

12 *Lee Mingwei: The Mending Project*, video uploaded by Virgil Wong, 2.10.2012, https://www.youtube.com/watch?v=kfduRgfMD_4.

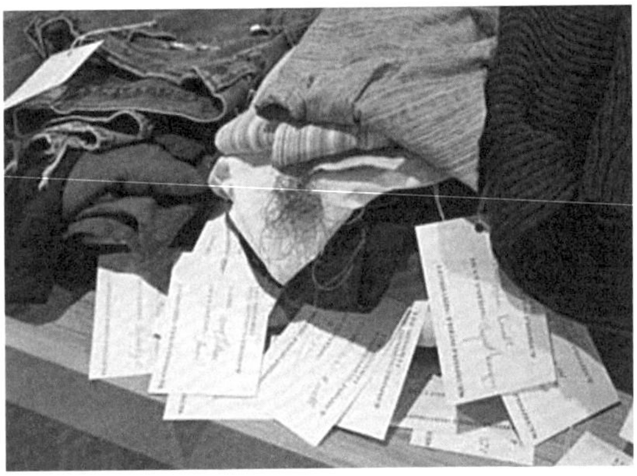

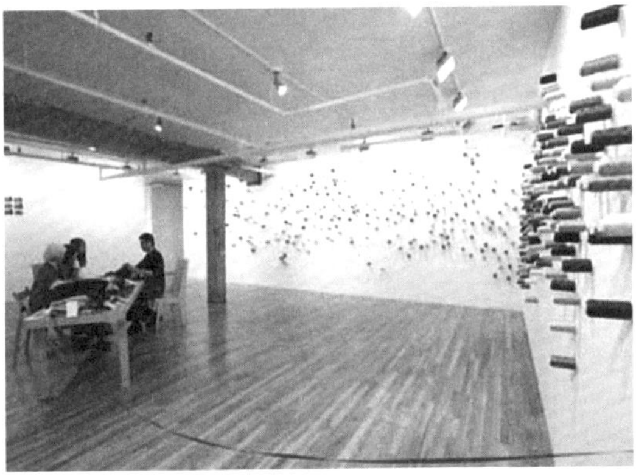

Fig. 11. The labels attached to the mended clothing for *The Mending Project* delineate the name and occupation of the owners, who could return to the gallery to collect their mended garments on the last day of the exhibition.

Fig. 12. Installation view of *The Mending Project* at Lombard-Freid Projects, New York, 2009, depicting a long table, two chairs and a wall of colourful cone-shaped spools of thread.

and vulnerability, as the threads were so thin and ephemeral (figs. 11-12., 60). In the middle of the room there was a table. A person sat in front of another person at the table. The idea of *The Mending Project* is that one person brings a piece of clothing that needs to be repaired to the "mender"; using threads and a needle, the item of clothing is then repaired and the visitor can pick it up after the end of the show. During the process of mending, a conversation takes place between the mender and the participant. Lee talks about this experience as being an intimate one, because it used to be done in the privacy of one's own home. He has also described how this process of mending has a personal meaning. When he grew up in Taiwan, the country was poor, and repairing and mending clothes was a common practice (rather than going to buy new clothes if old ones needed repair). Mending "brings me something very satisfying emotionally and visually", Lee says.[12] Cross-culturally, "we all wear clothes as our second skin" and even if he mends in a country where he cannot speak with exhibition visitors due to the language barrier, the experience of mending clothing is universal. Lee emphasises his idea of mending for strangers as a gesture of "care and repair, of giving a gift for somebody".[13]

The Venice Biennale is a very public exhibition, making anyone's experience less intimate and more exposed. When I came to *The Mending Project* at the Biennale, walking to it through multiple rooms, I noticed that most of the artworks were objects or media (video, audio, animation) about life, including human life. However, there were no *living beings* to interact with; all of the works were either inanimate objects or were shown on screens. Lee's work was the only one that I encountered that day that included a human being who was waiting for me to make the "magic" of art happen. Lee emphasises the interactive nature of the project too, that the work would not be possible without a person giving an article to mend and sitting down for a chat. In reality, Lee's purpose of creating intimacy in the middle of the chaos of public spaces was soothing because of its contemplative intentionality. The artist changed the environment, even if that environment initially was not conceived as a welcoming space.

Theoretical writing on welcome often takes a bird's-eye view on the scene of hospitality, whereby the writer does not disclose whose position they take or whose side they are on – the guest or host, both, or neither. Nonetheless, readers often sense that the position of an objective observer is an impossible one to take in presenting arguments in relation to hospitality. The harder one tries to hide preferences for a specific guest or a host, the less "objective" one becomes in relation to one's own biases.[14] Lee, however, refuses this comfortable, safe position of seeming neutrality. I learned this myself by writing about his work, that it is impossible to claim to experience Lee's art without letting oneself be welcomed by the artist and his peer hosts, whose singular modus operandi is, indeed, to host me. Lee teaches us that by implicating ourselves in the emotions, feelings, phenomenological obsessions and epistemological complexity of hospitality, we open ourselves to the full potential of his work. This specific point became clearer to me when I considered the question of documentation of Lee's work. Whose experience does documentation represent? After all, a good host would not want to use documentation as proof of their perfection in welcoming others. It is up to others to testify (as this volume also attests) to the quality of Lee's hospitality.

Thus, there is a certain tension between Lee's intention of creating intimate encounters with strangers and the customary photo or video documentation of contemporary artworks. This tension is demonstrated on Lee's website. Many of the listed projects do not lead to any "documentation" but for their titles and descriptions. One could even say that art (of welcome) exists to represent those moments that live only in our (collective) memory, because to record them otherwise would be unethical or, at least, somewhat intrusive. If we say to our guests that we want them to "feel at home", this implies the privacy and comfort of an intimate interiority of being, also being at home with oneself. Another potential problem with "documenting hospitality" is its failure to live up to the multi-sensorial and subjective quality of a hospitality scene. As such, when I look at myself in the video and photographic documentation of *The Mending Project*, which I experienced at the Venice Biennale, this documentation adds to my memory but also interferes with it. It adds what are considered "factual details", such as the colour of my shirt or the position of the hostess trained by Lee Mingwei who was mending my hat. However, those factual details do not add to my memory of *sensing* my host's *feelings* about that moment. Thus, documentation does not necessarily clarify

13 Ibid.

14 I develop this point in more detail in *Hospitality of the Matrix: Philosophy, Biomedicine and Culture* (New York: Columbia University Press, 2012), where I discuss how gendered differences in approaches to hospitality have remained the blind spots of major hospitality traditions and philosophies.

anything new in such hospitality. In addition, as much as I wanted to remember how I felt and how my host felt during our conversation at *The Mending Project*, what I cherish the most was that fleeting moment of the human connection that Lee created under the umbrella of "mending". More than documentation, I cherish my old hat that was "mended" with those colourful threads. As an object, the hat now has aura that is full of the materiality of time that hospitality takes – of care, preparation and anticipation. Lee's aesthetic both stretches and collapses time between past, present and future. His hospitality is as much always present as it is "to come".

Some artists refuse to document their art because they see documentation as a form of "objectifying" and "product-making." In that sense, documenting a work's processes of hospitality could be objectionable on the precise ground that it is supposed to be free, a gift. The authenticity of the aesthetic of hospitality is questionable if it is sold as documentation. An absence of documentation could also mean "giving each other space", or, in other words, being present in the moment of welcome without considering its consequences – its traces. It is important to give each other space and to consider the consequences for each person when we are allowed such space (visual and psychological). In the above interview with Mary, I used a pseudonym because even now the memory of hospitality and its intimacy could be too private for her when considering this text as "documentation". After all, writing is as public as being hosted in a museum. Documentation can arrest the multi-pronged unfolding of an artwork that mines hospitality; at a personal, existential level, documentation can interrupt the sharing of memories, even long after the encounter itself has taken place. It can mould and overtake the actuality of a lived experience.



Images are powerful too, as memory makers. It is the temporality of documentation that seems to want to bring us "back" to the event. That is one of its purposes: "this happened". Documentation produces a document, testimony, referent to the past reality. However, the work of hospitality resists such linear temporality because it lives within our bodies, within us. It stays with us. In other words, the art of hospitality, whether within the framework of contemporary art or not, has the capacity to become a part of us. Hospitality relies on our embodied experience. In Lee's work, we share food, shelter and time together. The artist creates the conditions that are external to us to enable this moment of sharing. And yet it also relies on our embodied experience of interiority, of the emotions that such sharing elicits, and in this sense, Lee creates a *shared interiority*. Lee's artworks of hospitality generate a complex transformation: not only is a person changed in the moment, they will continue to be changed as time goes by, in their present, past and future.

# THE SLEEPING PROJECT

## 2000 / 2020

Wooden beds, nightstands, personal items

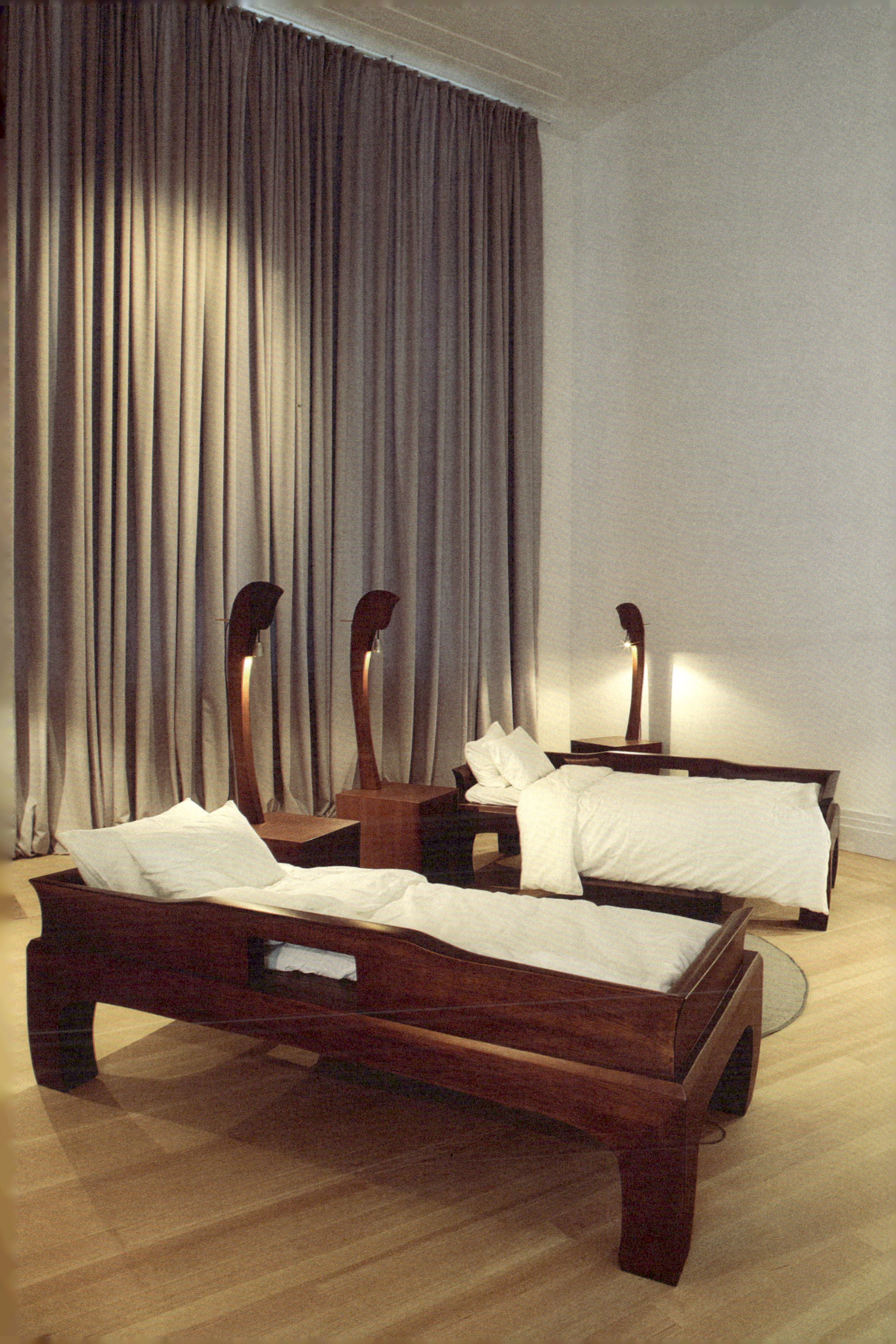

"The seed for *The Sleeping Project* was planted in my late teens. Right after I graduated from high school, I gave myself the gift of backpacking through Europe. On one of the night trains travelling between Paris and Prague, I shared a sleeper compartment with an elderly gentleman. We began having a polite conversation, but gradually, I learned that his whole family had perished during World War II. He was the only person who had survived Auschwitz; his grandparents, parents, siblings, cousins and everyone in his family had been killed. I remember he told me one of the guards was very kind to all the children; she was also the one who had closed the door and turned on the gas. After three hours, he hugged me and went to bed. I stayed awake through the rest of the night, imagining how many people were taken to these camps on the same train tracks.

The night I did *The Sleeping Project* for the first time, everyone told me that I have to be extra careful about my safety. The gallerist even placed a 911 auto-dial next to my pillow. I arrived at the gallery filled with fear and anxiety – staring at the beds, imagining the possible nightmares that could unfold. I woke up the next day extremely tired and sobbed all the way back to Brooklyn. I had to take a long walk in Prospect Park to calm myself and consider how to approach the next 19 evenings. I saw a young father holding his infant child, singing to her. I realised that the only thing I had to do was to be as open and as fragile as a baby. When someone sees a child the instinct is to protect, not to destroy. If we are armoured with emotional shields and weapons, this is when we are tested."

LEE MINGWEI

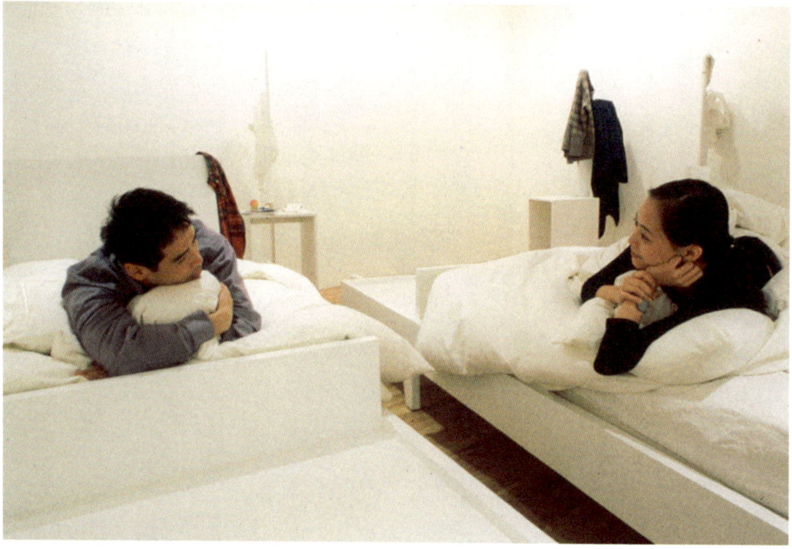

Lee Mingwei first enacted *The Sleeping Project* at Lombard Freid Fine Arts, New York in the year 2000, as depicted in these two images. Participants were chosen using a lottery-card system, with the purpose of two strangers (one being the artist) spending a night together.



People could place their items on nightstands next to their bed before they slept and these remained on display until the end of the exhibition.

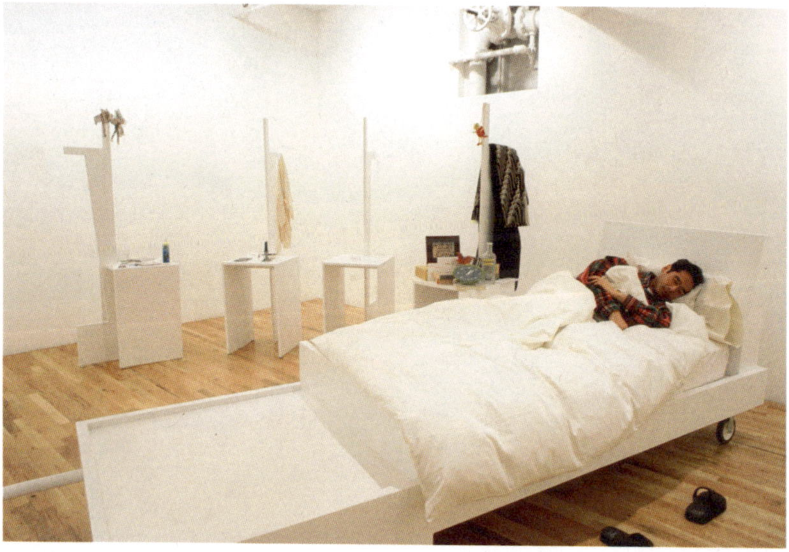

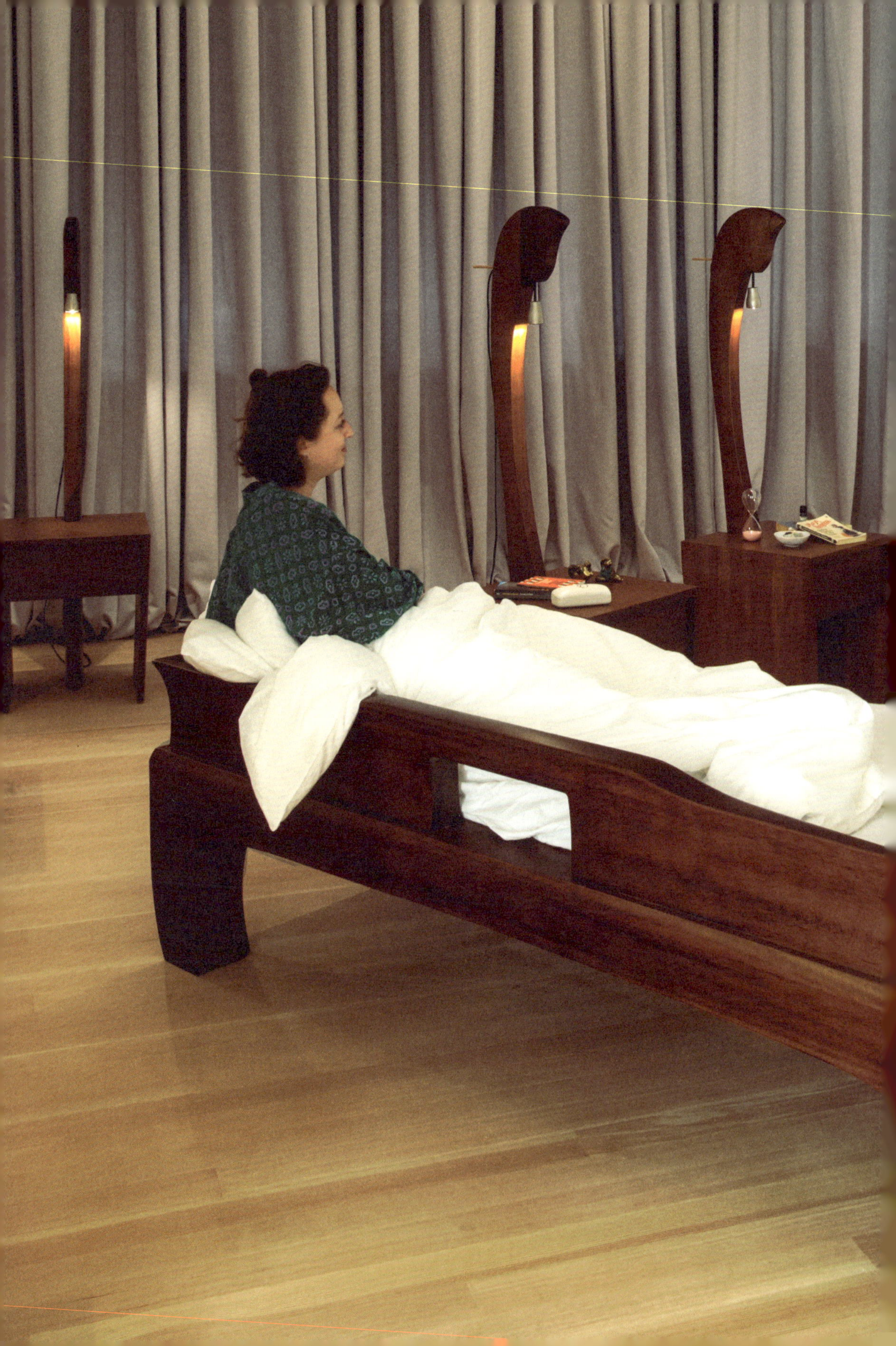

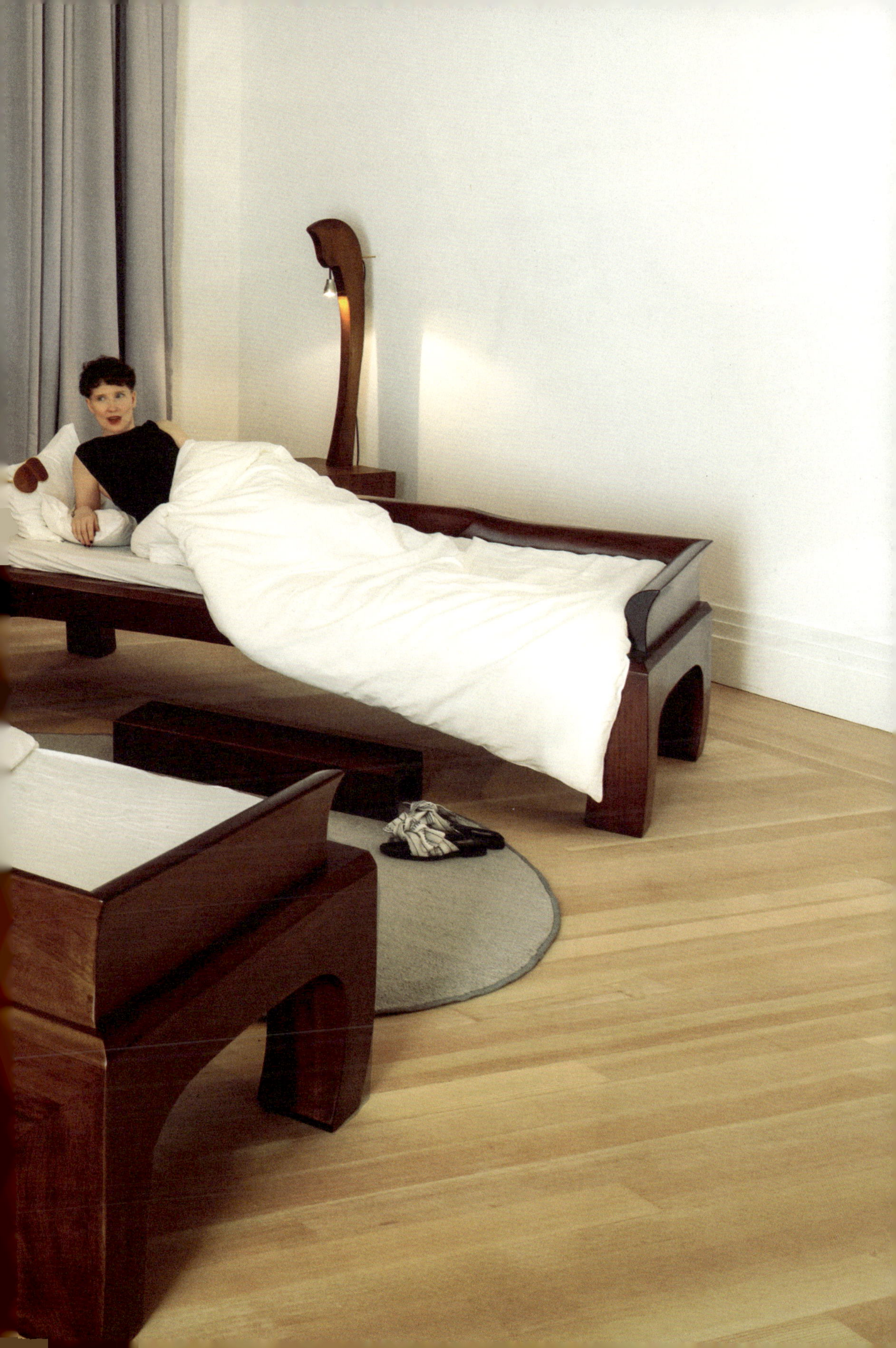

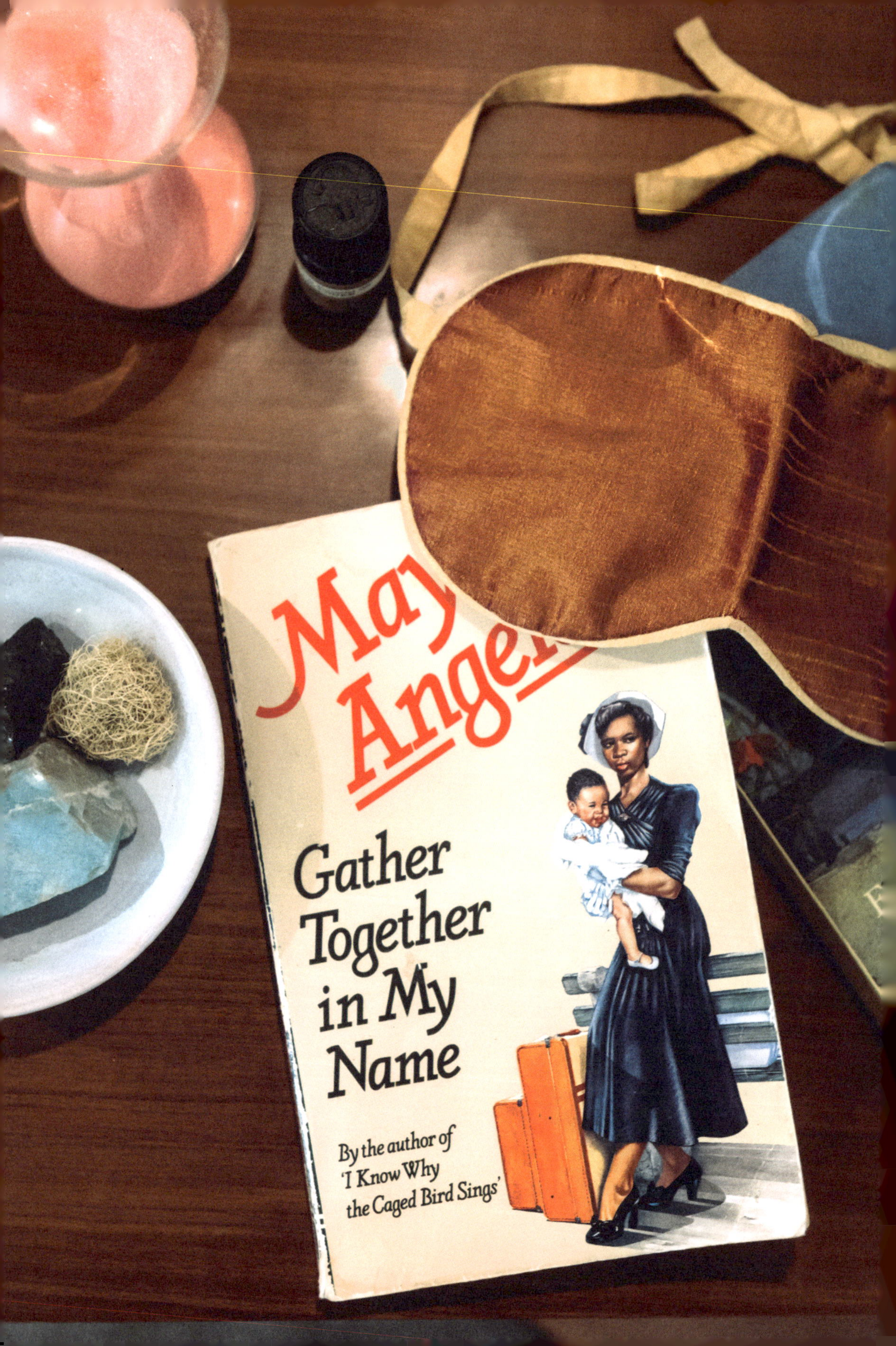
Gather Together in My Name
By the author of 'I Know Why the Caged Bird Sings'

"My sleeping companion was a young Japanese woman, a photographer studying art. We met in the Auckland Art Gallery Toi o Tāmaki at around 21:00, changed into our pajamas and lay awake talking about life, love and art for some hours. I remember the chimeric night shadows from the trees outside being cast into a tableau of forms on the walls. When we slept, I experienced a swarming of intense dreams. It seemed that the spirits came alive; hundreds of souls were busily making art and slipping from under the building into the gallery to fill the room. Although not threatening, it was as if the spectres of all those connected to the site had come alive in the darkness. I awoke at dawn to a pink light and enchanting anthropomorphic shadows dancing again from the trees into our room. My companion and I dressed, walked to the gallery's loading dock, embraced warmly, and walked our separate ways."

RHANA DEVENPORT

Former Director of the Auckland Art Gallery Toi o Tāmaki, New Zealand, which hosted *Lee Mingwei and His Relations: The Art of Participation*, in 2016

Lee Mingwei was inspired to develop *The Sleeping Project* after spending a night with a stranger in a shared train cabin, during which time he learnt about the man's very personal history. The subject of the work is, therefore, the intimacy or connection that can exist between two strangers who sleep together without sexual overtones.

# THE LIVING ROOM

## 2000 / 2020

Furniture, private collections, plants

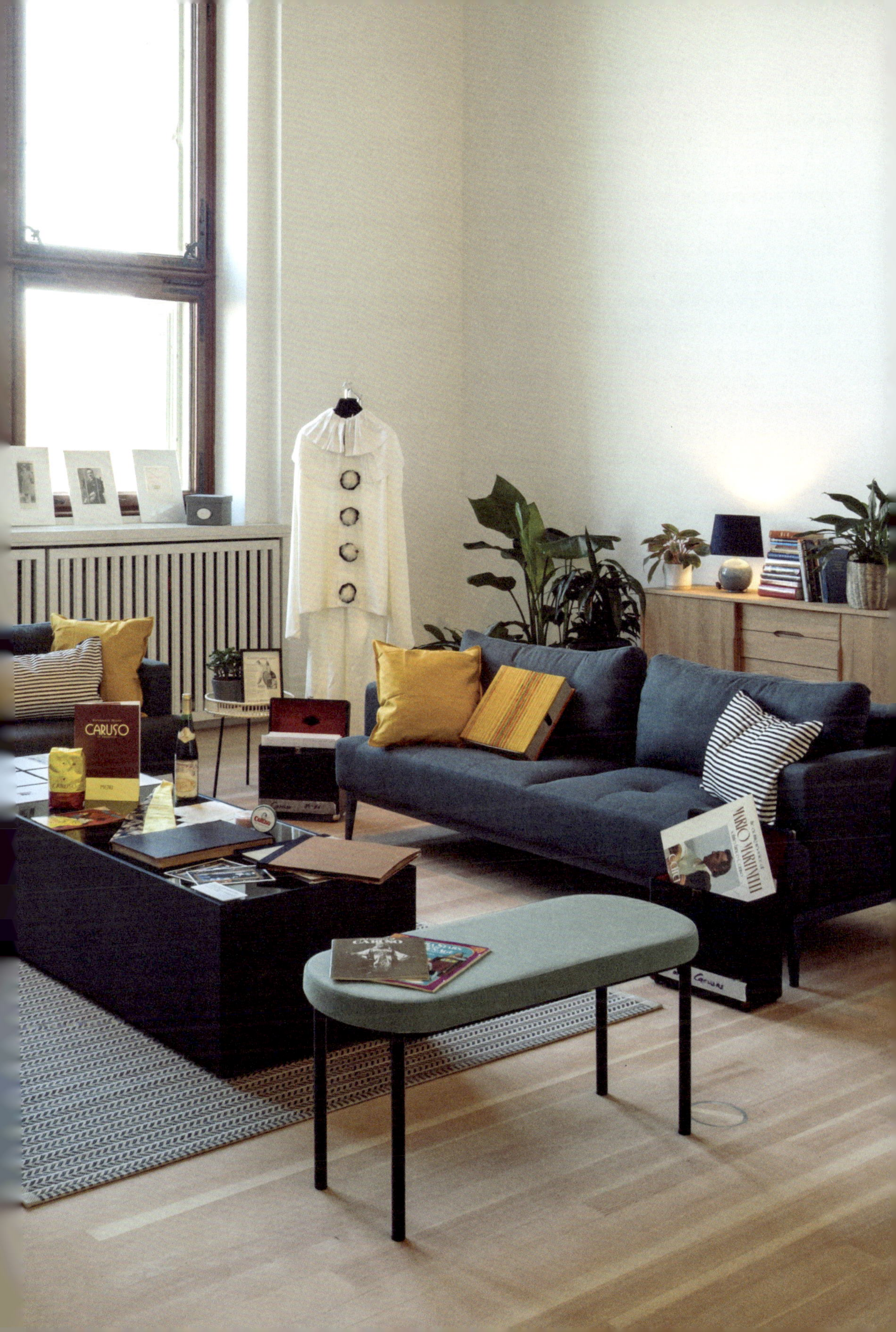
CARUSO

"I was invited by the Isabella Stewart Gardner Museum to be an artist in residence in 1999. That was my first experience of a residency programme, but after a few days I realised my project proposal was a simplistic intellectual response without much emotional spirit. I started talking to the guards and staff and each of them had a very interesting and thoughtful view on the collection and, indeed, on how Mrs Gardner might have been. I thought, wouldn't it be great if Mrs Gardner was still here to tell me more about her personal stories of acquiring the artworks? Then I thought, why not invite the museum staff to share their *own* collections. So in a sense, each of these hosts became Mrs Gardner.

She lived between 1840-1924 and was a celebrated arts patron of her time. Mrs Gardner opened her home to poets, artists, musicians and actors. According to her will, everything in the museum was to remain in the way that she had curated it. It is very interesting to consider what we collect, but moreover, to curate our personal collections and decide how these are shared with strangers.



In terms of my own collection, I have my grandmother's lacquerware, which contains some small odd object such as fossilised shells, personal seals, ancient ceramic shards, old passports, letters and photographs from my parents. This is the box that I will take if I ever find myself under extreme conditions and have to flee quickly."

LEE MINGWEI

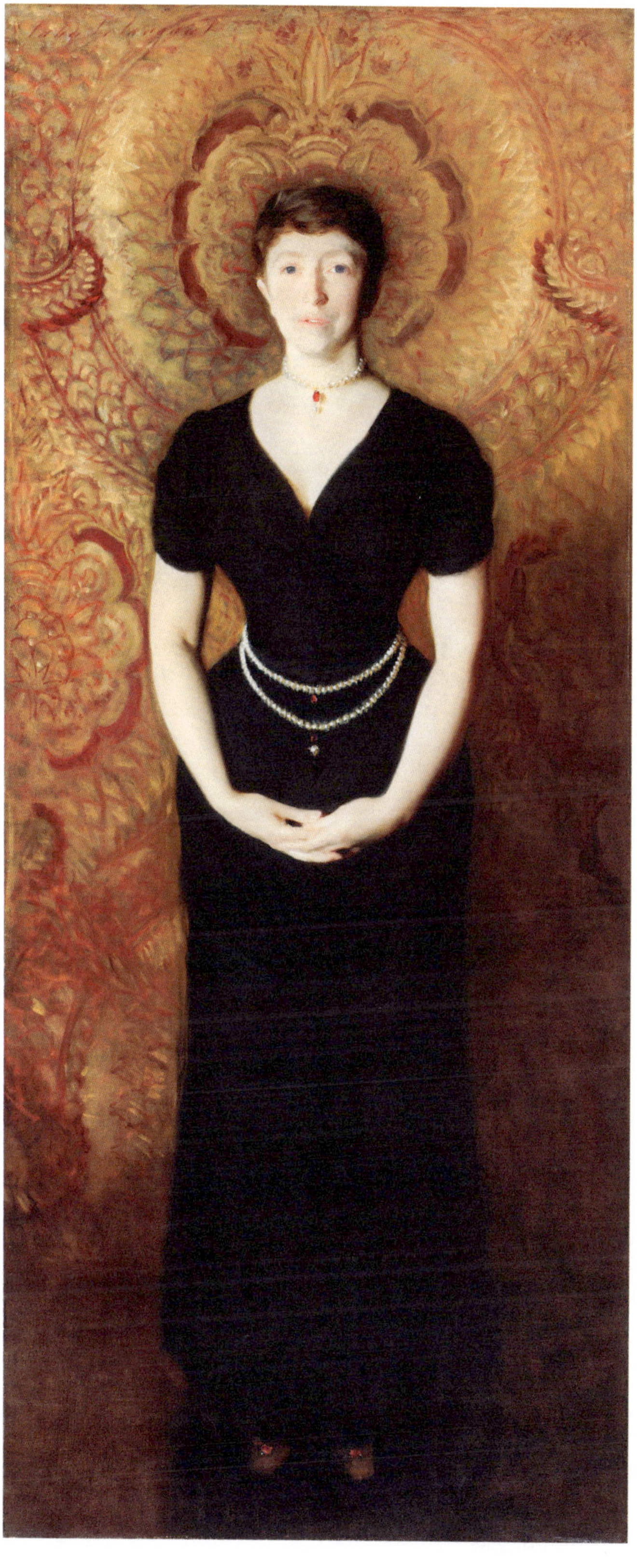

Isabella Stewart Gardner (1840-1924), depicted in this painting by John Singer Sargent, was the daughter of wealthy linen-merchant David Stewart and Adelia Smith Stewart, who became a leading American art collector and philanthropist. Initially growing up in Manhattan and travelling extensively in the Middle East and Europe, she founded the Isabella Stewart Gardner Museum in Boston in 1903, stipulating that even after her death, the permanent collection should remain unaltered. Singer Sargent is affectionately considered the museum's first artist in residence, as Isabella Stewart Gardner invited him to use the Gothic Room as his studio in 1903.

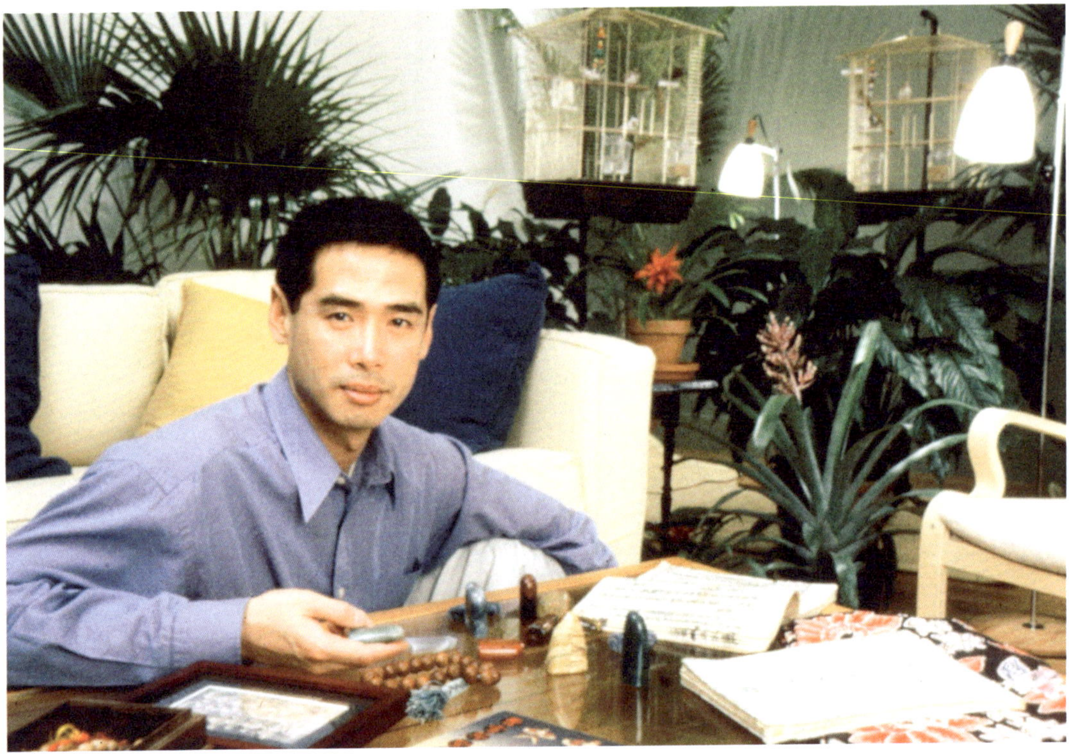



In 1992 the Isabella Stewart Gardner Museum's then director, Anne Hawley, started the artist in residence programme in order to connect with the spirit of the founder. In 1999 Lee Mingwei was in residence and his stay culminated in transforming one of the museum's galleries into a living room, allowing everyone from museum staff to local students to act as a host and share their objects of significance. Today this project is a permanent feature at the museum and enjoys a specially designed space in the institution's new wing.

"On a cold wintry morning in February 2000, I was a welcoming host in the *The Living Room*, waiting for someone to come. Four finches energetically chirped away in their cages, while I sat looking at the two paintings I had brought with me – one by Richard Yarde and another by Maud Morgan. I was eager to share my thoughts, but also felt quite exposed. The first visitors were a couple I knew: the Loves, who had been doing writing projects together since their retirement. They were warm and lively people. Although small in stature they were large in spirit. I also particularly remember a family from New Jersey with two teenage daughters. They wanted to know the dividing line between conversation with many points of view. After the second day of hosting I lost my voice. My experience had been rich and enjoyable. Mingwei's project forced me to slow down and make time for genuine conversations with visitors. The project made me forget my role as the museum's director and instead made me focus on my love for the two objects and the splendour of the people visiting the museum. *The Living Room* provided me with interactions that left a residue of deeply human connections."

ANNE HAWLEY
Director Emerita, Isabella Stewart Gardner Museum

"*The Living Room* illustrates so powerfully how small encounters, particularly between strangers, can have transformative effects. Simple shared acts of exchange help break down our unconscious assumptions about others and the world around us. Both parties are the giver and the receiver of the gift. Being a part of these personal exchanges has been a magical experience for me."

TIFFANY YORK
Contemporary Programs and Residency Manager at Isabella Stewart Gardner Museum

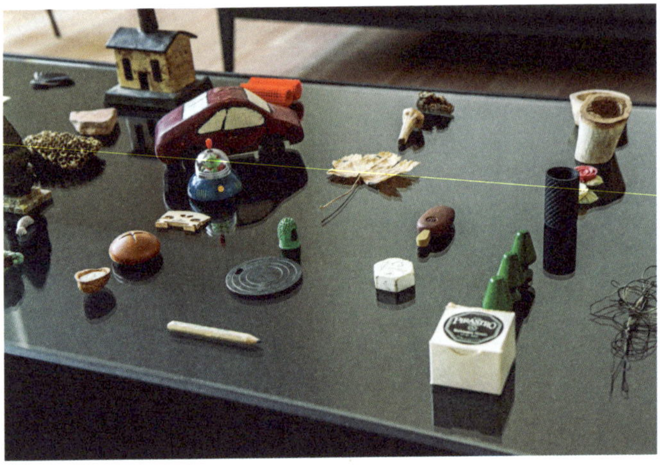

#DIESAMMLUNGEN (#THECOLLECTIONS)
Barbara Christin

My collection comprises everyday, trivial things that caught my attention: a carved toy car, a soldered house for a model railway, an egg-shaped tea strainer on a stick, a skeleton made of wire – little things that I found on the street.

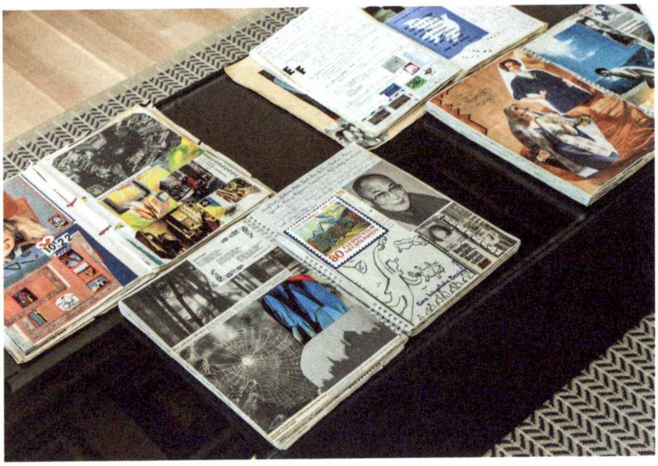

COLLAGE BOOK COLLECTION
Simon Haßler

The collection contains my grandfather's collage books; he recorded his visual impressions, ideas and experiences in around 300 books. Newspaper cuttings, personal pictures and texts are all mixed together in collages full of variety.



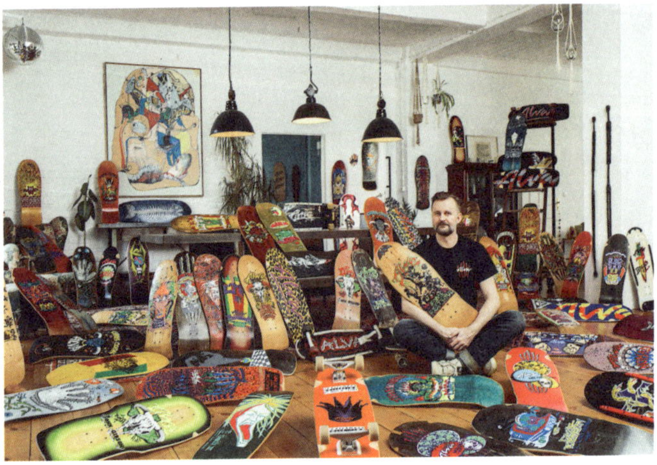

VINTAGE SKATEBOARD COLLECTION
Timo Hillbrecht

I collect old printed wood, vintage skateboards made by the ALVA brand. In addition to the history of the brand's founder, the team members and the designs, I'm fascinated by the manufacturing process and the art of the screen-print, which was used to print the boards in the past.

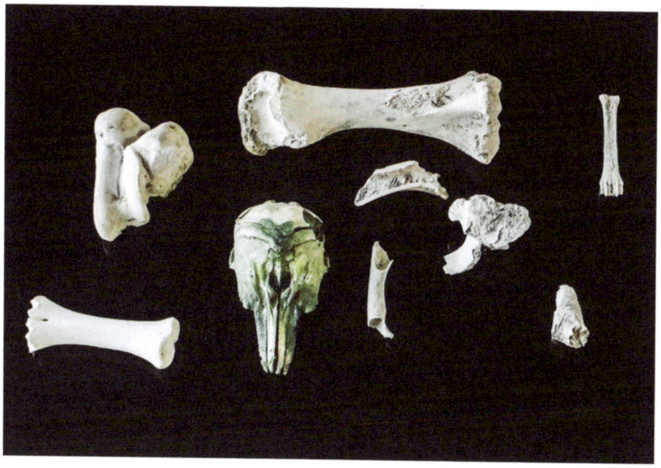

ANIMAL BONE COLLECTION
Petra Lehnardt-Olm

I collect animal bones and skulls. I am fascinated by the way structures and forms become visible during decomposition, as well as engrained traces of their "stories" and the location in which they are found, for example, the soil colour and remnants of moss. These are all items I found or were given to me.

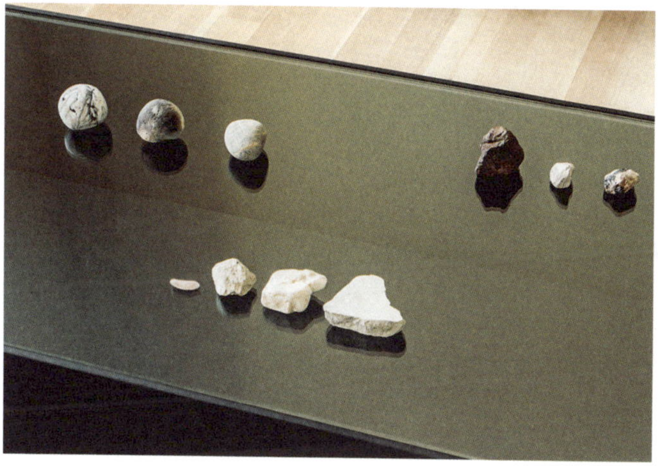

ROCK COLLECTION
Celine Loesche

My collection is of rocks. They were given to me from all over the world and I've collected some of them myself. They tell a personal story about me and the people around me. I have started a card cataloguing system for the rocks. The decision to select one particular rock always goes hand in hand with a decision against selecting another rock!



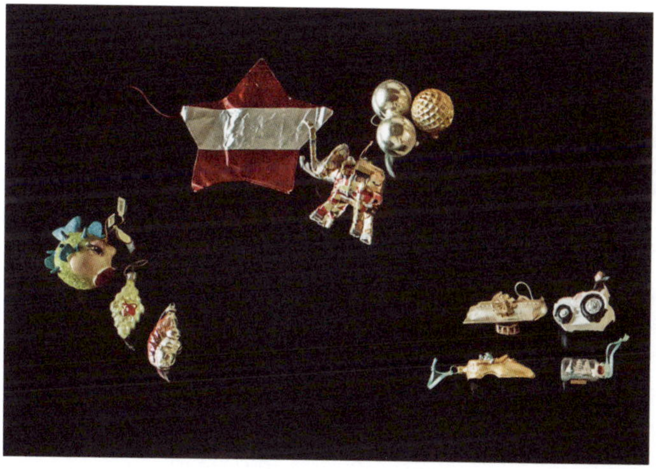

TREE DECORATION COLLECTION
Katrin Mundorf

No Christmas tree! My Christmas tree decoration collection hangs on a tree-sized wooden frame every year: old, new, tacky, home-made objects, gifts from friends, holiday souvenirs. Each piece has its own story, as does this special Christmas tree.

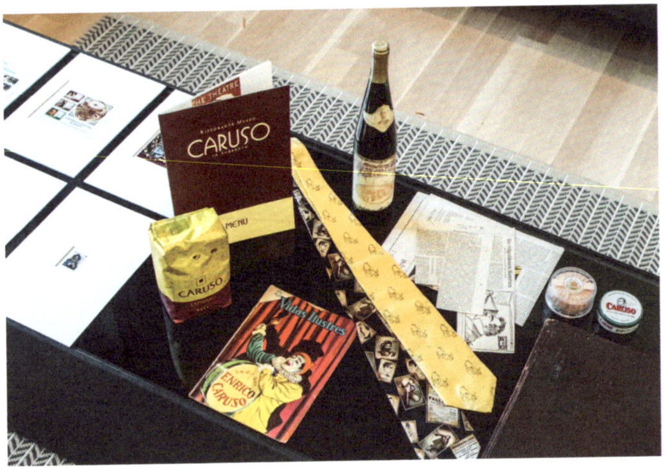


KRONENBODEN CARUSO COLLECTION
Karen Stuke

My collection's focus is Enrico Caruso: shellac records, gramophones, books, stamps, photos. It's not about whether Caruso was the best singer in the world, but rather why he has remained so iconic to this day and how his image has been handled in the past and today.

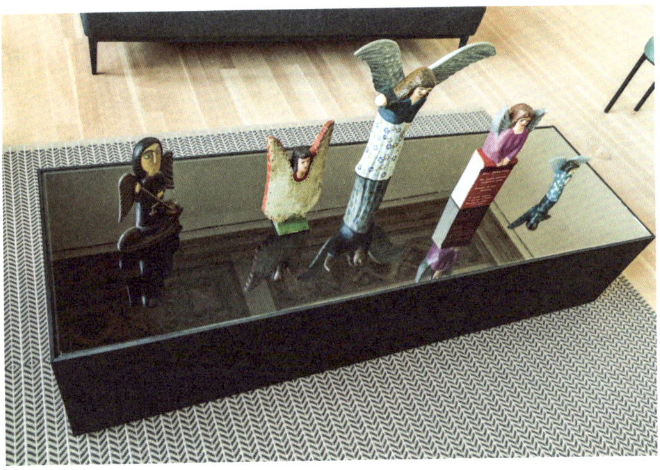

POLISH FOLK ART COLLECTION
Urszula Usakowska-Wolff

I would like to show a selection from my collection of Polish folk art, especially those items from the region of Kashubia. These are imaginative, painted figurines adorned with textual inscriptions, including fantasy-like angels with two or even four heads.

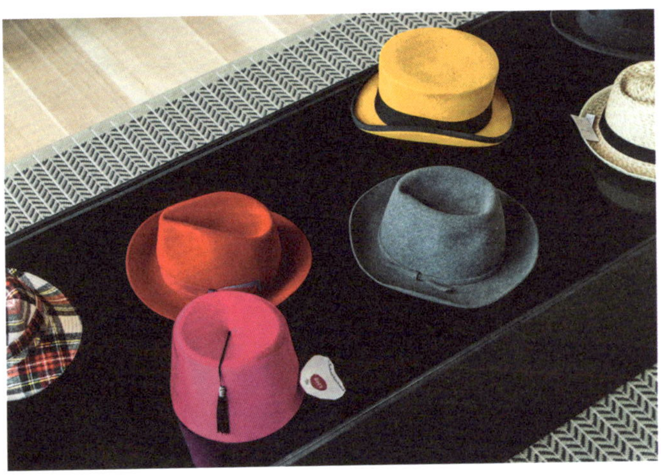

HAT COLLECTION
Stephan Wahner

I'm presenting my collection of hats. I try to purchase these hats in different cities and towns.

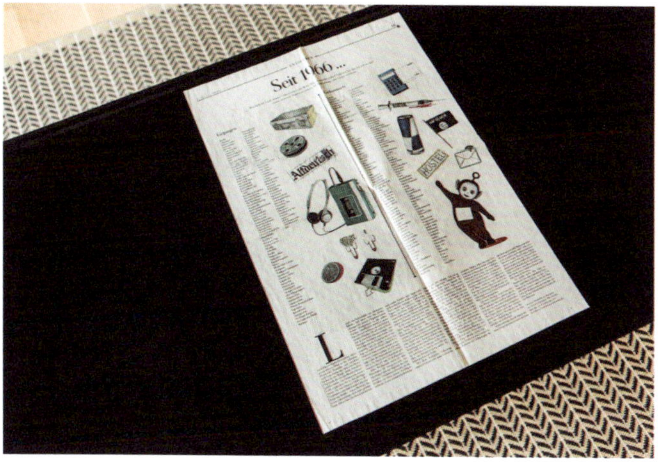


SINCE 1966 - TWO LISTS
Thomas Oberender

On my 50th birthday I began to make a list of things that have been invented since 1966, and another list of things that have disappeared from the world I live in since then. Things orientate us in time and also in society, they are associated with our origins, status and with our consciousness of ourselves.

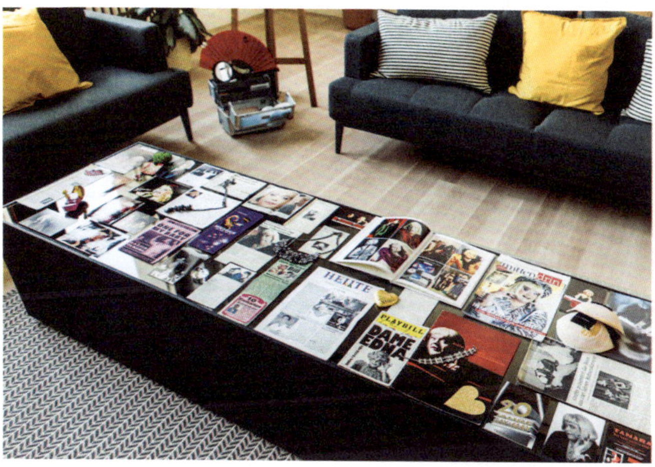


23 YEARS OF COUNTESS TAMARA
Jens Dierkes aka Countess Tamara

My collection displays memories of 23 years on the stage, with around 920 shows of my drag theatre act *Gräfin Tamara*. This special combination of 154 *chanson* numbers and 100% spontaneous interaction with the audience closed with a final show in the WABE in Berlin on 2nd May 2020.

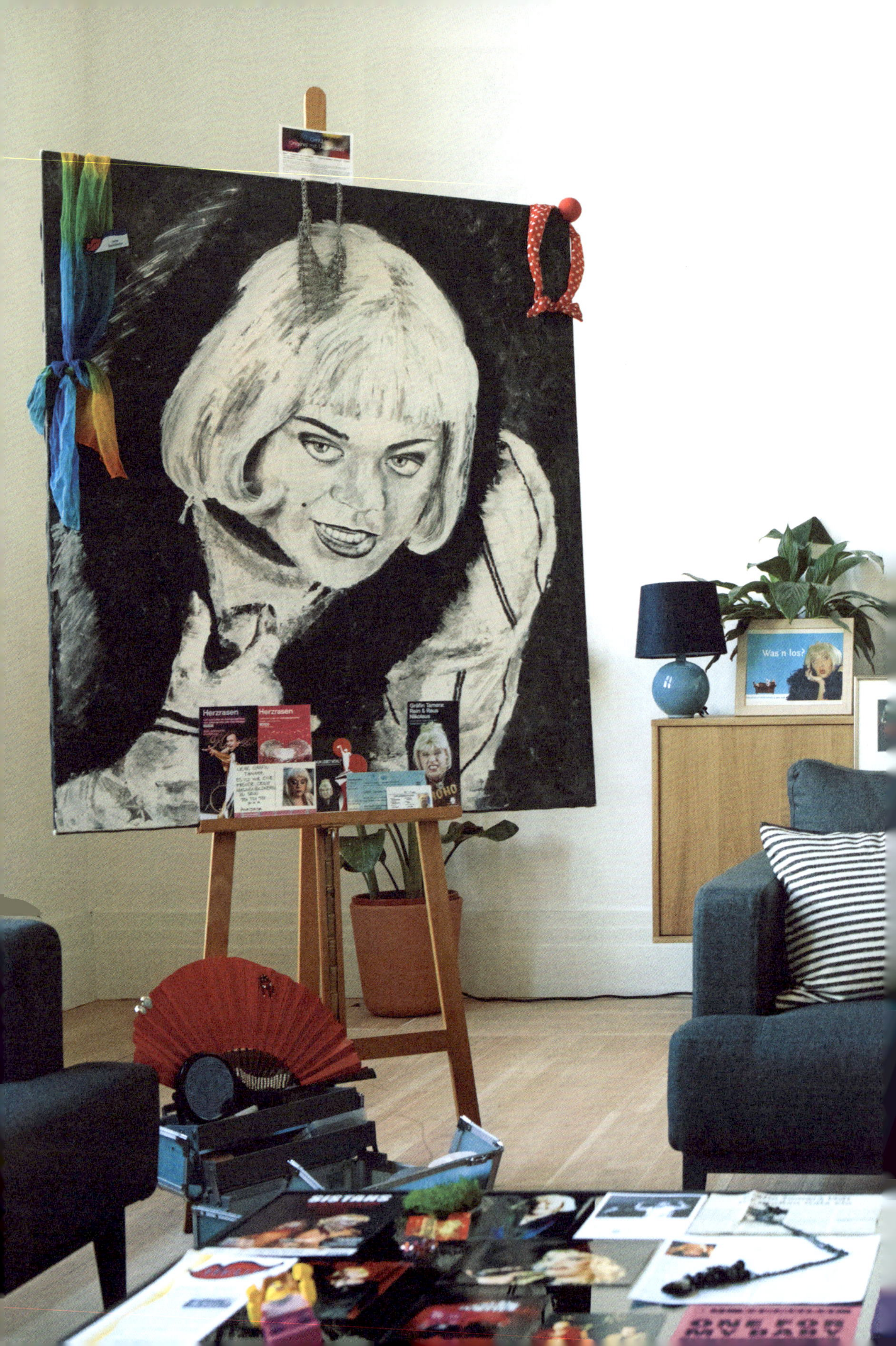
Herzrasen
Herzrasen
Gräfin Tamara: Rein & Raus Nikolaus
Was'n los?

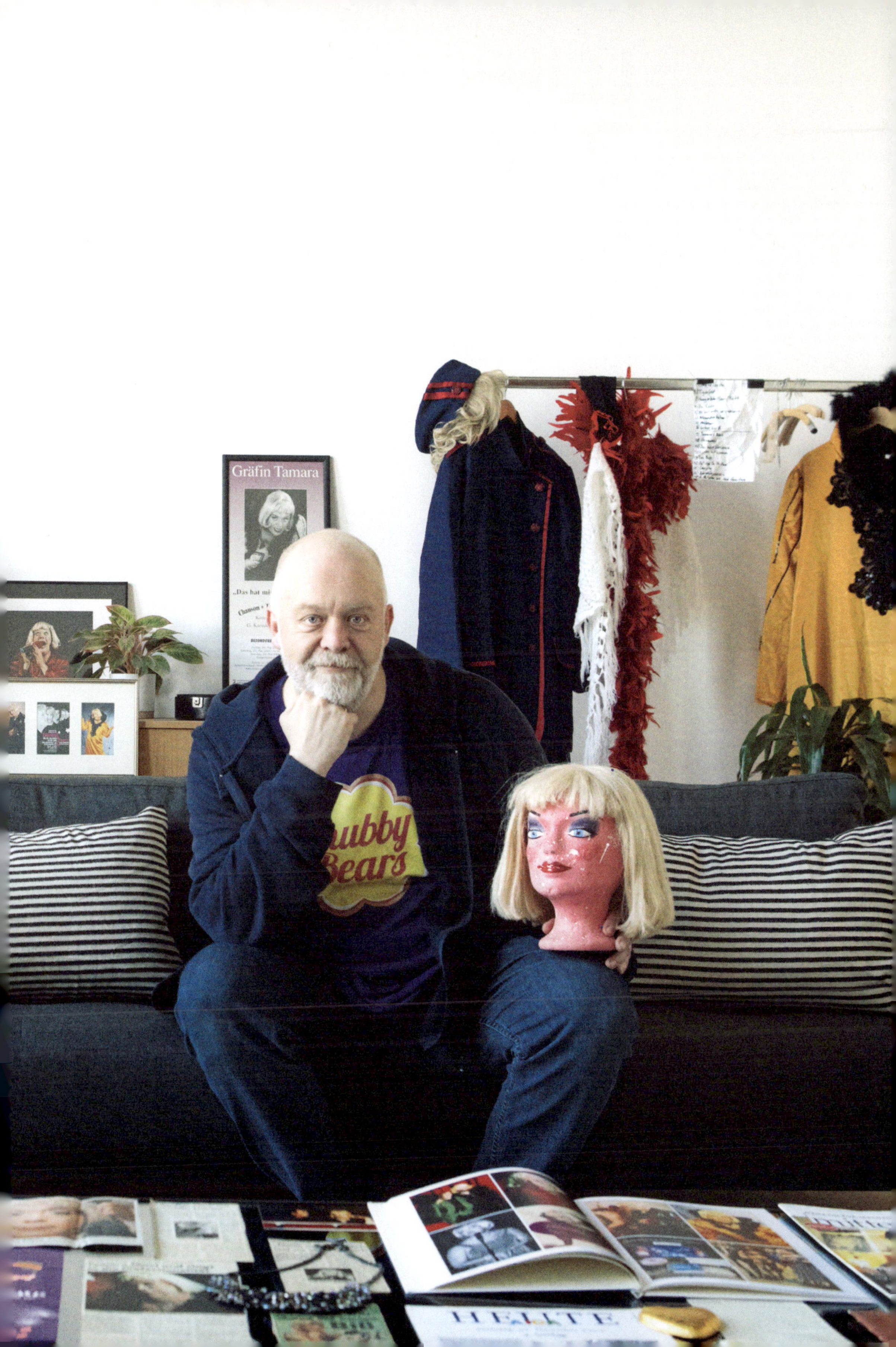
Gräfin Tamara

# THE TOURIST

## 2001/2020

Wooden vitrine, wooden boxes, personal items, two-channel video, sound
52 min., 30 sec.

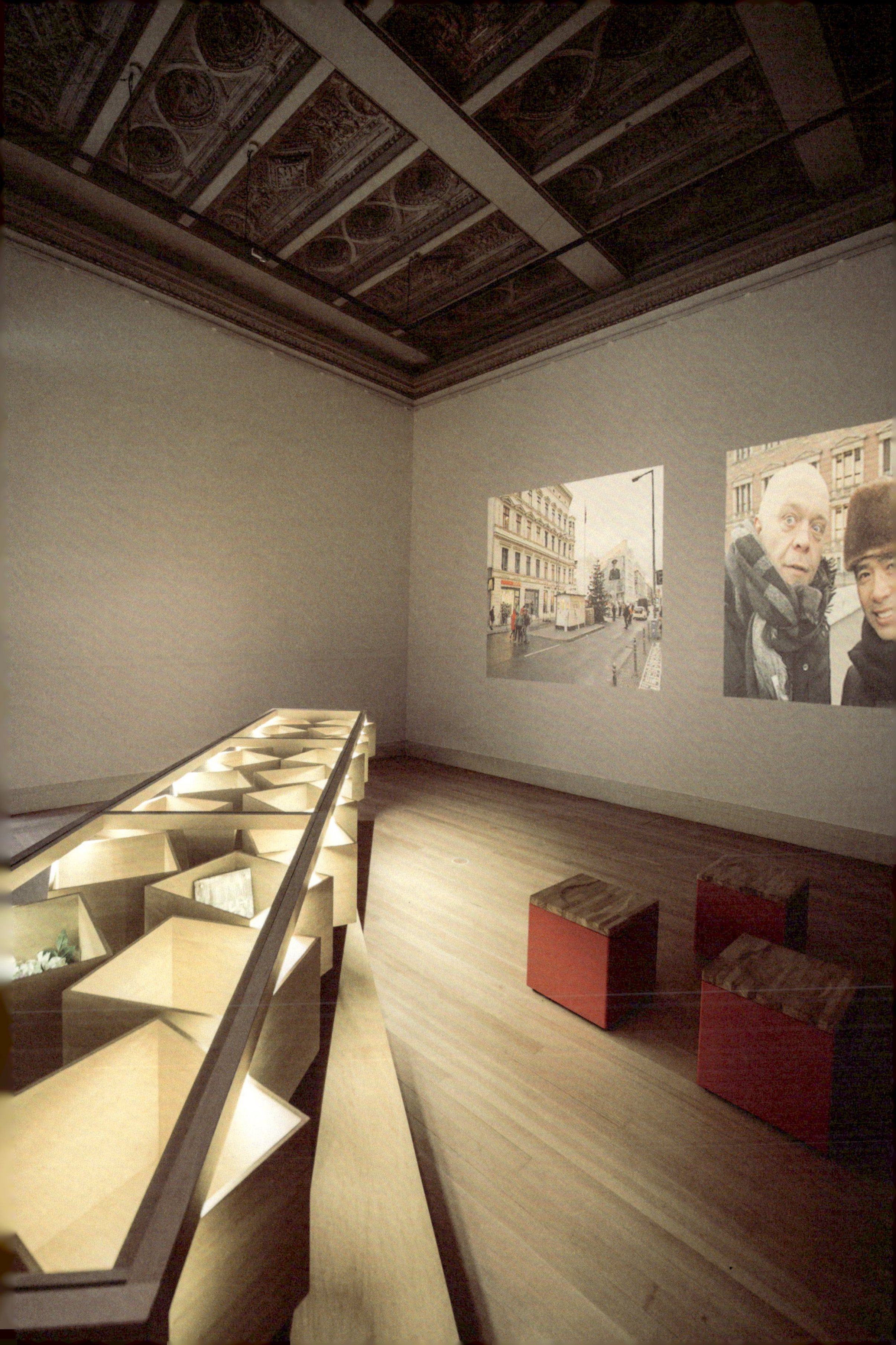

With the original idea for *The Tourist* beginning in Rome, iterations of the work have now taken place in numerous cities around the world, with individuals giving Lee Mingwei a tour in places including Tainan, New York and Paris.

"Sean, my nephew who grew up in Rome, took me to see the Roman Forum when he was very young. I was surprised by his way of guiding me through this historical site, which was directed by his mental map of where all the cat families lived. Instead of visiting the ruins, I was able to see a historical site through the eyes of a six-year-old boy. The ancient city came alive. *The Tourist* resulted. The work is about people seeing things that are familiar to them through a stranger's eyes.

If I am hosting a tour in Paris, I often take friends to visit the farmers' markets and the magnificent cathedrals. Another of my favourite things to do is to walk from our home in the Marais district to the Luxembourg Gardens, which passes historical sites such as Place des Vosges, Notre-Dame de Paris, Hôtel de Ville and Jardin des Plantes. We often stop by my favourite coffee shop for a break near Notre-Dame. As for New York, where I also live, I often take friends for a morning walk starting in Brooklyn Heights. We then walk through Dumbo and over the Brooklyn Bridge to have lunch in Chinatown. It is often about beautiful sites, delicious coffee, cakes and dim sum."

LEE MINGWEI



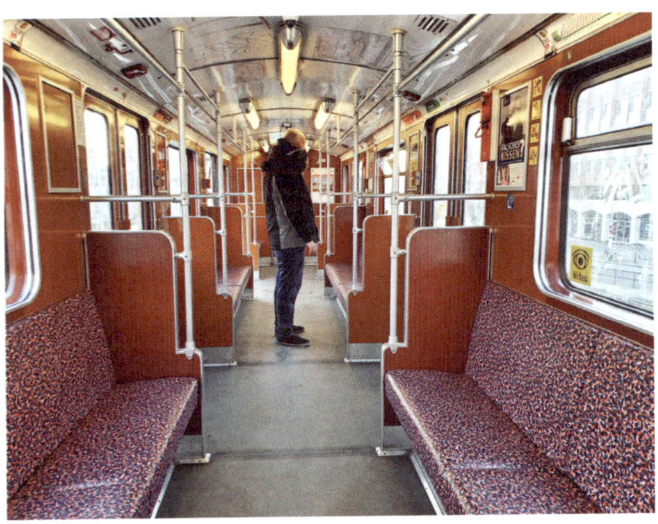

"I moved to Berlin 14 years ago. At that time I was working as an Assistant Director at the Schaubühne and I lived in Kreuzberg, on Nostitzstrasse. For our city walk in the context of the *The Tourist*, I decided to visit places from my past with Mingwei. Firstly I showed him Alexanderplatz, then Berghain or rather Panorama Bar, where I spend a lot of time with my husband. Afterwards we went to Warschauer Straße train station and parts of the Kreuzberg 61 district. These are all places that hold memories of my personal LGBT history here in Berlin."

JENS DIERKES

A member of Gropius Bau's Welcome Team / Secura Protect

In January 2020, Jens Dierkes took Lee Mingwei on a personal tour of Berlin in the latest iteration of this work. These photographs depict the artist standing at Checkpoint Charlie, a former crossing point between East Berlin and West Berlin during the Cold War, and Jens Dierkes riding Berlin's subway, the U-Bahn, in an otherwise empty carriage.

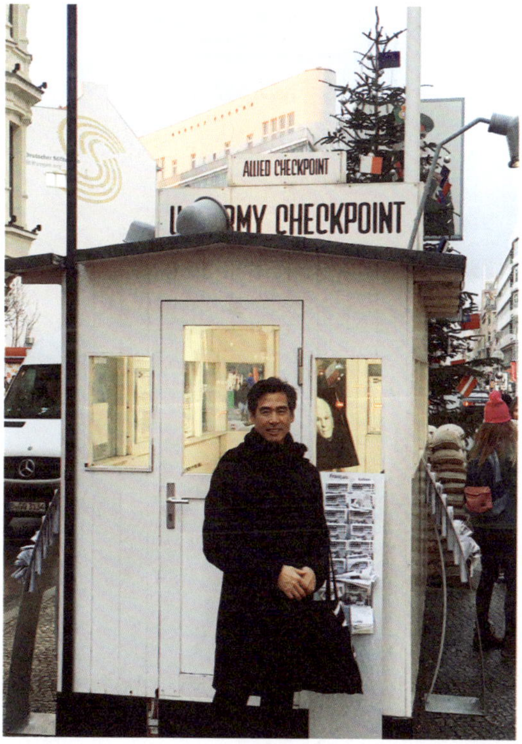

“I wanted to take Lee Mingwei to a place called Kunitachi, where I had a wonderful memory from my childhood. I hadn’t visited for a long time and for me it was a journey that allowed me to experience these childhood memories. The cherry blossom trees were beautiful at that time. It is a place where the Shinkansen bullet train was developed, as well as a place where I once played. I wanted Mingwei to experience an idyllic cityscape in a suburban residential area, far from the city centre. Of course it is part of Tokyo, but it is where the ordinary people of Tokyo live. Through this experience, and Mingwei’s kindness, I realised that you can walk the same cityscape and have a different perspective. Feeling different experiences in the same place and talking about each other’s impressions and experiences is, in a sense, giving a gift to each other. I wanted him to experience my tour as my poetry.”

TARO SHINODA

Host of *The Tourist*, who took Lee Mingwei on a tour in Tokyo in 2019 as part of the Perrotin exhibition

Placed in this wooden vitrine are personal items that were collected on the tours on which Lee Mingwei has been taken, and behind is a two-channel video that depicts some of the scenes encountered.

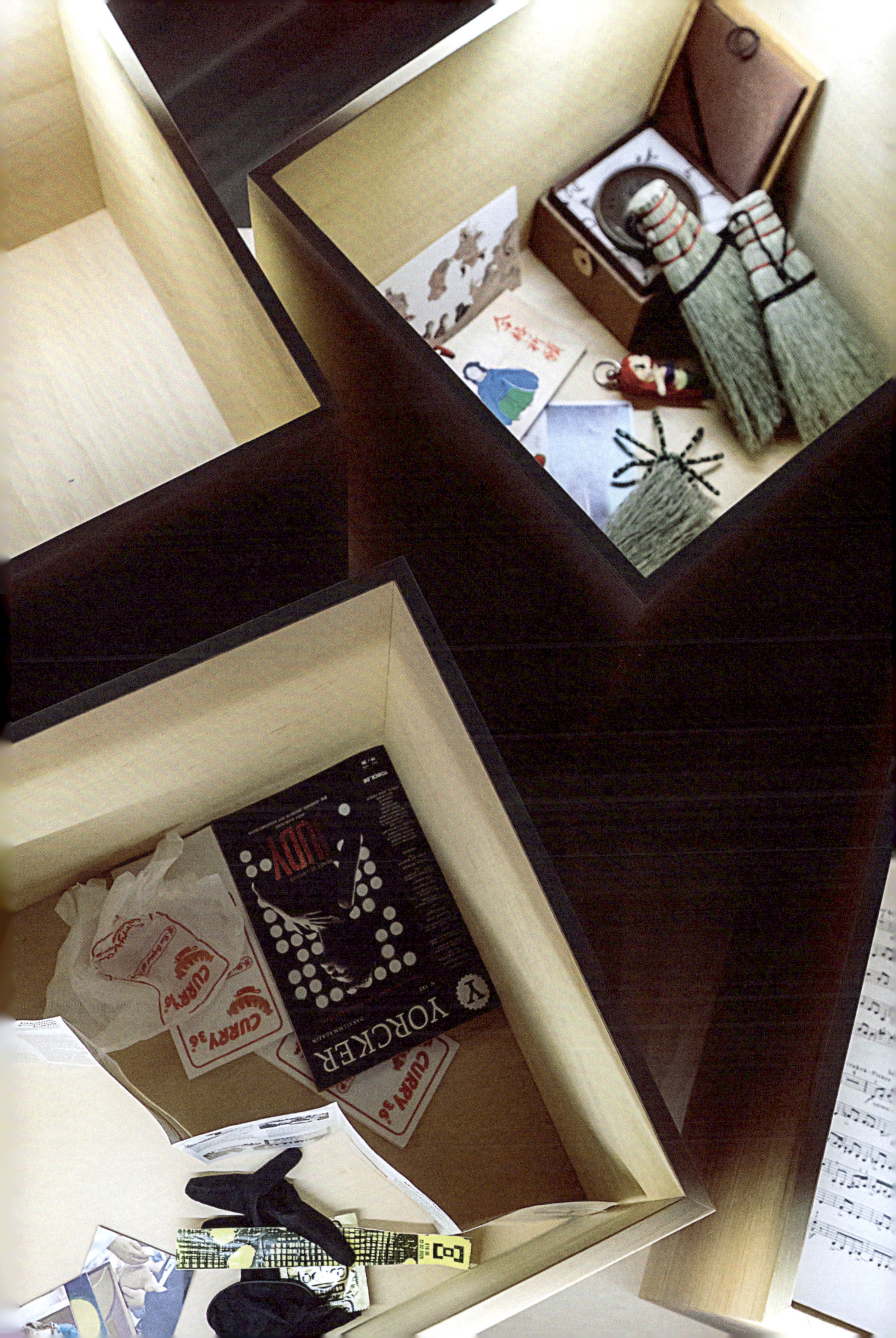
YORCKER
CURRY 36

# NU WA PROJECT

2005

Bamboo, silk, cotton thread, acrylic
350 x 112 cm

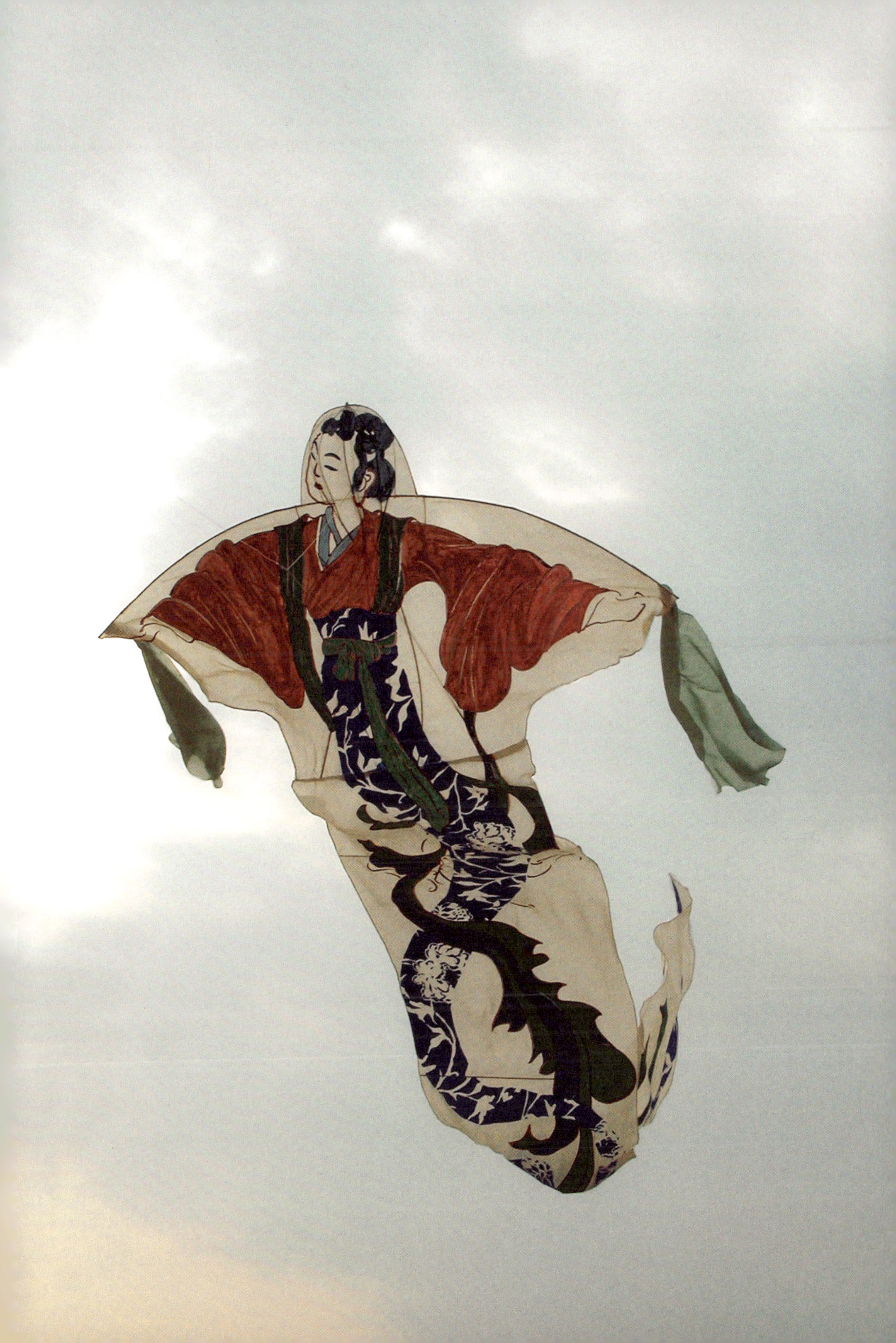

"Nu Wa was a Chinese mythical goddess who was both a creator and a maintainer. She patched up a huge hole in the sky by using the dreams she had collected from her children (and these children, in a sense, are us). The idea with the *Nu Wa Project* is that whoever owns this kite must write their dreams on the silk. Once it has been filled with their dreams, they must fly the kite as far as it goes and then cut the string, allowing Nu Wa to patch up the hole in the sky. I collaborated with the kite maker, Master Hsieh, creating one of his last large-scale works, as well as with Chao Yu-Hsiu, who painted the image of Nu Wa upon the silk surface. Master Hsieh had to teach me how to fly a kite made with hand-woven silk, which must be handled in a completely different way to polyester kites."

LEE MINGWEI

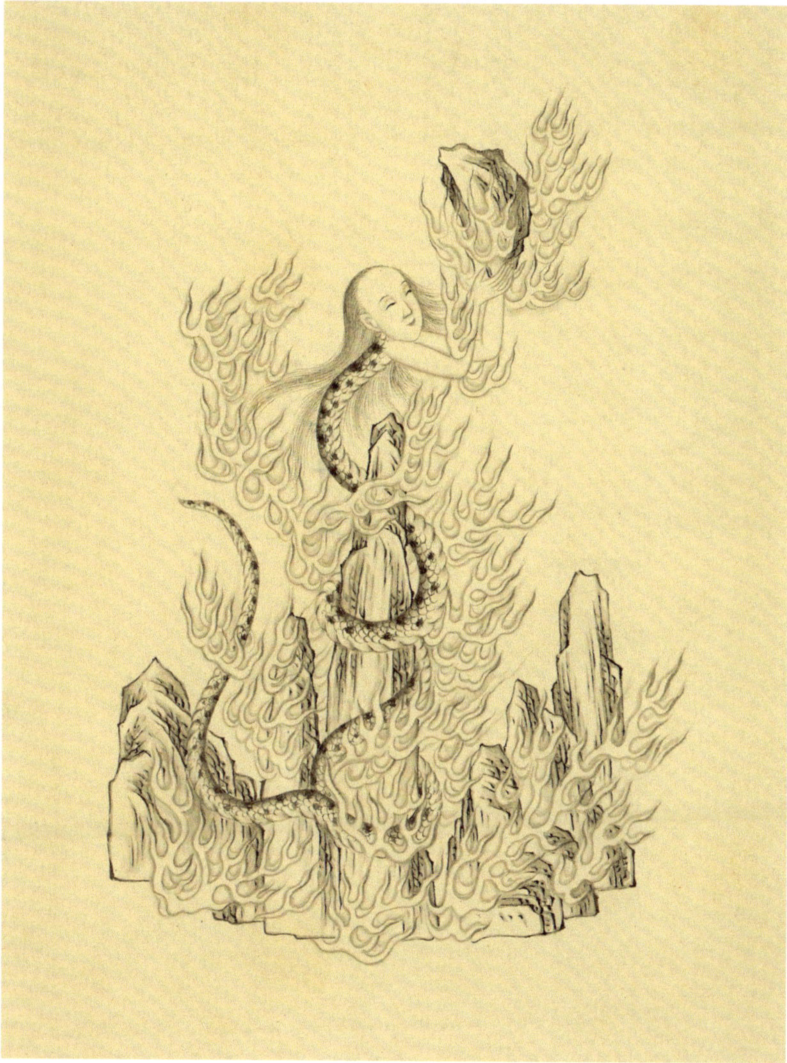

This print depicts the Chinese myth of Nu Wa, specifically showing the mother goddess repairing the Pillar of Heaven. An ancient Chinese text, the *Huainanzi*, describes Nu Wa at a time when the heavens and earth had been disrupted. As fires blazed and waters flooded, the heavens no longer completely covered the earth, and earth could not hold up the heavens. Nu Wa melted stones to a paste and repaired the sky and so protected her creation, humankind.

# FABRIC OF MEMORY

2006 / 2020

Wooden platform, wooden boxes, fabric items
485 x 485 x 65 cm

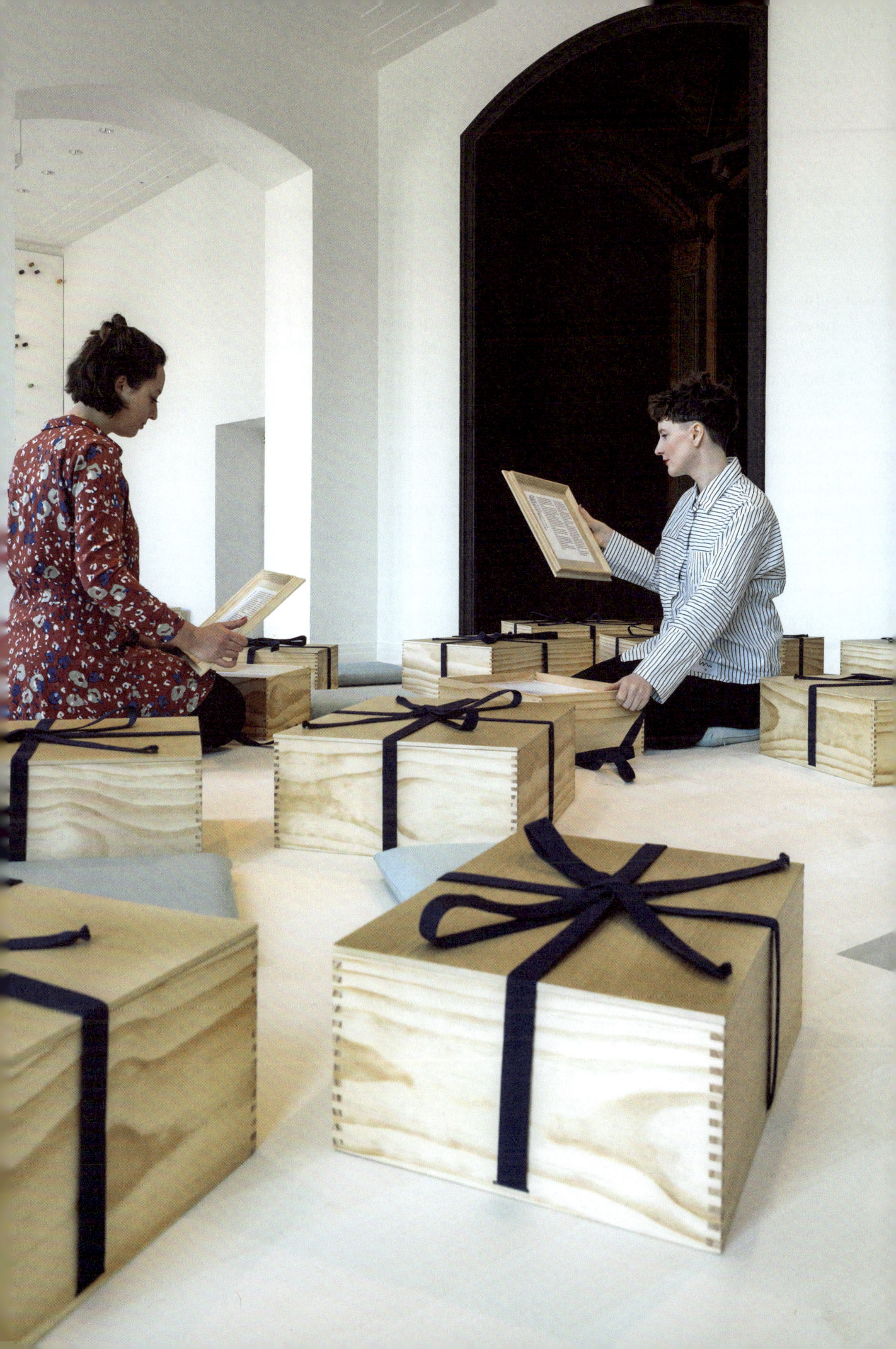

"For this work, I ask volunteers to provide a textile that has a personal story. Placed in a wooden box, when the audience opens this, they are able to read the personal story along with seeing the piece of textile. The platform installation is important: I ask each participant to take off their shoes before stepping on to the platform because this is a clear way to create an intimate physical and psychological space to experience these stories.

The work relates to my first day of kindergarten, which I can still remember. My mother was holding my hand. I have a photograph of the day and in it you can see I was in a bad mood because I didn't want to go to school. Being a clever and thoughtful person, my mum spent the six months prior learning how to sew in order to make what I was wearing that day. She said, 'when you miss mum, please imagine that I am holding you now, because you are wearing everything that I made.' I wish I still had these clothes; they were my second skin and gave me warmth and courage to go to kindergarten.

When this project was shown at Tokyo's Shiseido Gallery after the 2011 earthquake and tsunami, I remember vividly there was a water-damaged kimono. This was the only thing the lady was able to take with her when water gushed into her house. It was an heirloom kimono passed to her from her great grandmother."



LEE MINGWEI

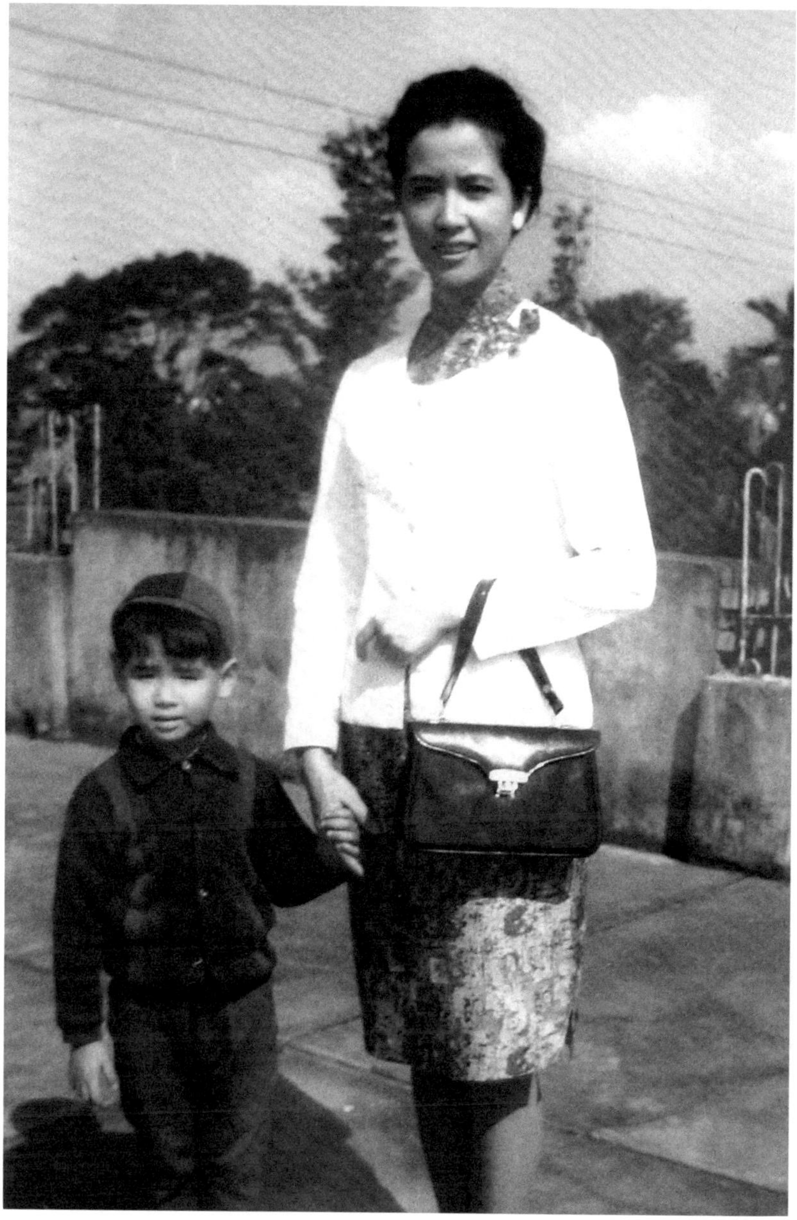

In this black-and-white photograph, a young Lee Mingwei stands with his mother on the first day of kindergarten, wearing the outfit that she had sewed for him in its entirety.

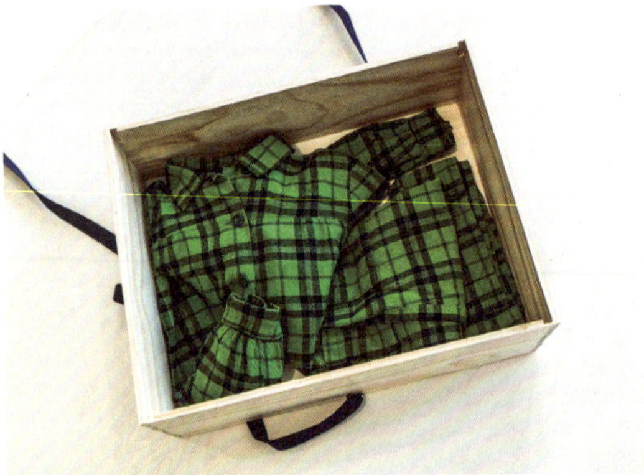

HOUSECOAT

This housecoat, upon which time has passed by without leaving a mark, was sewn for my mother by my grandmother 45 years ago. Back then, she sewed two housecoats from the same fabric: a big one for my mother and a little one for me. My grandmother had been taught to sew by a ladies' dressmaker in a Basque village. The large housecoat has survived every house move and every thorough spring clean since the 1970s. I've worn it many times and every time I wear it, it gives me strength.

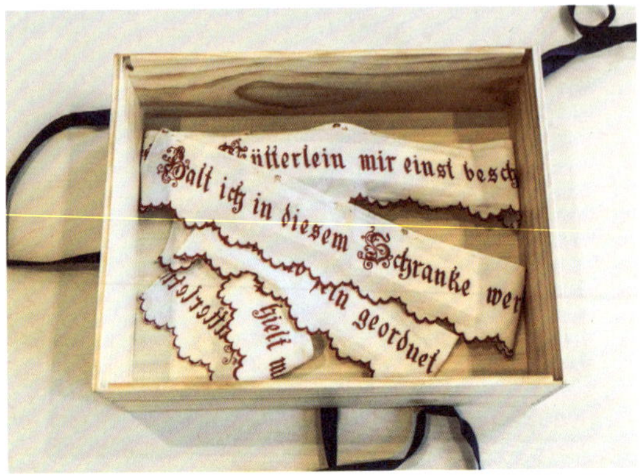

EMBROIDERED CUPBOARD TRIM

*This which my dear mother once bestowed upon me, / will keep all in this cupboard orderly, / evenly and carefully arranged here, / as' [sic] it once was kept tidy by my mother dear*

This embroidered saying decorated my grandmother's cupboard. When, suffering from dementia, she moved into a nursing home, my mother removed the yellowed trim and washed it. She gave it to me to take to my grandmother when I visited her. After that, my grandmother praised me effusively every time I went. It didn't register with her that she owed the thanks to her daughter-in-law. It's become a fond anecdote for us.

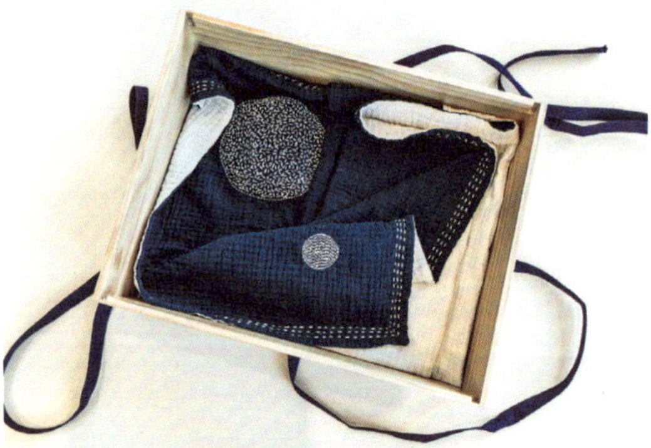

MOON BLANKET

This is my "moon blanket". It looks like a sky with moons made of rice and rain. A farmer in the mountains near the Mekong stitched the moons. My mom lived in Asia for a long time. Before my birth, she came to Berlin but could not sleep. She was lonely and wrote a story for me about a little sleepless rabbit that is picked up by the moon each night to travel through the sky. My Mami made my blanket bit by bit. I can wrap myself in it all throughout my life or give it to my baby later.

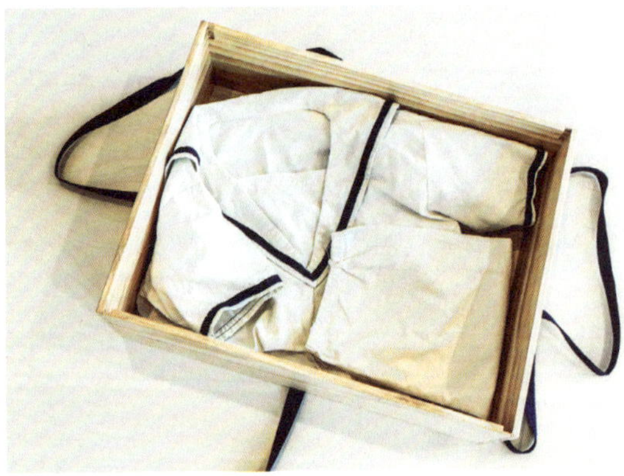

LITTLE SAILOR

When I was eleven years old, I was chosen to play the Baron and in the last scene of *C'era due volte il Barone Lamberto*. I had to enter the stage dressed like a child. My grandmother sewed for me the "little sailor" outift in one night. In my twenties, I applied to the Theatre Academy and I started to work as a professional actor. The pretty white sailor outfit now stays well protected in my drawer, reminding me of when I was a chubby, shy kid. When my grandmother died, I felt that she took the chubby dreamy child with her, for good.

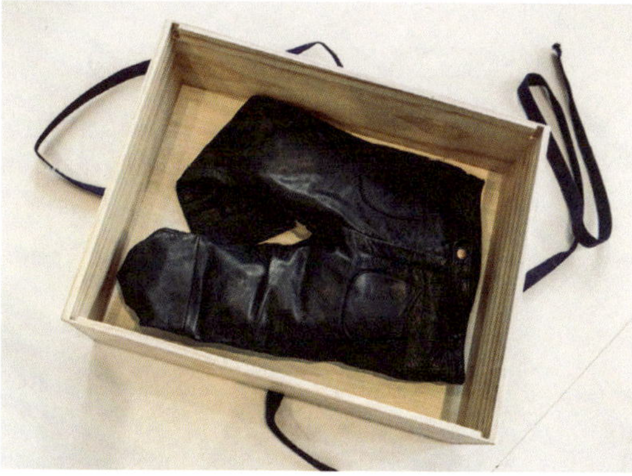

LEATHER TROUSERS

A sturdy pair of trousers that I only occasionally have to grease, that won't wear out when my child is crawling on his knees again – that's always been my dearest wish. My father made that wish come true. He made up a pattern and got the leather. My child had those trousers a long time and loved wearing them. They practically grew with him, we just kept folding the legs down. Whenever I see those trousers I think of my father and smell that scent that was so typical of him: a pipe, leather and saddle grease.

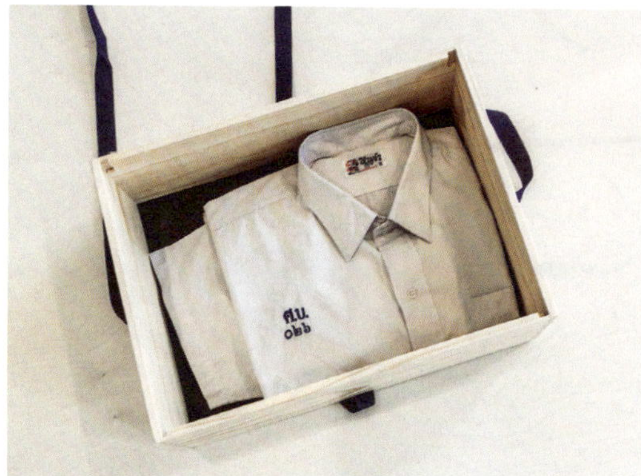

THAI SCHOOL SHIRT

This is the shirt from the school uniform that I wore from 1994-1995 as an exchange student at the Sri Boonyanon School in Nonthaburi, Thailand. My host parents bought it for me. The numbers 026 are embroidered on the chest, because I was the 26th student to come from abroad. My shirts were dirty and sweaty at the end of every day because I did a lot of sport in the breaks and after school. So I had to take care of the pre-washing process myself. It was my host father who first introduced me to the high art of ironing.

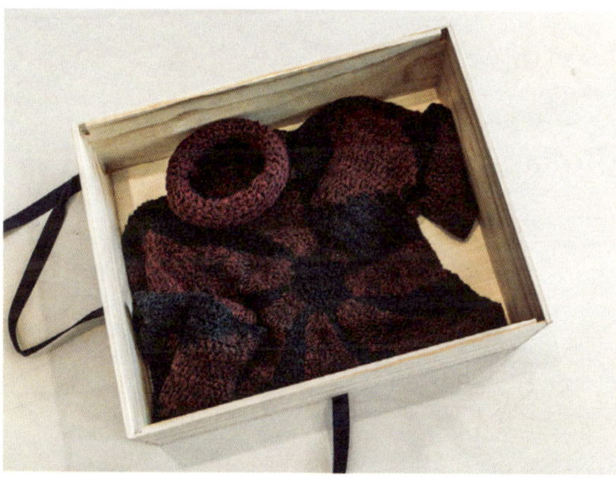

HAND-CROCHETED SWEATER

My mother knitted a sweater with the burgundy yarn for my father, shortly after they married, in 1961, New Jersey. It was passed on to me when I was a teenager in the 1980s and was one of my favourite pieces of clothing, travelling with me wherever I went. I then passed it onto a close friend who had fallen in love with it and subsequently moved to California. That is where I found it again years later. I brought it home with me to Berlin, where I unravelled the yarn and used it along with some newly purchased black yarn to make this spider-web-patterned sweater.

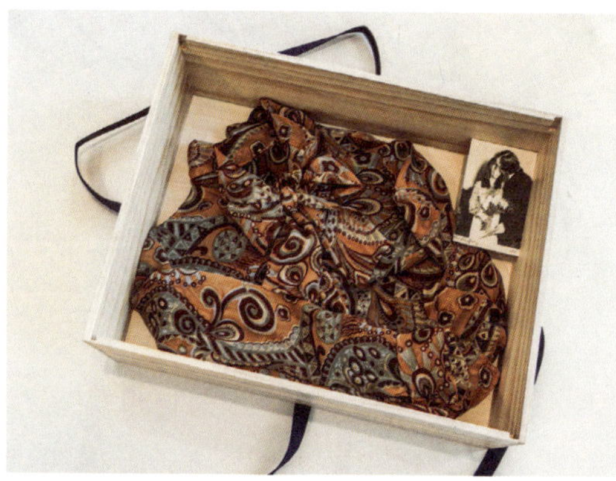

WEDDING BLOUSE

We married in Halle in May 1975. It was a small wedding, as we were students and didn't have much money, and our son was just two months old. A white princess dress was out of the question. We decided on a long, white skirt and looked for a matching blouse. We found a delicate, patterned silk fabric, but what to do with two metres of silk? My husband sewed the blouse together on the evening before our wedding using my mother's sewing machine – which I had never been allowed to use.

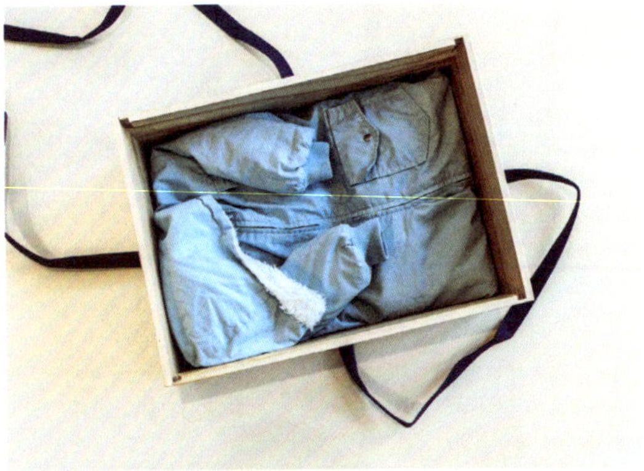

BLUE JUMPSUIT

This blue jumpsuit is the only piece of childhood clothing that I still own. It has accompanied me through the years. There are plenty of photos in our family album, in which I wore this jumpsuit. I was one or two years old. Now, after 41 years, when I look at those photos, the first thing I feel is safety. The jumpsuit was a birthday present from my uncle, who lost his sight when he was just six. I believe that my childhood jumpsuit tells a lot about the relationship between my mum and her older brother. Some years ago, she gave it to my wife. The blue jumpsuit still keeps us company!

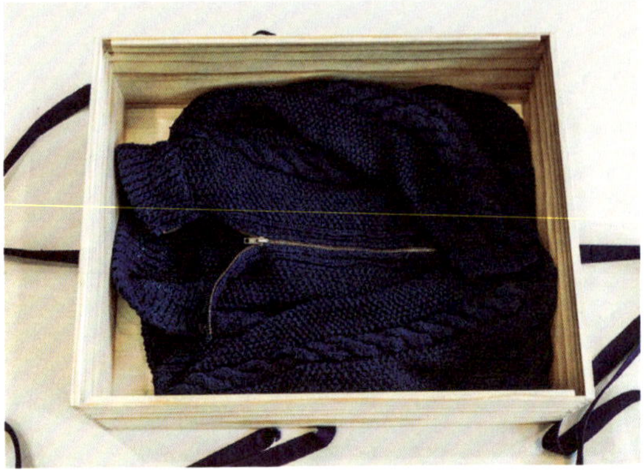

CARDIGAN

My mother knitted this cardigan for me one Christmas. I loved it right away: it sat perfectly, I was intrigued by the cable-knit pattern and she had taken care to work in a metal zip. My mother died suddenly after an illness. We had barely had any contact for a year, but fortunately, we had just started talking again shortly before her death. I wear this cardigan again now - so a little bit of my mother is still with me.



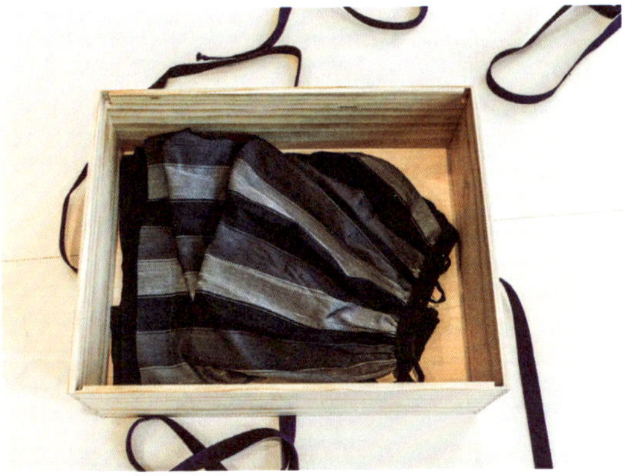

*GIRLS IN UNIFORM*-SKIRT

When I was around 14 years old, I was allowed to design a skirt that my grandmother would then sew for me. She was a ladies' dressmaker and I wanted a skirt like the costumes in the film *Mädchen in Uniform* (Girls in Uniform), 1958, in which Romy Schneider is in love with her female teacher. My skirt keeps alive the memory of my deceased grandmother, her dressmaking artistry and matriarchal authority, and also my first realisation that other girls also fall in love with their female teachers.

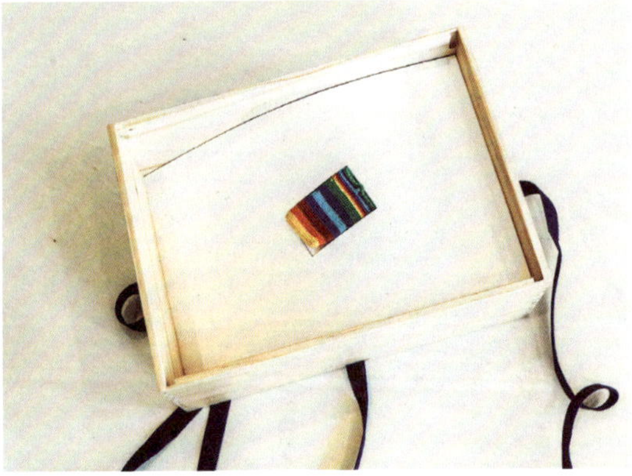

OCTOPUS CARD HOLDER

When I moved to Hong Kong, I lost my Octopus Card for the public transportation system many times before a close friend made this cardholder. While I lived in Hong Kong, I learnt to listen better, to care more, to jointly tell stories through exchanging words and small gestures of love. I also learnt that things change. My friends now leave their Octopus Cards at home as an act of resistance. They go on the streets to fight for their freedom, their love, their home. The fragile joy and the memories of the cardholder remind me that we are all relentlessly knitting and crocheting this world together.

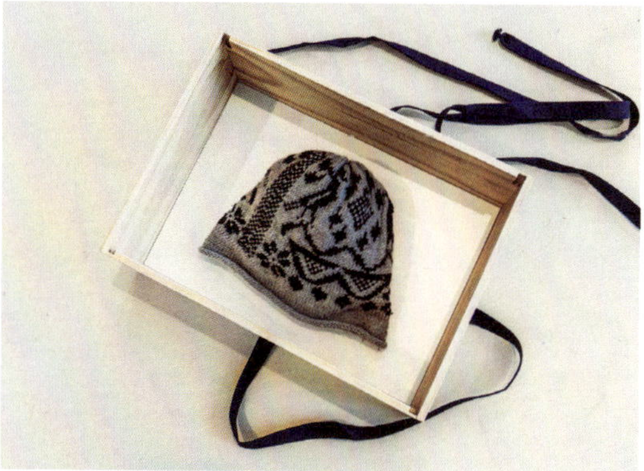

HAT

Katja lived a few doors down, she was just one year younger than me: we would run across the street and play together. It was all very simple. I hadn't lived there for a long time when she became ill with leukaemia. My mother recently found Katja's knitting pattern. She had worked on it during her chemotherapy: birds, flowers as big as trees, lots of sky. What do you do with something handmade in which every stitch is so entwined with hope? My mother sewed a hat out of it. This winter I wore it while out walking.

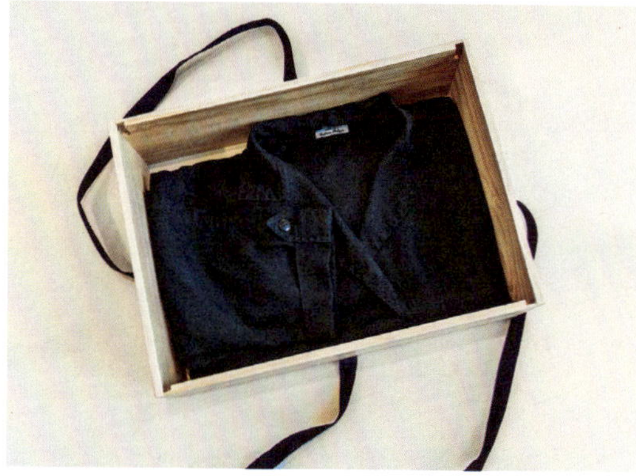

BLOUSE

At 20 years old I was given a blouse that had belonged to my grandmother. It was made by my mother during her dressmaking apprenticeship. On the label on the collar there is a name that isn't familiar to me. My mother sewed her name with a "C" instead of the usual "K" and used her maiden name. I wore that blouse with pride at the same age as my mother had been when she made it. It has something of the feeling of being able to lead one's own life independently.

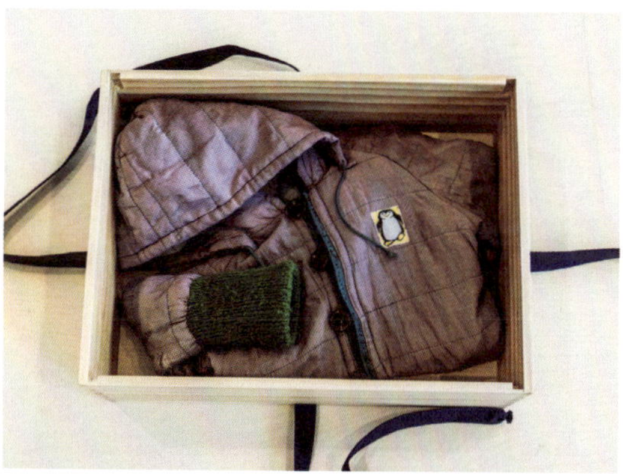

FAVOURITE JACKET

This jacket was my "favourite jacket". I was born in Šiauliai, Lithuania, then still an unwilling part of the USSR. When I moved to Germany as an artist after the fall of the Wall, I just had a few of my art objects, this jacket and a few photos as mementoes in my luggage. My art objects were sold or "disposed of" in performances through moving around or even burned, but the jacket was always there, a fetishised fixed point in my life.

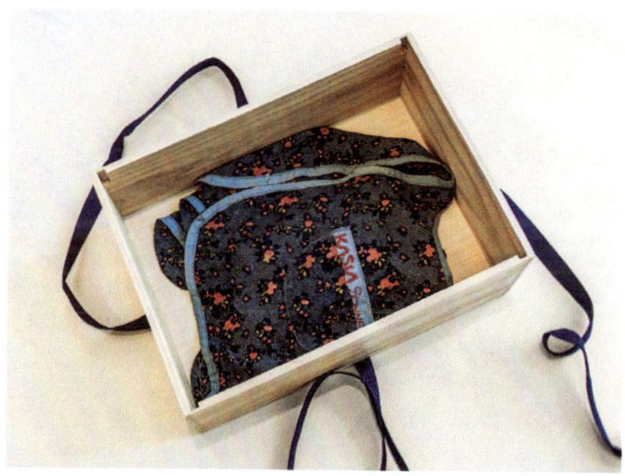


KINDERGARTEN APRON

In Poland, a *fartuszek* is a small apron that children had to wear during Communist times in the socialist kindergartens. My mother was an art student at the time and sewed my apron from the left over bits of fabric from her wedding Wdress. When, in 1980, we escaped to West Germany, with me hidden in the boot of a car, my mother took this little apron with us, which I never needed again because in Berlin everybody was allowed to wear whatever they liked to kindergarten.

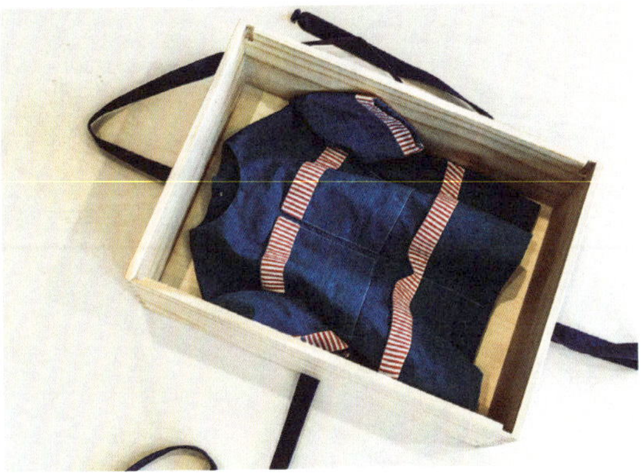

SMOCK

I had a fascination with breasts as a baby and and there is a story about me putting croquet balls down my small shirt. As a safer solution my mother sewed me a small smock with two large pockets at chest height. She used a sturdy blue cotton and trimmed the pockets and sleeves with a red and white striped pattern. I would wander around the house, picking up lost socks or panties, stuffing them into the pockets of my smock until I had gathered enough material to form two lopsided forms at the top. Nothing I have worn since has ever made me feel so loved or protected.

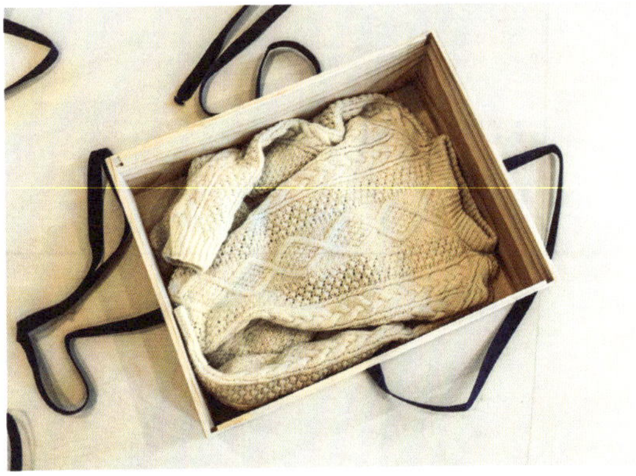

ARAN SWEATER

This is my Aran sweater knitted by both my maternal grandmother and my mother in the early 1980s. My mother knitted the body and my grandmother the arms. I remember them always having a project on the go. I would tease my grandmother who would stick out her tongue when she knitted. I would complain that my mother would click the needles too loudly and distract me from the telly. My grandmother has passed and my mother now no longer knits. She says it makes no sense to knit when buying the wool costs more than buying the finished article in the shops.



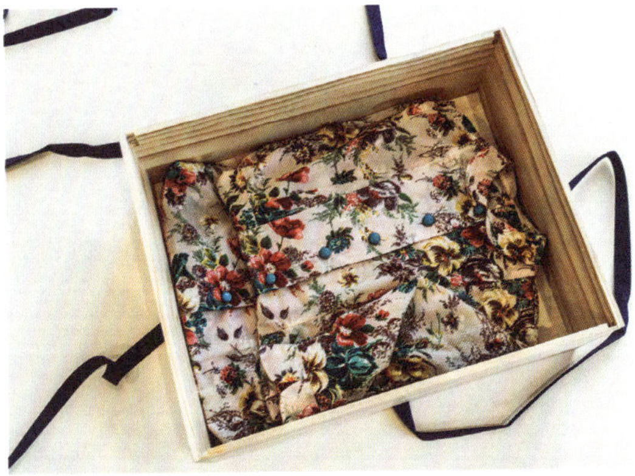

DRESS

My mother, Ethyl Gooch, made the nylon seersucker dressing gown for my wedding trousseau in 1956. For a year, she was sewing wedding dresses, bridesmaid dresses, summer dresses and skirts, as my sister's wedding was six months later in the year. Many yards of fabric and thread were cut; it was the 1950s. Unfortunately, Mother died in 1983, but she would have said that making clothes for her two daughters was a sheer pleasure and that it was rewarding seeing them on their wedding days walking up the aisle.

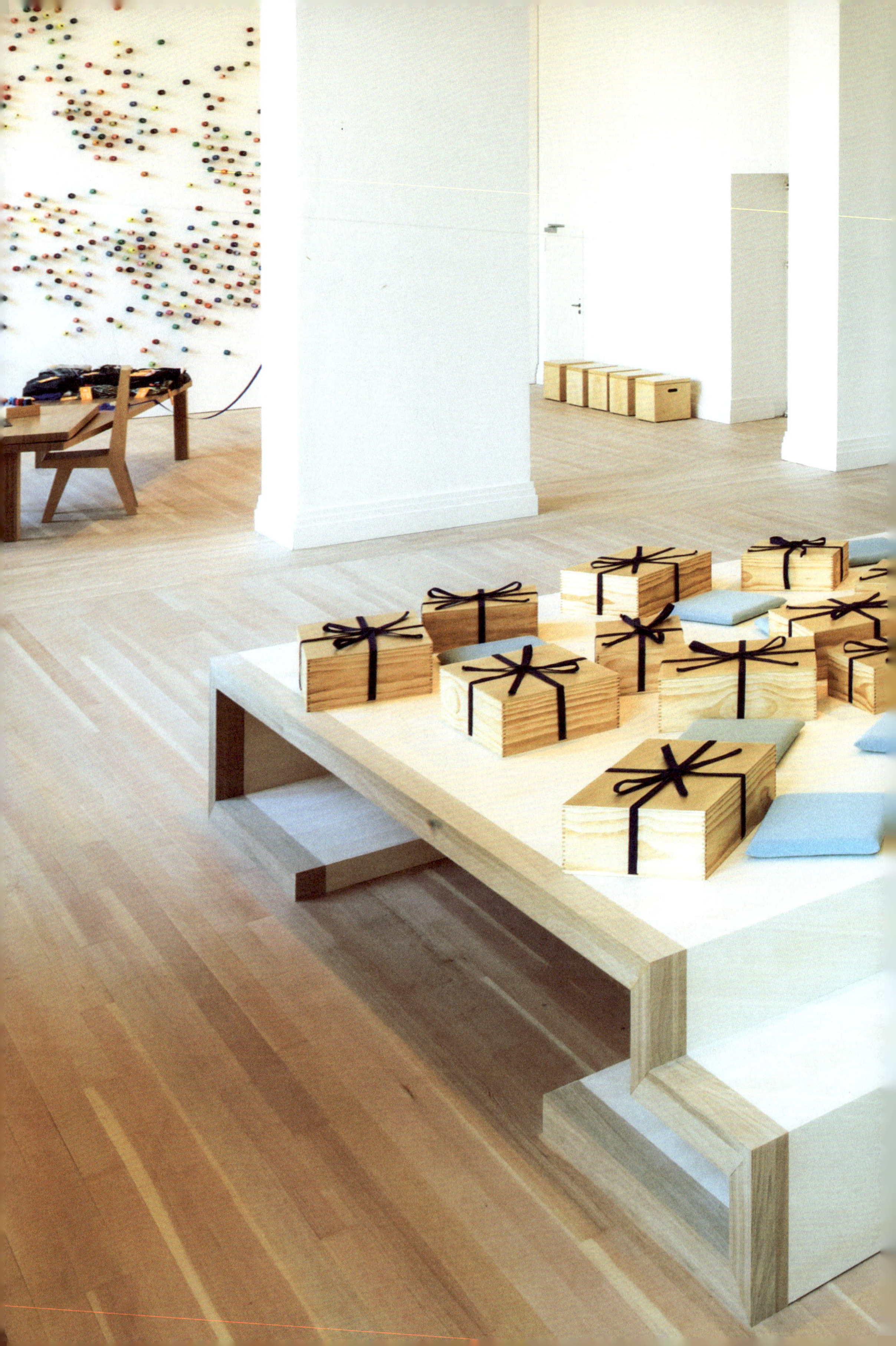

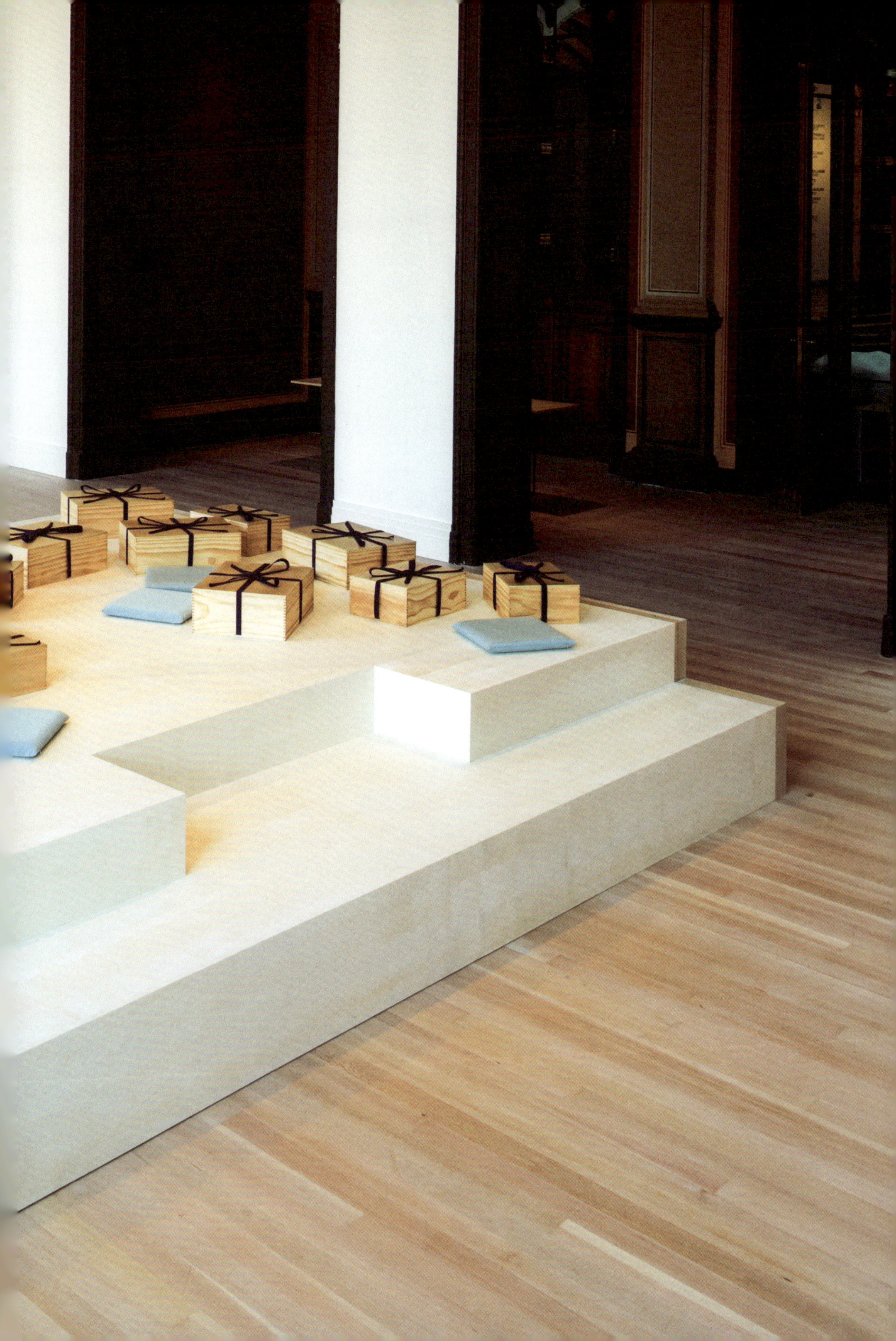

# GUERNICA IN SAND

## 2006 / 2020

Sand, wooden island, light
11 x 23 m

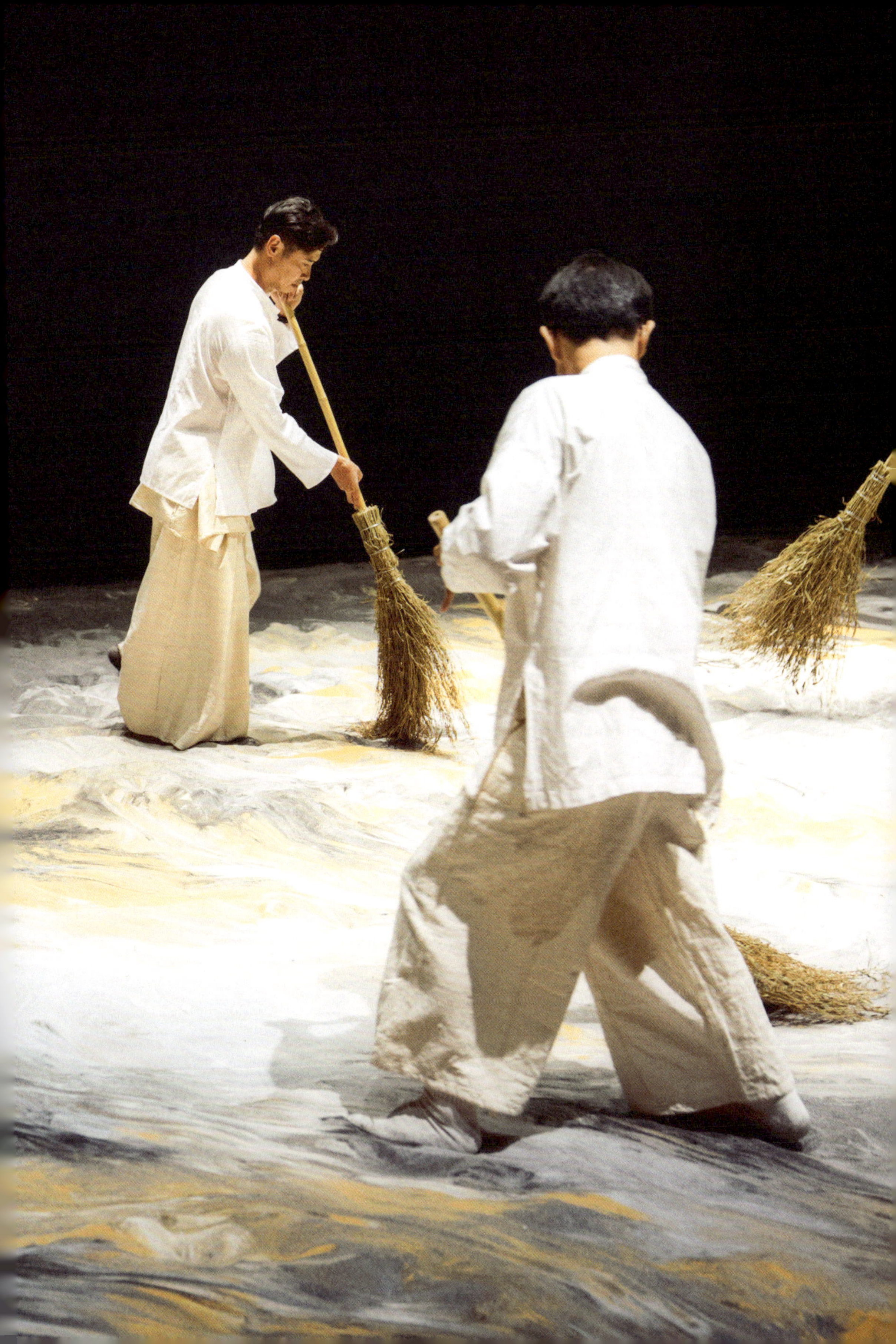

“I remember my first encounter with Picasso’s *Guernica* at New York’s Museum of Modern Art. I was twelve and was on my way from Taiwan to live in the Dominican Republic with my family. I was overwhelmed by its size, the abstract images of animals and the mother and the child, as well as the obvious violence and pain emanating from the painting. My parents told me that it was created by Picasso in response to the bombing of a small town in Spain. Living in Taiwan, most of my encounters with paintings came from visiting the National Palace Museum. Here I saw painted birds, flowers and palaces on silk, but nothing like *Guernica*. It opened up my eyes to a different dimension in art, beyond just beautiful scenery.

I once had an idea for a large-scale performance project where robotic machines would clash with each other, which an audience could watch from a tower. Around this time, I travelled through Bolivia’s Altiplano and got caught in a sand storm. Once the storm had passed, I remember standing in what felt like the middle of nowhere, looking at a sky, which was sparking with celestial entities, complete silence surrounding us. It looked like the trace of a snake as the sand moved across the desert. This inspired me to create a painting that evoked the Tibetan Buddhist practice of sand mandalas, which speaks to the concept of impermanence. In relation to my original idea, the tower became an artificial island on which people could stand or sit, and the battling robots evolved into the person creating the sand painting and the person walking over it. The tension between these two people is obvious and extremely important because it speaks about change.



A grain of sand was a part of a rock formation millions of years ago. Because of the rain, water, sun, heat and wind it retuned to being a grain of sand again. This piece of sand combined with an infinite number of other sand granules to become my artwork. Once the show is over and millions of years have passed, this grain of sand will be a piece of rock again.”

LEE MINGWEI

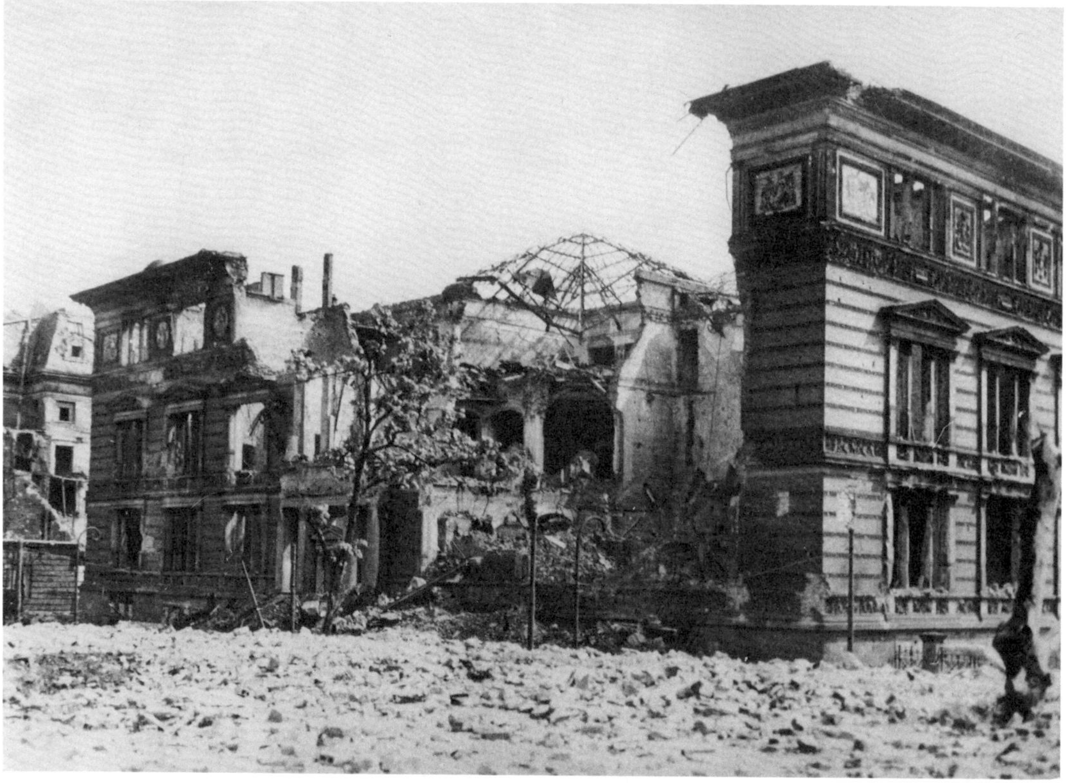

Designed by Martin Gropius in close cooperation with Heino Schmieden, the Gropius Bau initially opened as a Museum and School of Decorative Arts in 1881. In 1945, the building was heavily damaged during one of the last major bombing raids on Berlin. The north façade and the upper floors were almost completely destroyed and the museum holdings in the cellar were decimated. The Gropius Bau was ultimately designated a historical landmark building in 1966. Reconstruction began in 1976 and it was officially reopened in 1981.

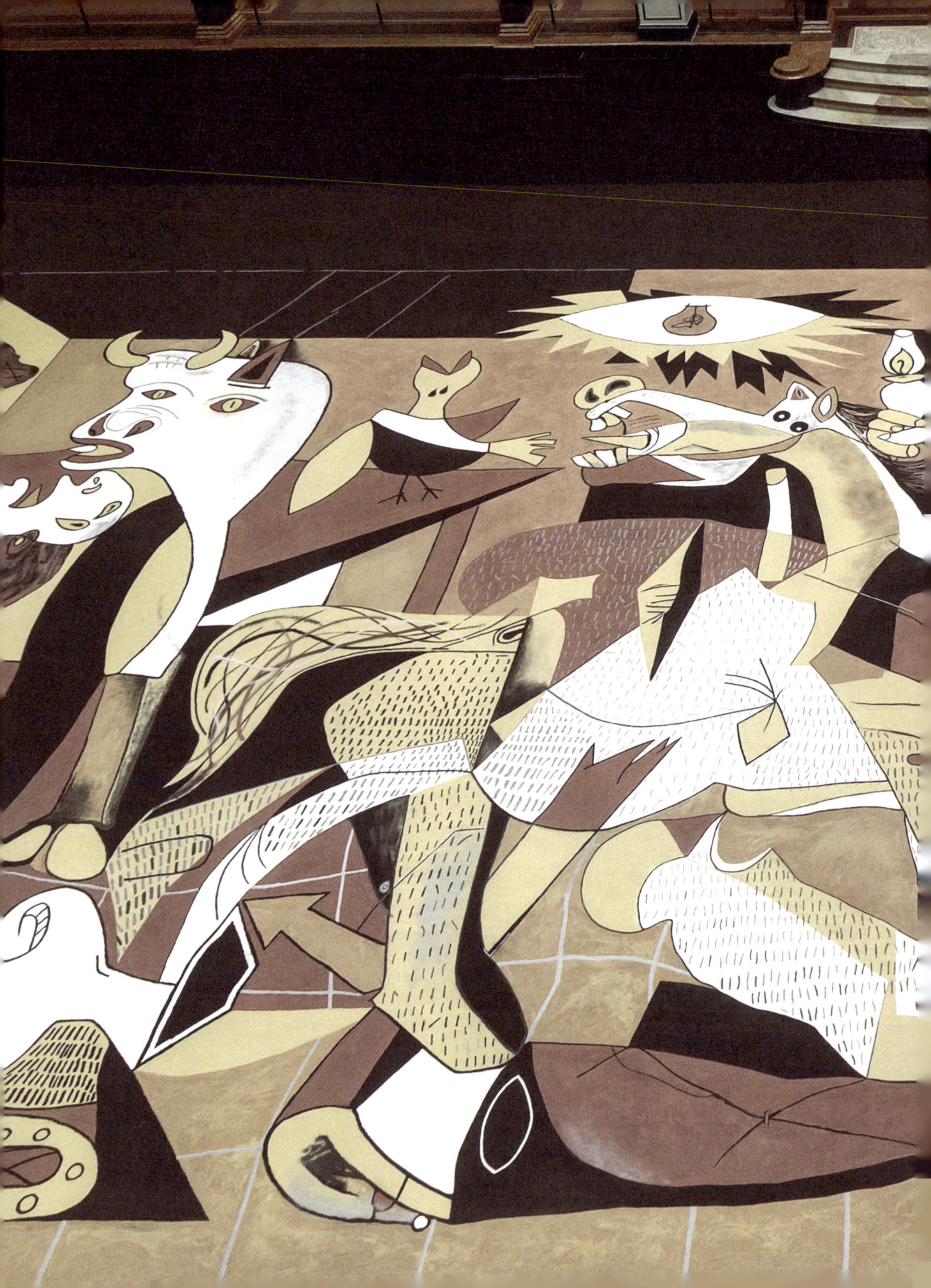

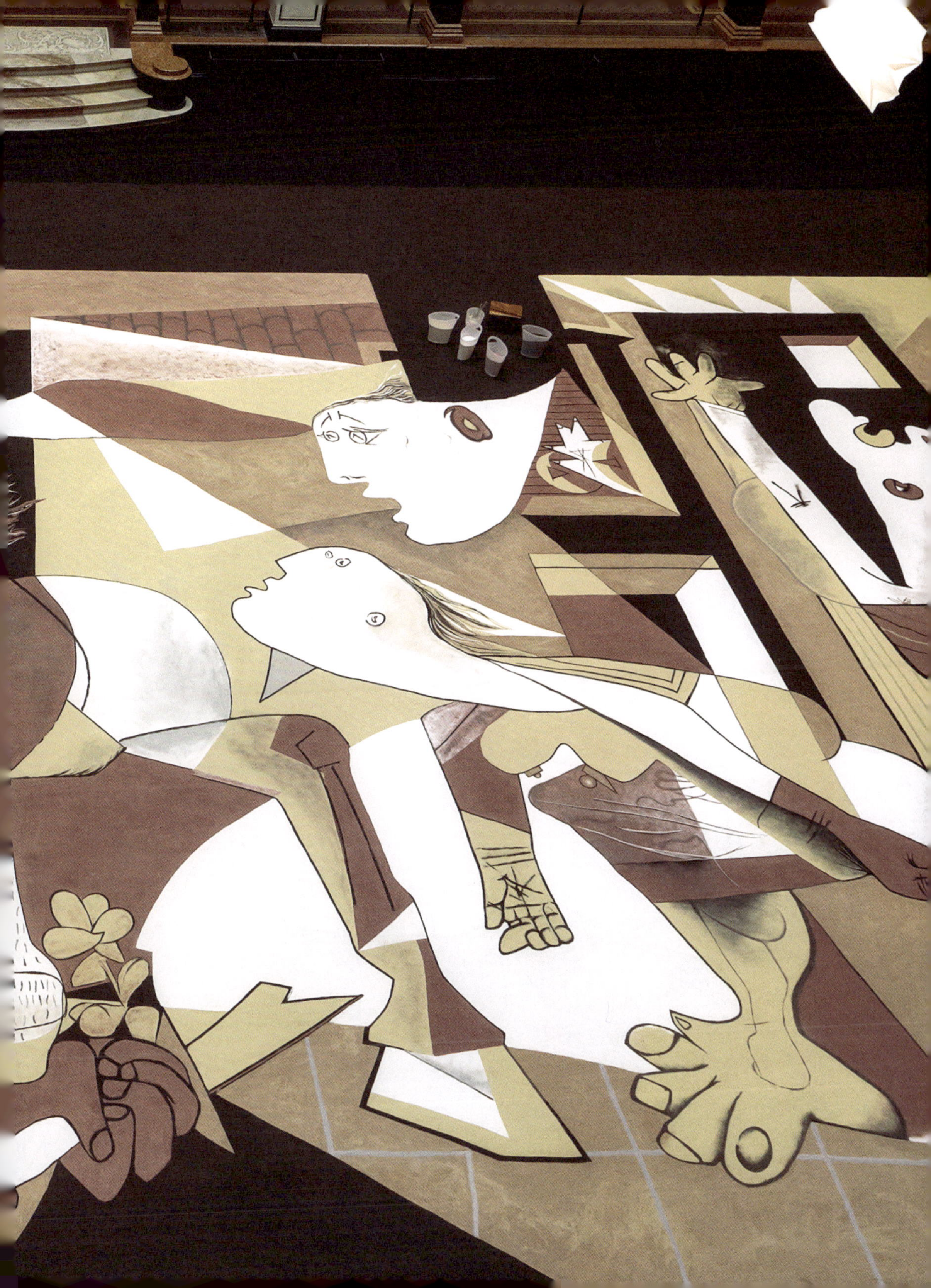

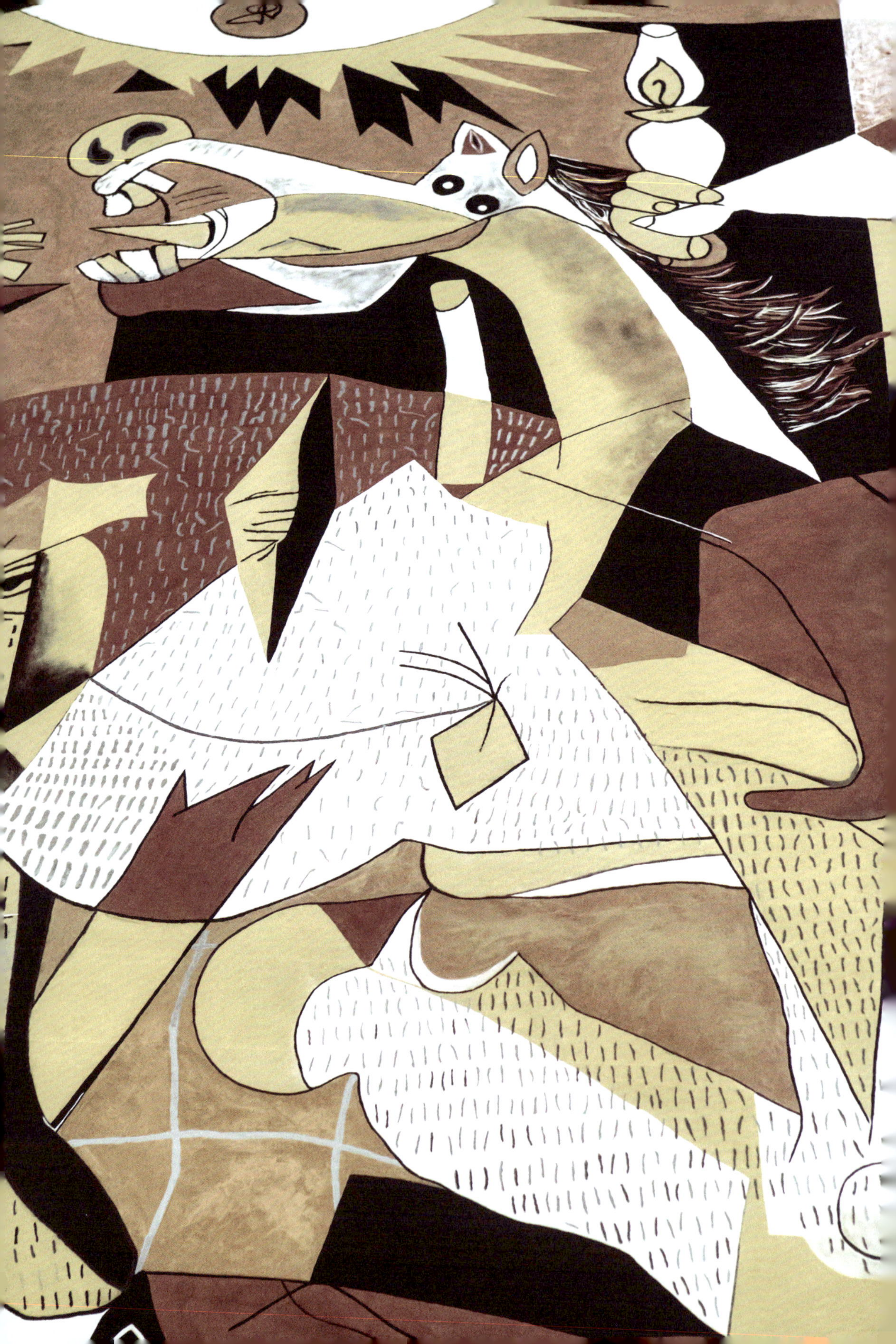

"In 2005, Mingwei and I were at 14,000 feet approaching the Laguna Colorada in Bolivia – a shallow salt lake that mirrors thousands of flamingos, framed by a desert of sand and stratified rock. We were suddenly surrounded by the red and yellow of a sandstorm that swiftly passed on. Mingwei started to talk of ideas of a sand work. Participating in *Guernica in Sand* in London, the performance day was emotional, combining creation and destruction, care and continuity. To complete the work, I had to look down, although I did have a strong consciousness of the other participants and how they were walking on the sand. Many people took quiet care; some less so. Not everyone knows the story of Guernica; participants bring their own meaning to the work. The pace started slowly and then accelerated. For me, the day of making *Guernica in Sand* mirrored the increasing intensity of Guernica's destruction as described by the journalist George Steer who first reported the bombing of the town to the world in 1937. As the performance concludes, the final sweeping of the work is a release; this is not an ending but, rather, a breath of life and an invitation to continue. The work is a meditation; the ephemeral 'gift' combines an invitation, space and moments to think."

JOHN RIVETT

Performer in several iterations of *Guernica in Sand* including the Queensland Gallery of Modern Art in 2008, Taipei Fine Arts Museum, 2015 and Gropius Bau, 2020

"I was a fascinated bystander when *Guernica in Sand* was staged at Queensland Gallery of Modern Art. As Head of Australian Art at the museum, I knew of careful planning over preceding months and was an early visitor to the installation. I noted the tons of sand blocking out the great painting, observed the punctilious labour, tried out visitor seating. I saw *Guernica in Sand* almost every day: from initial composition to completion, to the eventual sweeping-off of Picasso's image to give birth to new life in the great expanses of black, silvery, grey and golden sands. Picasso's *Guernica* commemorates the first airborne slaughter of civilians. *Guernica in Sand* in Brisbane – transposed in time, size, medium – was a Zen-like sand garden, a site for meditation: I found myself pondering the many armed conflicts across the globe today, and the complicity of we who live at a safe distance from sites of war. The best gifts are unexpected but necessary. In the Brisbane museum we were simultaneously gift-givers and receivers: we rejoiced in *Guernica in Sand*'s extraordinary gift to visitors, in which we also shared, and we understood its gravity. Such are the joys, and responsibilities, of hospitality."

JULIE EWINGTON

Former Head of Australian Art at QAGOMA, Brisbane

"One of the most memorable moments in my life was the instant I first saw Picasso's *Guernica* at The Museum of Modern Art, New York. I turned from the lift and there it was, so much larger and more demanding than I had expected. I've never forgotten its power. As one of four performers who added to and destroyed *Guernica in Sand*, I loved the ideas Mingwei introduced into the work 80 years after the original was made – the ephemerality, cultural references, scale, floor placement, moments of performance and participation and the destruction and regenerative hope that comes from the beauty of the 'new'. In Mingwei's practice, the notion of gifting is both explicit and implicit. Once one engages with the idea of the gift, we tend to see some expression of this in many otherwise mundane social interactions. I enjoy this almost ritualised formality as it engenders small flashes of self-awareness, which for me at least tend to accumulate during the lead-up to each installation and performance."



MICHAEL SNELLING

Performer in *Guernica in Sand* at QAGOMA in Brisbane in 2008, The Biennale of Sydney in 2016 and Museum MACAN in Jakarta in 2018

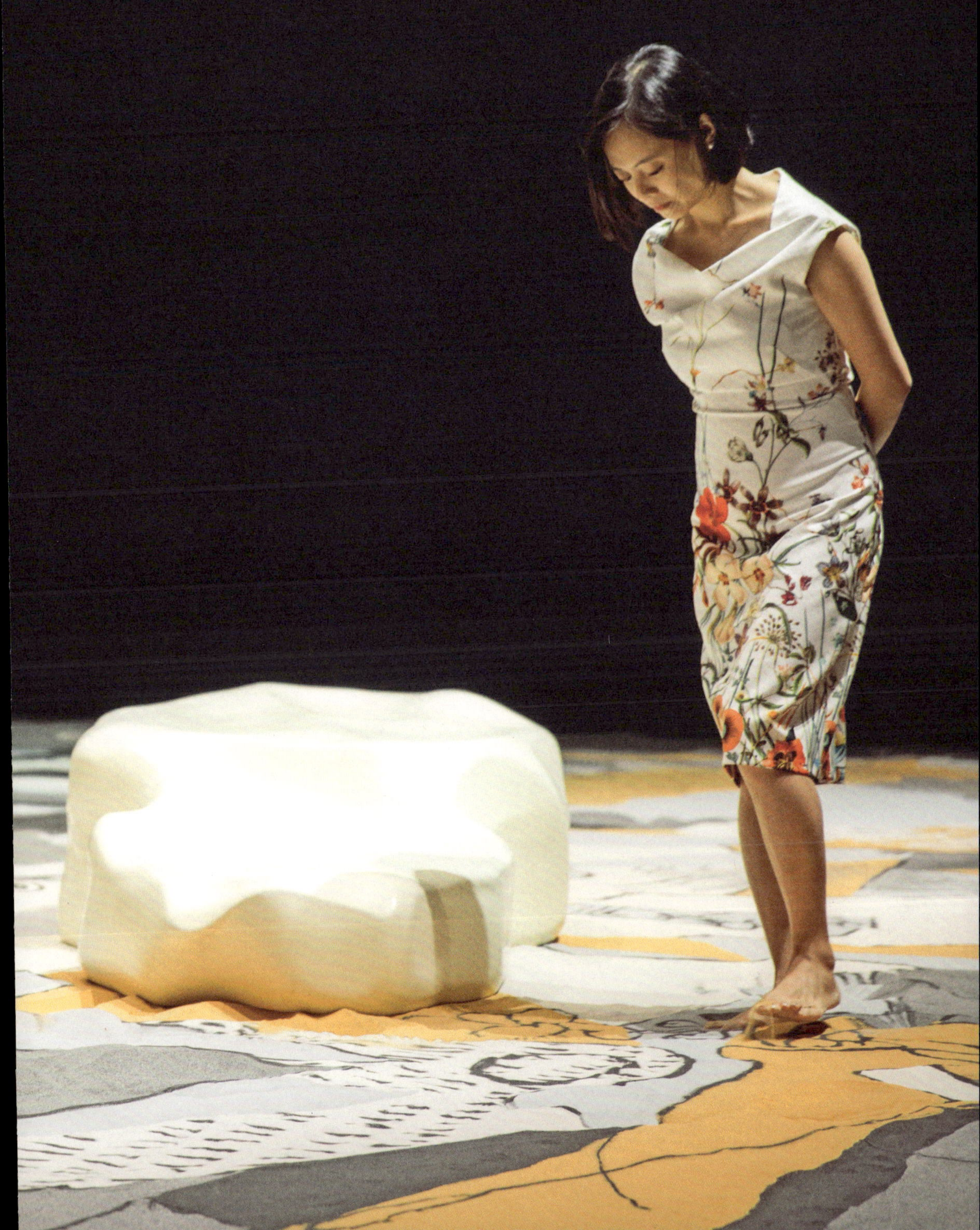

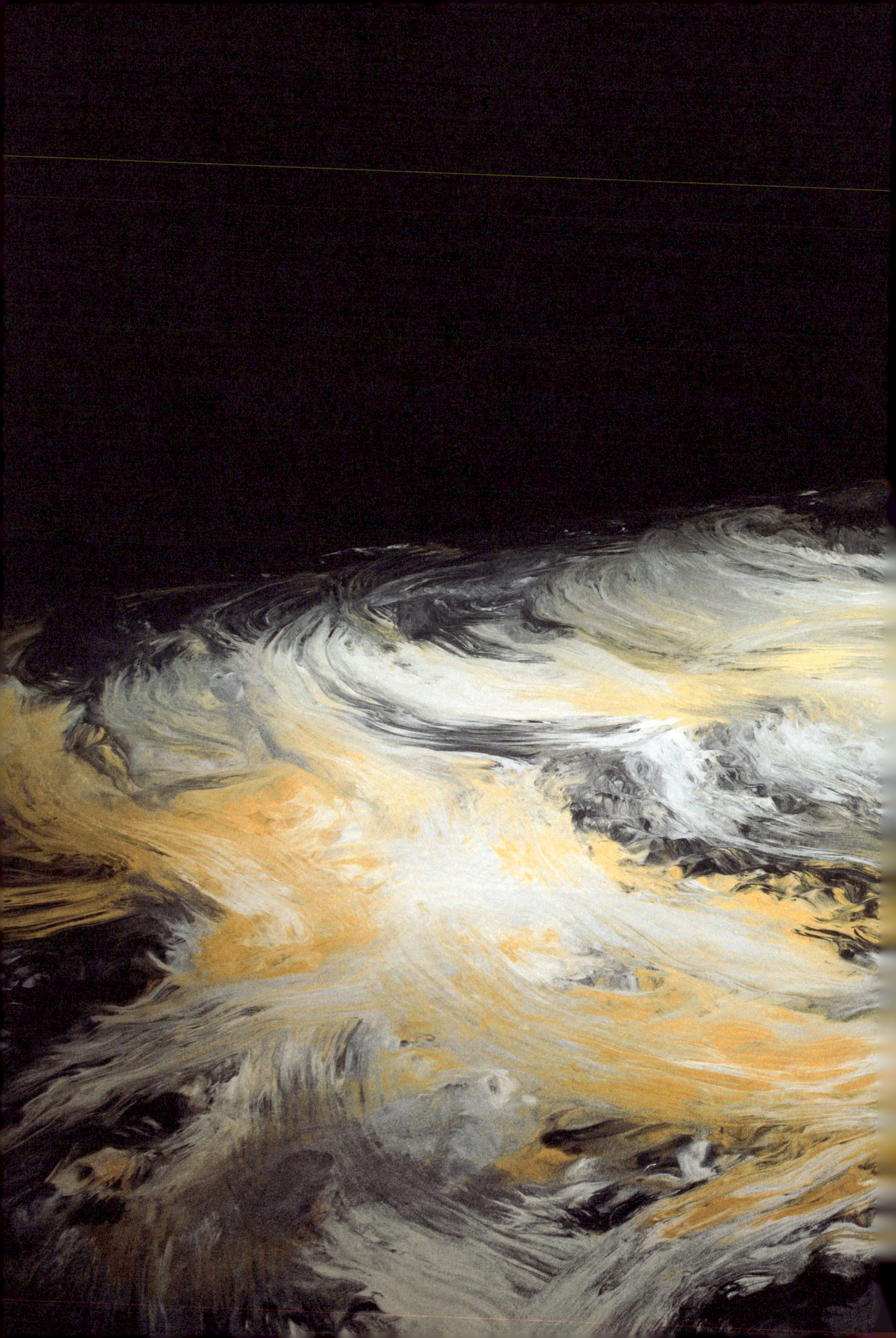

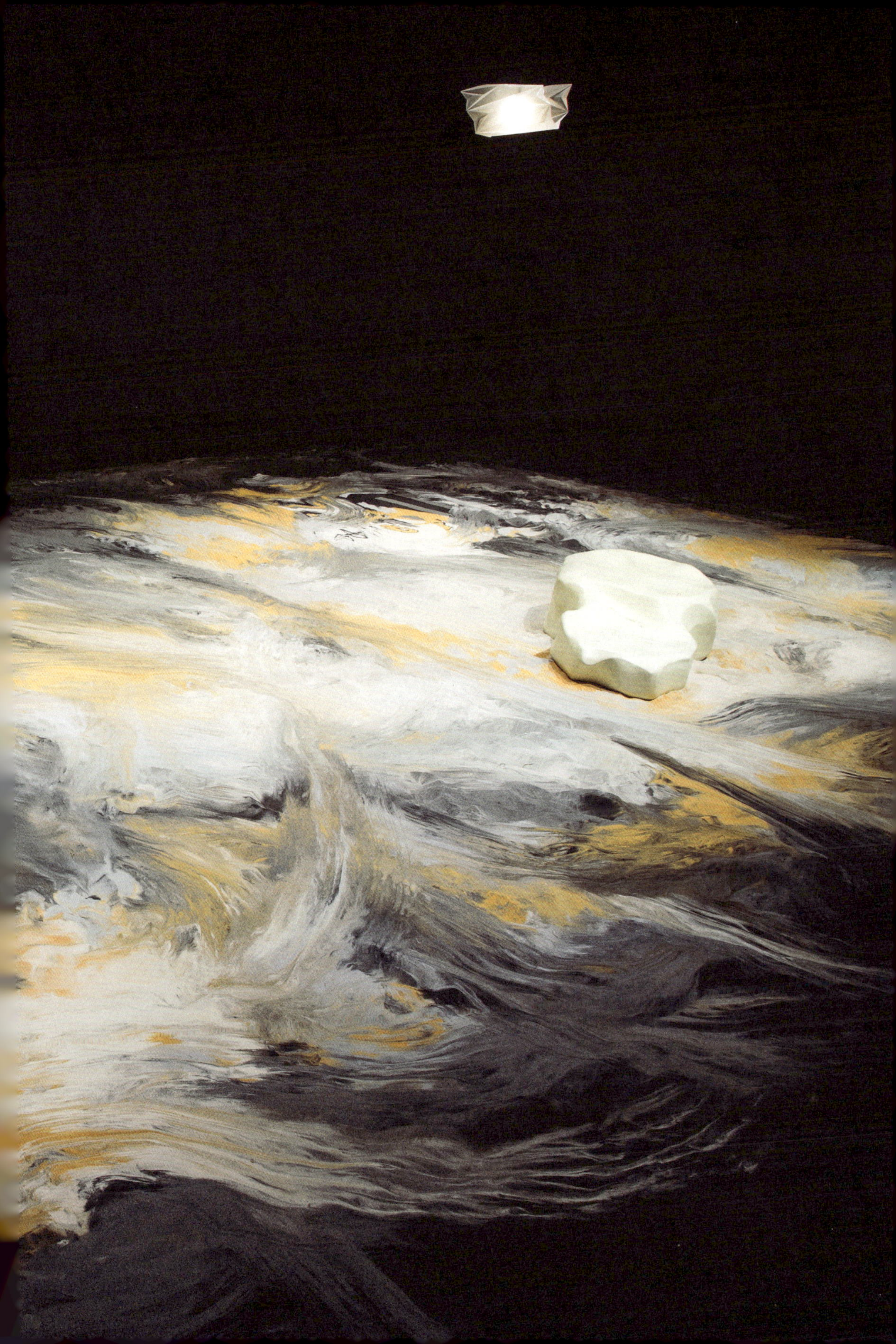

# AN EXCHANGE THAT HAPPENS IN DIFFERENT DIRECTIONS

## AN INTERVIEW BETWEEN STEPHANIE ROSENTHAL AND LEE MINGWEI

STEPHANIE ROSENTHAL: When we began thinking about your exhibition, significant words and terms were exchanged as part of our discussions. Three of those words that interconnect are "faith", "chance" and "impermanence". Let's start with chance: how does this play out in your work?

LEE MINGWEI: When I think about the idea of chance, it's the main thread that runs through everything I do and, in a sense, through everything that *anyone* does. I say this for a specific reason: if you imagine a family lineage, you are at the very end of that line. Your parents are the previous dot on that line, your grandparents before that, and so on. Eventually you reach a point where one of your ancestors is "in between" – which is to say that they are human and non-human. Continuing our dot-to-dot logic, you soon realise that one of your ancestors could be a creature between mammal and amphibian. You can trace that dot all the way back to a single cell. One of your amoeba ancestors could have been eaten by another amoeba, but that didn't happen; one of your insect ancestors could have been destroyed by a drop of rain or a falling meteorite, but that didn't happen. The chance of us having actually survived really is a miracle. For me, that says a lot about chance and faith: we are all at the mercy of both.

SR: And faith? When making art or presenting exhibitions, are you drawing attention to your faith in the fact that your ideas will find their form at the right time? Or is faith something that simply operates in the background of your work?

LM: I think it is both; faith and chance are the essences of my work. I ask faith and chance to help me create artworks, which makes the works much more complex than I alone could imagine. This is a more vulnerable and challenging position for me. All of my projects are like two people dancing the tango. When one person moves in one way, the other has to move with them. We really don't know where we'll be ten steps from now; however, I do have a bigger picture. The real step in this tango is that of depending on faith and chance.

SR: It seems that faith and chance play an important role in the how and when the first seed of an idea is realised. Equally, you don't seem to want to force the work's timeframe. Do you think about your projects years before they come into being?

LM: Yes, that is exactly the case. The seed of the project often comes from my personal experience. I only notice this seed if an experience has such power that it never goes away; it holds onto my spirit and soul so strongly that it drifts within the subconscious. When the project shifts into my conscious mind, I think, "Oh, there's something. Could this be a worthwhile story to share with people?" Sometimes they are so delicate they're not ready to be shared.

SR: We have been thinking about Arnold van Gennep's concept of rites of passage together. Originally he wrote in French. There are the *rites de séparation*, letting something go; the *rites de marge*, which are about the in between, the liminal; and the *rites d'agrégation*, in which one approaches a new state. I have always been most interested in the *rites de marge* as the most creative space because it takes place in a liminal space, where one has already let go of something but has not yet reached the new state. It's the space where you reach beyond your own experience, an entirely unknown space that is difficult to put into words. You spoke about knowing something but not wanting to put it into words: that's the *rites de marge*. Artworks allow you to be in that space.

LM: I realise that if I apply words to these very delicate states too early, that it somehow cages and kills the magic. I really need to pay attention to precisely when these states of mind are ready to be shared – verbally or conceptually, with myself or with friends.

SR: It's interesting what happens when you have to put an idea into words. I also feel that you can write a text in your head and on the page it can read differently. On the one hand language can free ideas by making them concrete. On the other it can hinder them from unfolding. There can be fluidity between the two poles. Some ideas simply fall into place and some ideas resist the linear order of language. What does it mean to you to put ideas into words?

LM: Sometimes I do need words to solidify these very ephemeral things because they can be too fluid – to the point where there's almost nothing there. On the other hand, in this fluidity there can be something that I need to protect, something I don't want to cage. I have such admiration for poets because they are magicians; they are the ones who know when and how words become the magic ingredients of the imagination. I'm slightly scared of words because they can cage ideas. However, poets or writers can liberate with words.

SR: Do you use exhibitions and the new environment of the institution to grow the seed of an idea that you've had a long time ago, in order to realise a new work at a later stage? Can art institutions provide such a space for rites of transition (*rites de marge*)?

LM: My last travelling survey show was from 2014-2016, which was six years ago. Everything has changed – even I have changed, but there is a steady stream of consciousness running through my practice, which you can see alongside my new work. I think this Gropius Bau show has already become a pivotal point of reflection for me: reflecting on myself, on my work and on Europe. When I was living in America I was truly American-Taiwanese. Now, after having lived in Paris since 2015, I'm very interested to see how this exhibition will be received and responded to by an audience in a European context.

I can already feel another artwork in a fluid, nascent state; this will come into being later, and is inspired by the collective effort and energy at the Gropius Bau.

SR: A new work which you will be on show at the Gropius Bau relates to the Quaker minister and painter Edward Hicks' series of paintings the *Peaceable Kingdom*, c. 1820–1849. When did you first start looking at Hicks and why did you choose this location to realise your new project, *Our Peaceable Kingdom*, 2020?

LM: I really started looking more deeply at Edward Hicks' *Peaceable Kingdom* around early 2000s, when I was living in New York. The world changed so much after 9/11. Something was triggered because of this violence. I started researching the Quaker's spiritual view and came upon Hicks' series. I wondered what it would mean to ask artists from different ethnic, cultural and spiritual backgrounds about their views of peace and to question whether ideas of peace have changed since the 1800s. Indeed, are they different if you are Buddhist or a non-spiritual practitioner? Nearly 20 years after that singular event in New York, we can reflect on how it has impacted humanity – probably not in a particularly kind or generous way. Reading about this building, the Gropius Bau, its site and Berlin as a city, it seemed like a good opportunity to bring this idea of different visions of peace into the show. The new work is called *Our Peaceable Kingdom* instead of the *Peaceable Kingdom* because I've invited 27 artists to paint their views of what peace could be in response to Hicks' painting. These artists are from places including Singapore, Indonesia, China, Taiwan, Australia, India, Pakistan, Afghanistan, France, Germany and the US and are of different races, genders, ages, spiritual practices and artistic practices.

SR: You've been visiting and engaging with the Gropius Bau building since 2018. I'm fascinated by your approach to creating *Our Peaceable Kingdom* – that the project was fluid for so long and now it's time for it to materialise. It's as if you made it for this building.

LM: Because this building was built in the 19th Century, its architecture makes the museum feel classical. The experience of seeing the paintings will also feel classical. Although there is a participatory component to *Our Peaceable Kingdom* as a way of making of the work, it's not about the audience's participation per se. The question I want to ask is: what is peace for you? What do you think? If you were invited to make a piece like this, what would you paint? There is one particular painting in *Our Peaceable Kingdom* that, for me, has no visual connection whatsoever to the original Hicks painting – not even the colour or the theme. The artist has decided not to trace any part of the original. That's the beauty of the project – the liminal space between how one person can conceive of peace, and another.

SR: The site of the Gropius Bau is incredibly politically and historically charged. During the Nazi period, the headquarters of the Gestapo were located next door. Across the road was Hermann Göring's *Haus der Flieger*, where the House of Representatives (*Abgeordnetenhaus*) is today. Next to that building was the Ministry of Aviation, the home of the Luftwaffe. In 1945 the Gropius Bau was extensively bombed; you can still see World War II shrapnel damage and bullet holes. In the late 1970s and early 1980s, restorers left the building's injuries so that they remained tangible. The building bears witness to the injury and trauma of its own history and, in turn, to all of our histories. Due to the building's history, we are engaged with the concepts of care and repair. Repairing relationships is the focus of several of your works, particularly *Guernica in Sand*, 2006/2020. What influenced you to create this work for the first time?

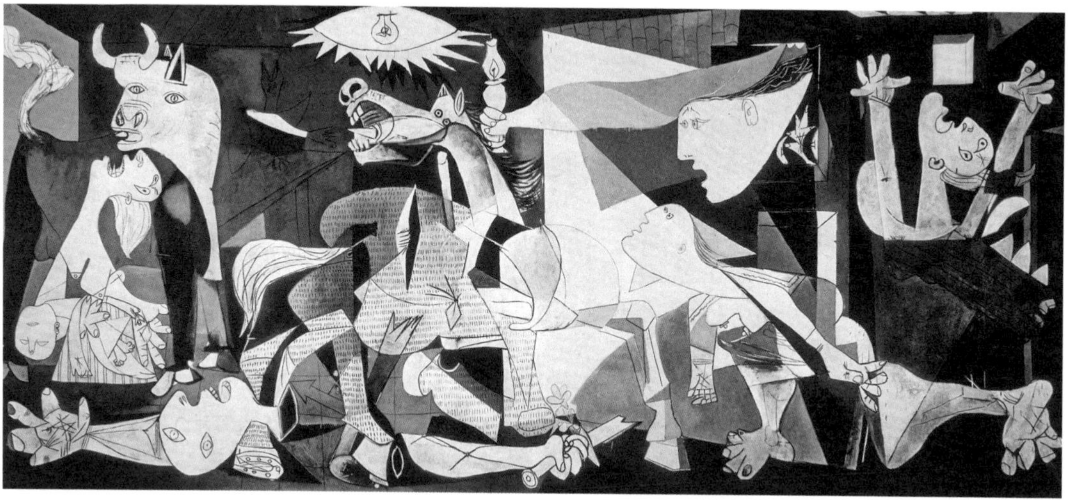

Fig. 13. Pablo Picasso's *Guernica* (1937) was painted in response to the bombing of the Basque Country town of Guernica, in the north of Spain, by the forces of Nazi Germany and Fascist Italy, as requested by Francisco Franco. Lee Mingwei wanted not to recreate this work exactly, or to focus on these violent events, but to use it as a means of exploring the concept of impermanence and the creative power of transformation. One of Lee's key concerns is models of peace in contemporary times and *Guernica in Sand* connects with the Tibetan Buddhist tradition of sand mandala, which are practiced to usher in world peace.

LM: *Guernica in Sand* is a project, superficially, about East and West. It's my homage to two different traditions and practices. One is the history of Western painting – recreating Picasso's iconic modernist painting *Guernica*, 1937. It is also my homage to the practice in Buddhist temples of creating mandala sand paintings. People can see it as a political statement or not. *Guernica* was a very direct response to the bombing of the Spanish town, Guernica, which was carried out by the Luftwaffe in collaboration with the Italian Aviazione Legionaria. They used a campaign of carpet bombing and set a precedent for intensive destruction during World War II. Within one day the city was brutally flattened. Picasso was, to put it mildly, angry and overwhelmed with sadness and he created this painting in a very short time while he was in Paris. He said that until Spain became democratic, the painting would not be shown there. The creation of sand mandala in Tibetan Buddhist practice takes weeks and involves four to eight monks making extremely delicate sand paintings. They are heavenly and extremely defined depictions of where Buddha lives. At the end, a ceremony to brush the sand painting together takes place; it is not destroyed, but transformed into something else. On one single day in the middle of the exhibition's run, from noon until sunset, I try to finish the last part of *Guernica in Sand*. Simultaneously, one person in the audience is allowed to walk onto the sand. Then a second person takes over and this continues until the day's end. We conclude the performance as a group of six. Each of us has a broom and we brush the sand, gesturing towards the middle of the work, and then we leave *Guernica in Sand* in this state for the remainder of the exhibition. I remember when I was presenting this work at the Mori Art Museum, one guest said accusingly, "Why are you destroying the greatest painting in the world?" I could feel and see her anger. She only saw the destruction; she didn't see the transformation. This work has a political backdrop, but I wish to talk about us as humanity: how do we move on after destruction?

SR: Presenting and performing *Guernica in Sand* at this site and in Berlin feels like part of a process of healing. How do you approach care, repair and healing in your other works?

LM: Care and repair are present in *The Mending Project*, 2009/2020 and even in *Sonic Blossom*, 2013/2020. The process of healing is part of the work. I want to be careful with the word "healing", as I don't assume that people are broken or damaged. For example, sometimes people are so moved by the gift of song that they cry, but not necessarily because they are broken – and if they are heart broken, that's also perfectly fine. I don't want to suggest that the singers are superior or can cure us. Being the mender in *The Mending Project* is incredibly healing for me, personally, because of the beautiful stories that people share.

SR: In terms of the link between crafts and mending, and the related shifts in meaning, we could also discuss the Japanese tradition of *kintsugi*. Is this an approach that interests you?

LM: In Taiwan we actually also have a technique for mending ceramics known as *juci*. It's not as elaborate as the mending in Japan, where cracks in ceramics are mended with gold. The repairs to Taiwanese ceramics are rougher: rice glue is used and cracks are nailed together. The idea is that when something is broken and you have a personal relationship to it – to a piece of clothing or a bowl – then the repair makes it even more beautiful and also functional. *Kintsugi* and *juci* are similar traditions in this sense – this way of thinking is deeply embedded in East Asian cultures.

SR: That undermines the capitalist ideal of the consumption of goods. Currently an awareness is re-emerging that questions this "ideal" and instead celebrates the repair of objects. Another facet of *The Mending Project* or *Sonic Blossom* is the way you consider them to be gifts – the gift of repair or the gift of song. Many philosophical traditions make us aware of the underlying power relations of gift giving. By giving something, someone is indebted to you. How do you feel about this?

LM: As someone from a Confucian society, I have a very different relationship to gifts. One of the five virtues of Confucianism is *li*, which could be translated as "rite", "ritual" or "gift". So when we say *liwu*, which means "the object of the rite", it means we always prepare a gift when going anywhere. In Confucianism, the gift is a way of me gratefully saying, "thank you". It's not about what you can do for me in return. It's the same with *Sonic Blossom*: the person who is offered the song has the right to say, "I don't want a song to be sung for me," or they could openly receive a Schubert song. Usually, the gift is quickly reciprocated back to the singer and, within a few seconds, the singer is also emotionally moved – sometimes they can't finish singing because the gift is returned in such a powerful way.

SR: How do the politics and economics of gift exchange manifest in the exhibition?

LM: My work is underpinned by a very different point of view. Today, when I was standing in front of the Gropius Bau, the wind came and I saw the leaves falling. I thought, "That's such a beautiful gift, but from whom? Is it a gift from nature?" Maybe we can think about the show like that: the wind just comes. The exhibition is not a gift from a particular person – it could be from Schubert, the Gropius Bau, the artist or the singer.

SR: How much have texts by Marcel Mauss, Jacques Derrida or Lewis Hyde inspired your practice with theories of gift giving?

LM: When I was in graduate school at Yale University, my professors pointed me to these three iconic writers and philosophers. I could comprehend them, however I come from a very different environment having grown up in Taiwan. There, I simply started reading about gift giving and became increasingly interested in this practice. I was very lucky that the theory came later – the ideology, the inherent power dynamic would have scared me and created a critical dialogue within my head.

SR: Was *The Dining Project*, 1997/2020, your first work with this idea of gift giving?



LM: Actually, the first work was a project I have barely talked about. I don't have a name for it. It was one of the three projects I included in my MFA application – another was *Money for Art*, 1994/2020, which is included in the Gropius Bau show. The unnamed work allowed me to honour three very important literary, artistic and cultural icons in my life. They were all alive at the time and somehow I found out where they lived. I spent three months hand sewing each a *hakama* from one of my grandmother's kimonos, during which I chanted a particular Buddhist sutra. A *hakama* is a garment similar to skirt-like trousers, the kind worn by samurai. It was a meditation for me. I wrapped them in such a way that it was clear they were a gift and sent them to these three people.

SR: Can you tell us who these three people were?

LM: Anonymity is essential for this project, the packages just arrived at their doors and that's it. Someone asked me if they ever received the gift. I don't really know.

SR: Would they have been able to reach you to respond?

LM: No, they never knew why they received a *hakama* in their mailbox. I simply left a note saying, "thank you for the beauty you bring to my life".

SR: In *The Dining Project*, it's not an anonymous gift per se, but an exchange:

you invite strangers to dine with you and there is the expectation that you will get to know them in return. It's therefore a different proposal.

LM: At Yale, my professor asked how I was going to show the work in my thesis show. We had read so much about Joseph Beuys, Marina Abramović and artists from the 1960s and 1970s that I thought, "I'll create a handmade book and after the meal the person will write their feelings in the book". The first diner actually became a dear friend of mine, Hubertus Breuer, who now lives in Munich. He was studying philosophy at Yale University and I remember he said, "I'm not going to write because I'm a writer; I get paid to write". That actually helped me a lot. I realised that I didn't want to create a project that involves homework.

SR: You studied with Suzanne Lacy. For many years you have been understood as creating participatory art in Lacy's lineage. How does this feel to you?

LM: Museums often struggle to categorise my work. Twenty years ago I was very much described in terms of relational aesthetics. Sometimes my art has been understood as performance. I think that here we return to the idea that words can never fully describe an artwork.

SR: Despite your work being so immaterial – *Sonic Blossom* is literally a song – it is present in many institutional collections. I am hugely influenced by Allan Kaprow's ideas about art as life and life as art. There has been critique of many participatory artworks, saying they "instrumentalise" by telling people how to enact the score of the artwork. We want to lift this framework to instead think of your works in terms of gift giving and, indeed, hospitality. What is your ideal scenario for an art institution and how could institutions learn how to be better hosts?

LM: I always think that institutions are transformed by hosting my work. I really see transformation within the teams. Often people talk about my work in terms of the idea of hospitality. For me, when I am living in this world I'm always being hosted by different things. When I'm taking the subway I'm hosted by the metro staff; when I'm in the house I'm hosted by the architect; when I'm in a restaurant I'm hosted by the chef. I'm also a host of the cells living in my body. So the host and the hosted are in a symbiotic relationship – it is fluid.

SR: The idea that institutions could be hosted by visitors already equates to a very different way of thinking. Whereas institutions can feel so static and fixed, this feels fluid and open to the possibility of change. Hospitality also feels like osmosis: an exchange that happens in different directions, like a form of translation. Indeed, your work often translates your personal experiences into the form of an artwork.

LM: I think the transformation that happens in *The Dining Project*, *The Sleeping Project*, 2000/2020 or *The Letter Writing Project*, 1998/2020, is a translation of a quotidian activity into a ritual. These are not rituals that you learn at school; they come from our parents and, as we digest them, they become personal rituals. I am interested in transformation – this feels even closer to my work than translation. Though they are linked, the translation of a text such as *The Pillow Book*, c. 1002 CE, by Sei Shōnagon, which I read in Mandarin despite the original being in Japanese, allows me to understand the connections between Chinese and Japanese literature at that time. So in essence, translation allows for transformation.

# THE MENDING PROJECT

2009 / 2020

Table, chairs, thread, fabric items

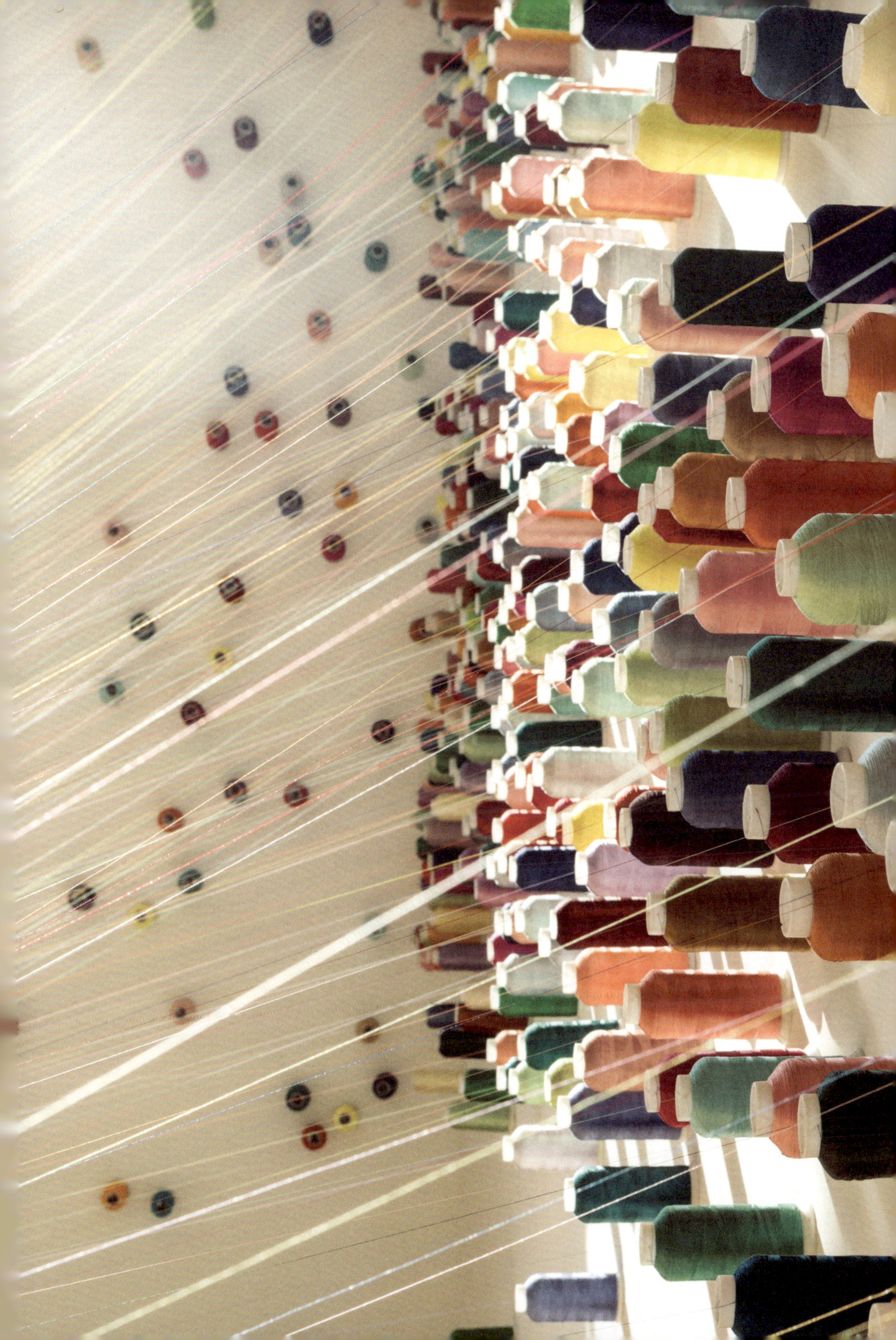

*The Mending Project* is based on an act of sharing between Lee Mingwei or a mending host and a stranger, mediated by a garment that needs to be mended. As the artist darns the fabric using colourful cotton thread, he shares conversation with the participant. The visibly mended article is then placed on the table along with other mended items, forming an ever-growing installation.

"The seed for *The Mending Project* was sown on 11th September 2001, at the moment when the two aeroplanes hit the World Trade Center. It took me nine years to have the strength and courage to create a project about how humanity can move forward with grace and kindness. The work is about the offering of gifts between strangers. The visual aspect of the project, with the connecting cones of thread, was inspired by a butoh performer tossing threads toward the audience to create a tangible connection so that a social fabric is formed. One of my childhood memories is of a young woman showing up in our village on her bike, which she parked underneath a huge bodhi tree in front of the temple. She would ring the small bell and let the villagers know that she was here if anyone had something to be mended. She also had a Siamese cat in her sewing box, called Naomi. I loved playing with Naomi while she mended clothes and listened quietly to the stories about the villagers.

Over the various iterations of the project, I remember a particular encounter with a tailor who came to visit the performance. He observed my interactions with the visitors for a few minutes and the only word he said was before he left: 'rubbish'. Another encounter was with a group of young kids, who came into the gallery daily before school – one of them was even finishing his maths homework while I was mending someone's sweater.

In Venice, a young lady came in with a heavy winter coat. She had a pair of different coloured eyes – one was ebony black and the other sky blue. She told me she was born in the Amazonian jungle, but because of her appearance, her parents considered her a bad omen. They put her in a small basket and let the river take her away. It just happened that a young German couple were swimming downstream and received the basket (just like Moses). This couple adopted her and became her parents. She told me that she wished it was her biological parents mending the coat. Before I could finish the mending process, she grabbed the coat and ran away."

LEE MINGWEI

"I first visited *The Mending Project* in December 2014 while in Tokyo. Mingwei invited me to be a mender for the morning, after which he asked me to repeat this by becoming a mender at the Venice Biennale during the summer of 2017. I spent six weeks there and mended garments for hundreds of visitors from all over the world. I quickly became aware that the project was really not about mending per se, but about getting to know another person. I recall with most clarity the visitors who clearly enjoyed sharing personal information and experiences with me, despite any barriers of language or culture. Several people gave me small gifts of their own – a koala keychain from Australia; a handmade ring; a photograph of us together; an invite to lunch. Many people stayed to have extended conversations, despite all the art they could have been viewing. They became *my* hosts. Mingwei creates 'situations of sharing' by inviting participants to reveal or offer themselves to others, and by doing so, people can create new bonds and enrich one another's lives."

GREGG RICHARDSON

Mending host for *The Mending Project* at Mori Art Museum, Tokyo in 2014 and the 57th Venice Biennale, 2017

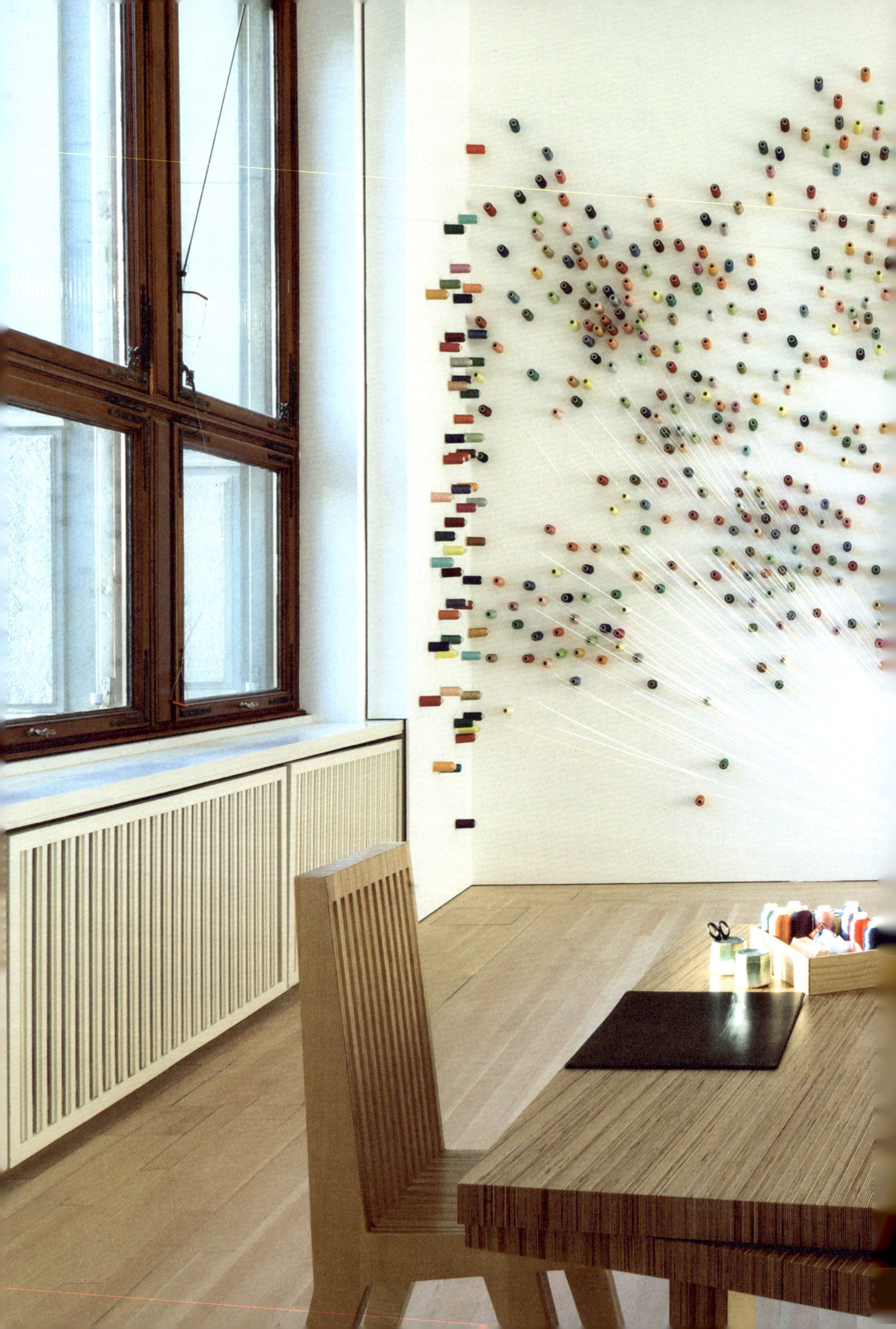

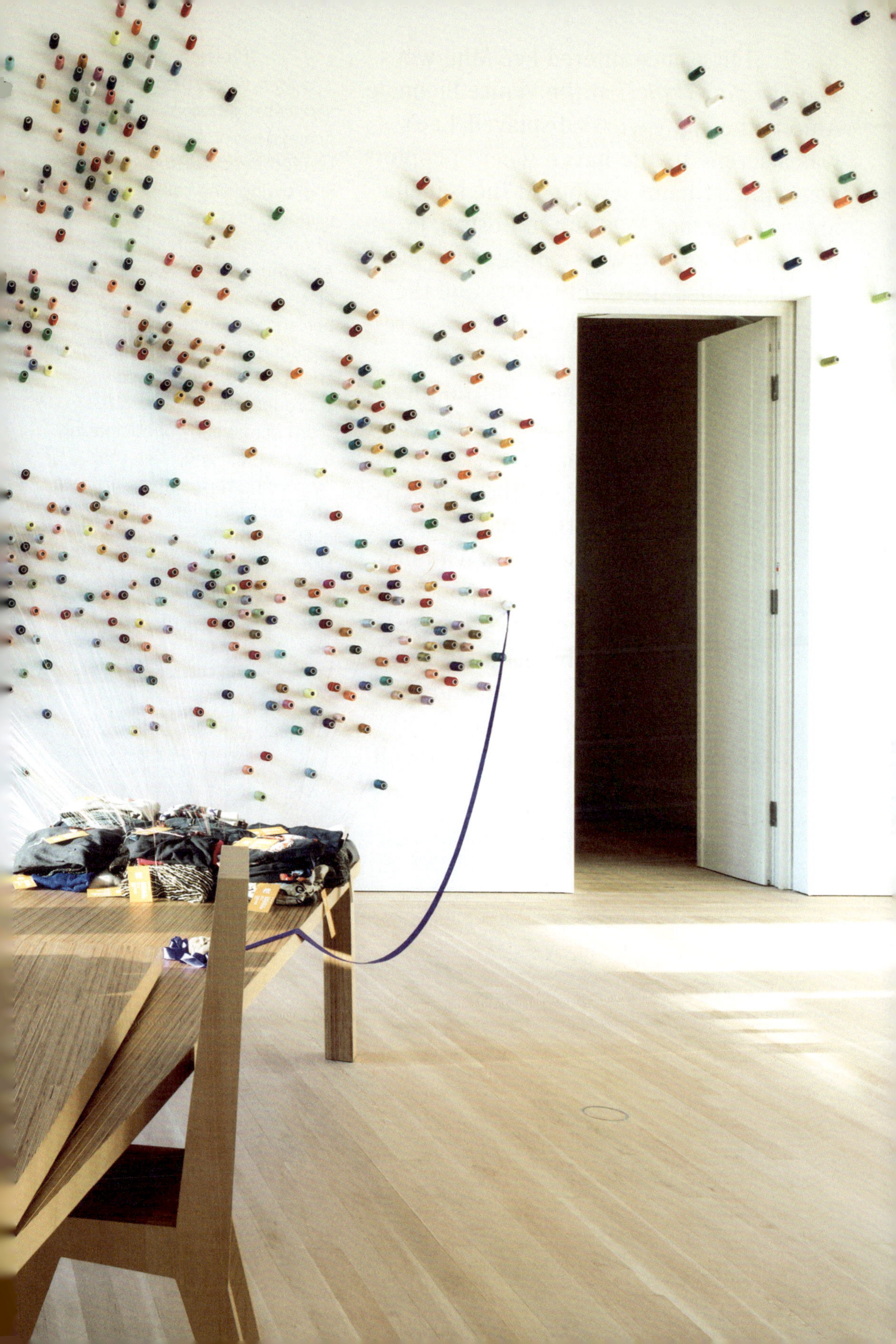

"I first encountered Lee Mingwei's *The Mending Project* at the Venice Biennale. Among the many works displayed, Lee's was a serene textile haven where people were quietly hand sewing. At the Isabella Stewart Gardner Museum in Boston, I was part of a team who managed the daily mending schedule of volunteers and the visitors we hosted. Each day became a remarkable experience of quiet kindness. Visitors were struck by the colourful threads that were strung from the wall to the garments and they were amazed to witness the personal gift of mending. As they sat across the table with their offering, they each recalled the people in their lives who had sewed or mended for them. Each one commented on how satisfying it was to have their clothing renewed by hand stitching. We shared experiences of giving and receiving – from the act of mending to the stories and threads exchanged. It was joyful."

MEEGAN WILLIAMS

Team member at the Isabella Stewart Gardner Museum, Boston, who managed scheduling for *The Mending Project*

"I have encountered *The Mending Project* on four separate occasions, seeing the project becoming hugely extended in scale. I observed it growing: the table gradually filling up and the matrix of threads becoming denser. As a mender for two days at the Venice Biennale, my experience involved acts of engagement with the audience that proved unexpectedly profound. I received a gift from Mingwei by participating as a mender and I felt that by telling stories I was giving a gift to the audience. Especially in the context of Venice, there were moments of respite, intimate engagement and also contemplation."

TIM GRUCHY

Encountered *The Mending Project* at Lombard-Freid Projects in 2009, the 18th Biennale of Sydney in 2012, Auckland Art Gallery Toi o Tāmaki in 2016 where he received mending, and the 57th Venice Biennale in 2017, where he was a mending host

"Being part of *The Mending Project* was extremely magical. I would sit in the most beautiful gallery and people would bring me a piece of clothing to mend. It felt like being at dinner with an old friend, skipping all the small talk. You would learn things about each other and have really touching moments. I felt like a host every time I mended and I also felt like I was being hosted when an individual shared a personal detail about the garment or their life. Each sewing fix felt like a gift in so many respects: it was a gift to me to share a little piece of art that I had created, a gift to the garment that became wearable once more and a gift to the person sitting across from me. Another gift was the friends I made along the way. Many of the menders at the Institute for Contemporary Art in Richmond, Virginia, have kept in close touch."

LISA HUTCHINSON

Was a mending host for *The Mending Project* in 2018 at the Institute for Contemporary Art in Richmond, Virginia

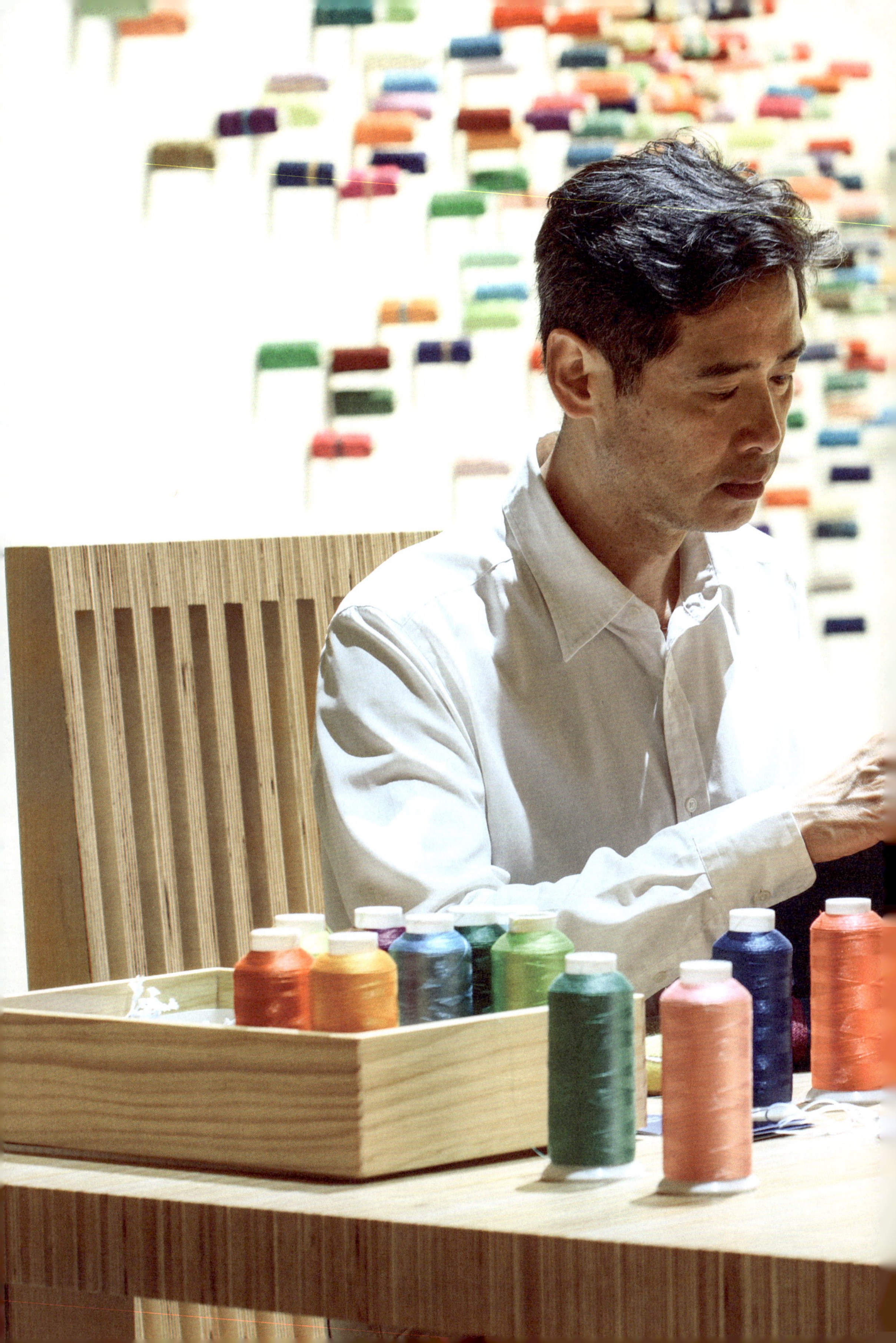

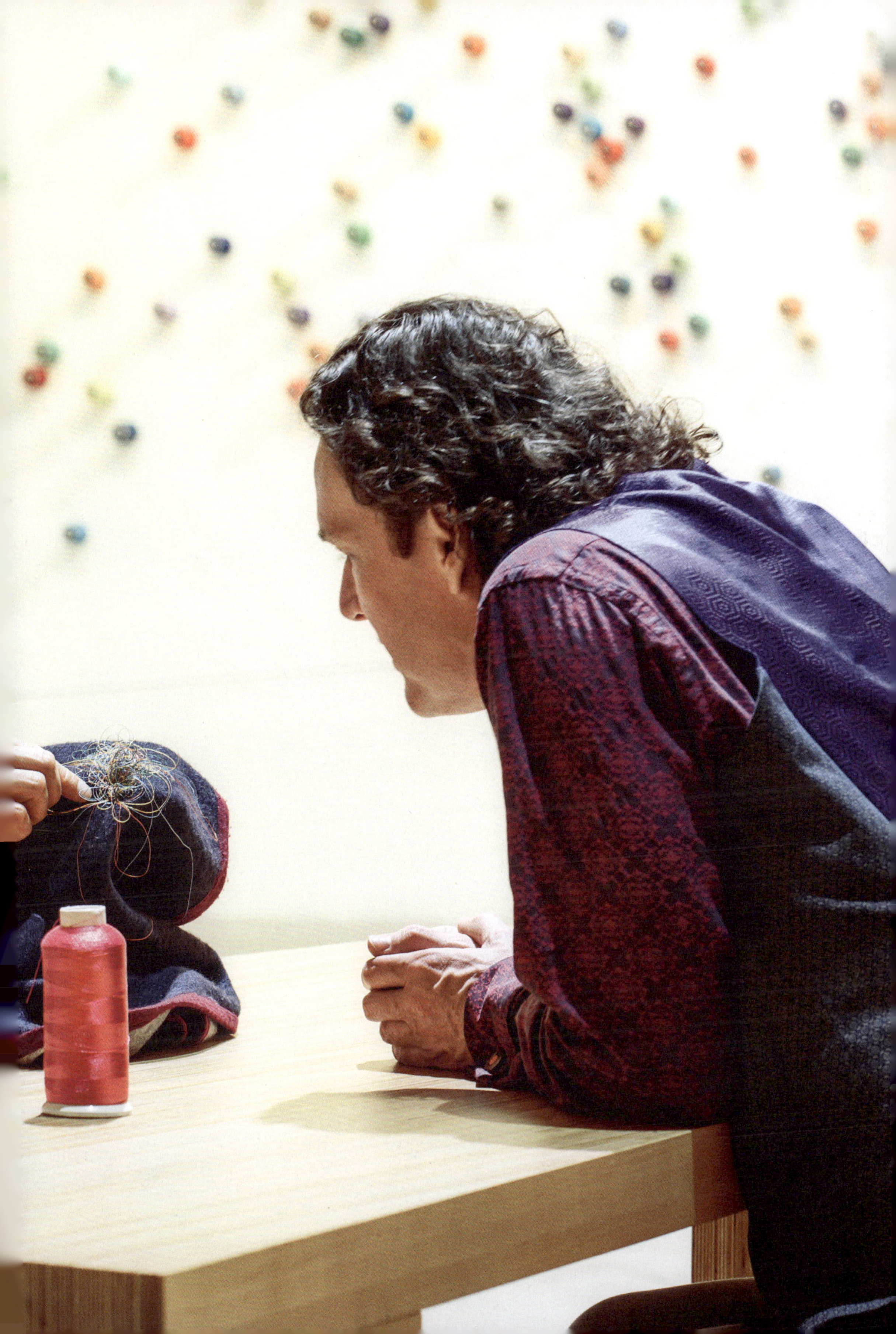

# STONE JOURNEY

2010

Glacial stones, bronze, wood
9 sets from an edition of 11
Each 10 x 50 x 15 cm

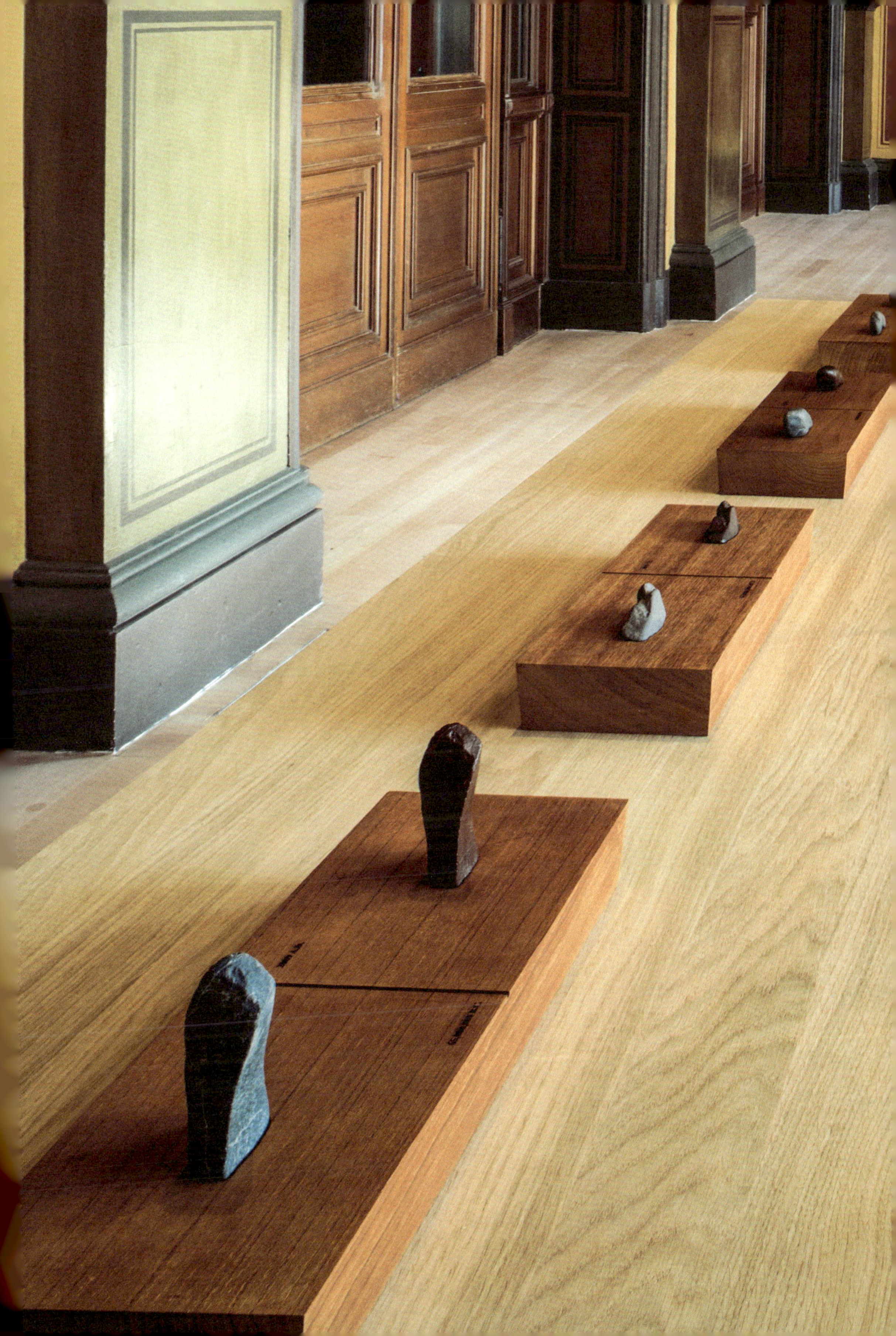

"When I went to New Zealand's South Island, I arrived at a glacial park and was stunned by the beauty and purity of the landscape. I was especially taken with the delicate stones, which have been polished by the glacial river for the past millennium. While standing there, I randomly selected several stones, which were in the close proximity to one another. I was very much aware that just by picking them out of the river-bed, this small gesture would change the content of the river forever, as well as the life of these rocks and my life too. Interestingly, the Chinese tradition of scholar rocks has a similar appreciation for stones that have been sculptured naturally by a process of erosion. Often formally displayed, these too embody the dynamic transformational processes of nature.

Being in such a Jurassic landscape, my imagination escaped into an expansive space and time. I decided to bring the stones that I had collected back and make a bronze cast to create a twin of each stone. I wanted the project to focus on the idea of ownership, raising questions such as: when and how do we own a memory, object or experience? With every collector who has acquired the work, I have asked them to choose when, where and which one to *discard* when the time comes – the natural stone or the bronze cast. It is really up to them to decide when this task happens.

One of these collectors saw me the other day and asked: 'If I decide to perform the task, could I sell the work afterward and, if so, for what price? Would the price of the project be more than when I purchased it, less, or would it even be invaluable?' 'Good questions', I said, and continued, 'It's similar to having a bottle of rare champagne which has been opened and consumed by a celebrity on her 80th birthday. Could the empty bottle be sold and, if so, at what price? Could it be sold at the same price if the person was not well known?' 'It all depends', he answered, leaving with more questions than when he arrived.

None of the collectors have done their 'homework' yet."

LEE MINGWEI

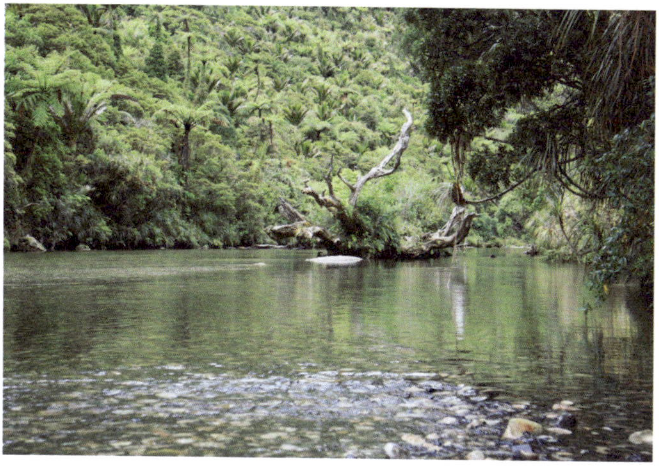

Lee Mingwei gathered the original stones for *Stone Journey* in the lush landscape of Te Waipounamu, New Zealand's South Island, where he walked in the Pororari River Valley, which was sculpted by glacial movement 70 million years ago.

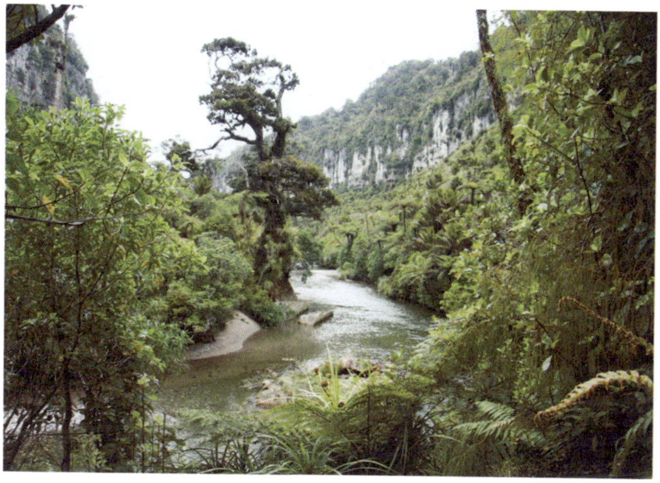



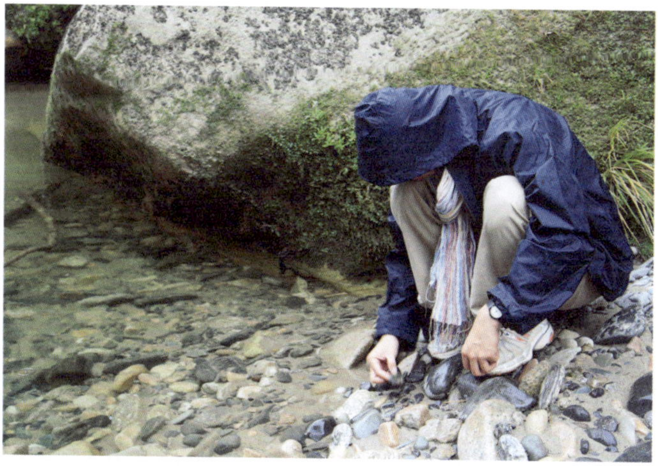

Selecting eleven rocks as souvenirs, he later cast them in bronze. Those who collect a pair of stones are challenged to choose one of the rocks to discard, either the original or its copy. The work functions as a score, waiting to be enacted.

“We understand the idea behind *Stone Journey*, but executing the act of discarding one of the stones can be hard. Instead of having the struggle of deciding, we have delayed the decision altogether. We want to be constantly engaged with the piece, constantly deciding which stone to discard. The piece should be most powerful with one piece missing, but it also feels like at that stage we will have ended the journey, and we want to stay in a state of connection with the piece. The stone is a gift from nature, constantly reminding us to respect what we often take for granted.”

SOPHIA & LEON TAN
Collectors of *Stone Journey*

“As a collector of *Stone Journey*, I became the first person to ‘choose’ a rock. At the time, I felt that these rocks looked like the rocks that appeared in the studies of the Chinese literati, the stones akin to *lingbishi* stones. I haven’t decided on what to do with *Stone Journey*, but I feel Mingwei’s artistic works and explorations all revolve around traditional Chinese Confucianism – the six arts that form the basis of ancient Chinese culture, which were practiced by gentlemen. These are *li* (rites), *yue* (music), *she* (archery), *yu* (charioteering), *shu* (calligraphy) and *shù* (mathematics). Mingwei has an old soul, which is invaluable in the 21st Century. Confucianism developed from the teachings of Confucius, who grew up in the tumultuous spring and autumn period, but formed a transcendent philosophy. Through Mingwei’s work, visitors enter this era of *li*, which is no doubt an ‘ancient gift’ that Mingwei is bringing to us today.”

RUDY TSENG
Collector of *Stone Journey*

"It is not an easy decision to discard one of the pair of stones in *Stone Journey*. On the one hand, it makes the work feel incomplete, but on the other hand, that is the thing you *must* do in order to complete this installation. The collector has an internal fight. Should they discard it? Which one should they discard? What will happen afterwards? I thought, 'Maybe I should hide the stone'. Honestly, I have yet to discard mine because I am finding a good place to do so; maybe in New Zealand's Antipodes Islands."

LEO SHIH

Collector of *Stone Journey*

"The artwork plays on my philosophical inclinations: that to truly love anything is to feel a tension between two things. *Stone Journey*'s proposition that the collector discards the stone – which in turn creates meaning – is impressive because it is novel and thoughtful. I wanted to be a part of it. I have not discarded either stone. I do sometimes wonder whether I should go through with it. One of the most beautiful themes in Mingwei's work is gift giving. I have a strong respect for his use of this as a medium by which to understand relationships and trust. Whereas art normally provides a material and intellectual exchange between people, Mingwei also allows an emotional exchange between people and for that I feel he offers us something more credible and real. I have loved *Stone Journey* because it is a gift to my family and me: it helped us see art in a completely new and fresh way."

CESAR REYES

Collector of *Stone Journey*

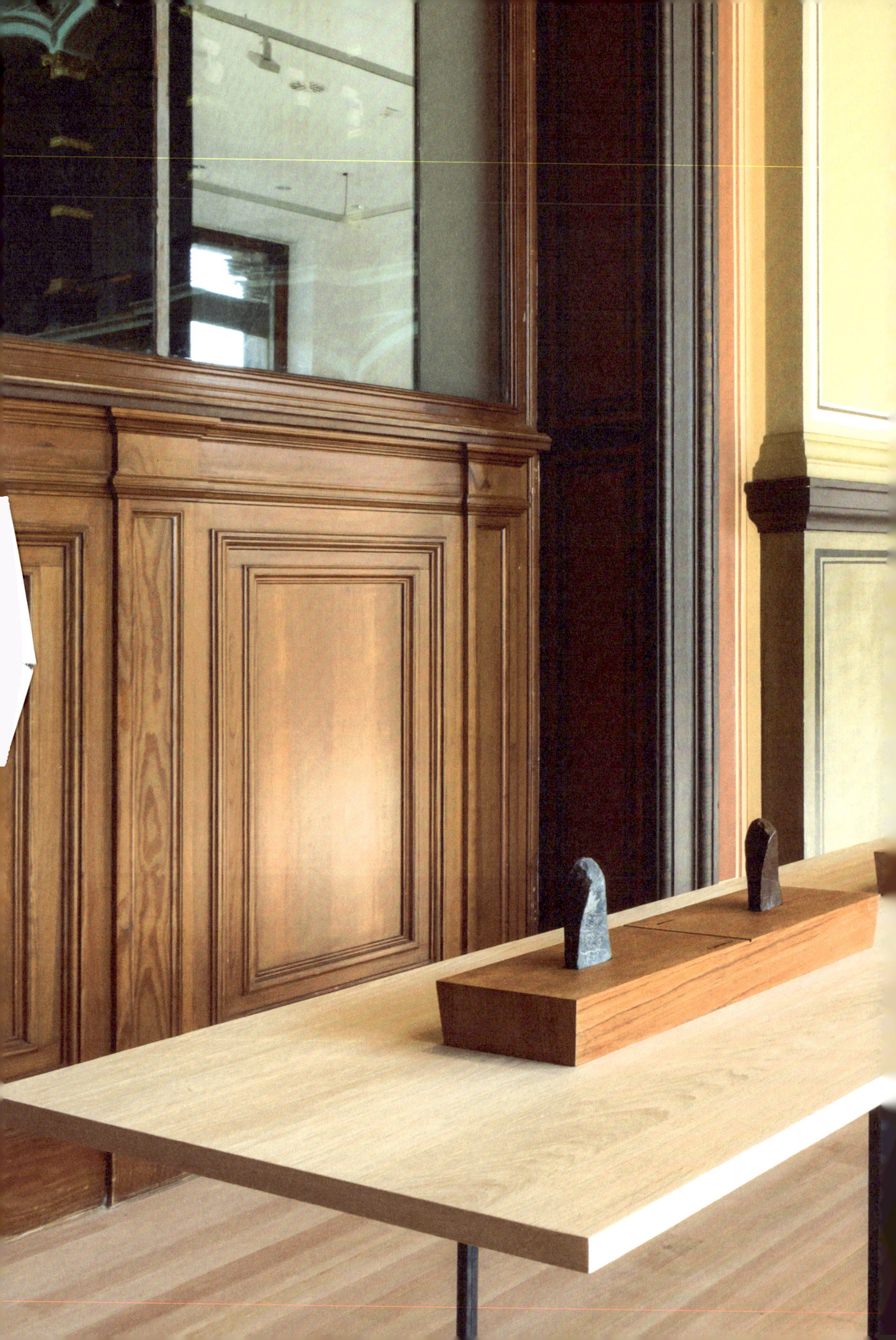

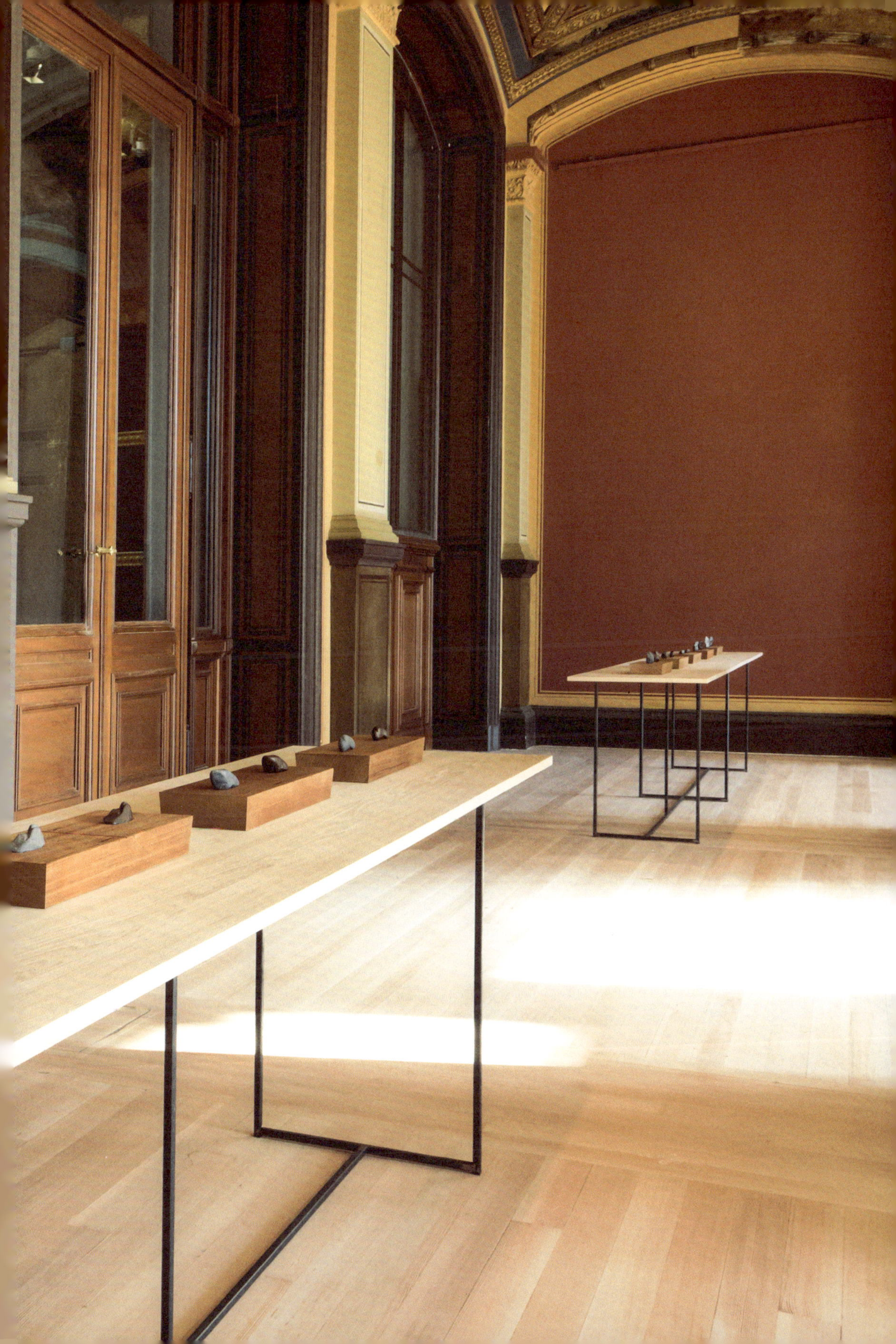

# READER

The common reading of Lee Mingwei's artistic practice has been to see it as part of the tradition of participatory art. However, the Gropius Bau's exhibition identifies the impetus behind the artist's works as lying within traditions of giving and rituals of receiving. *Lee Mingwei: 禮 Li, Gifts and Rituals* demonstrates how the combination of aesthetic and philosophical concepts of giving, as embedded in Eastern and Western traditions, have influenced his work. As such, this reader brings together a selected group of reprints; not only do these reflect the influences, ideas and themes of the artist Lee Mingwei, they too express the thoughts and discourse explored during the curatorial process. One of the priorities when selecting these texts was creating resonance with the atmospheres that Lee Mingwei's works evoke. As you will read, these range across time and geography: from the poems of Paul Celan, one of the major German-language poets in the post-World War II era, to French anthropologist Arnold van Gennep's *Rites of Passage*, 1909, which looks at how individuals transform through rituals of transition, as well as Sei Shōnagon's *The Pillow Book*, 1002, observations recorded in the late-10th Century by this court lady to Empress Consort Teishi in Heian Japan, a literary work that fascinates Lee Mingwei, and Guy Keuleman's analysis of the geo-cultural conditions of *kintsugi*, the Japanese art of repairing broken ceramics using liquid gold. Together these texts lay the theoretical foundations for how one might read the art of Lee Mingwei or further explore the concepts that his practice introduces.

# THE PILLOW BOOK

## SEI SHŌNAGON, 1002

*The Pillow Book*, translated by Meredith McKinney (London: Penguin Classics, 2006), 41-43. 

[36] Seasonal palace festivals – Of the five seasonal palace festivals, none is better than the fifth month's. I love the way the scents of sweet flag and wormwood blend on this day, and another striking thing about the day is the way everywhere, from the "nine-fold palace" to the houses of unmentionably common folk, people compete to spread their roof thick with all the sweet flag and wormwood they can lay hands on. After all, when has this ever been known to happen in any other festival?

The sky is generally heavy with cloud. The Bureau of Clothing sends across to the Empress' palace the little decorative herbal balls that are hung for this festival, with a colourful array of braided threads dangling from them, and we put them up on the pillars to the left and right of Her Majesty's curtained dais in the Inner Chamber. We tie them up in place of the chrysanthemums that have been hanging there, wrapped in plain gossamer-silk cloth, ever since the Chrysanthemum Festival in the ninth month, which we now throw away. I wonder if in fact the herbal balls in turn shouldn't stay up till the next Chrysanthemum Festival, but in reality the coloured threads all get pulled off before long and used for tying things.

Her Majesty is served special festival food, and the younger girls put sweet-flag herbal balls at their waists, and special sweet-flag abstinence charms in their hair, and tie delightful little sprigs of seasonal plants on to long sweet-flag stems with dappled cord and attach them to their Chinese jackets or over-robes. Of course I can't claim there's anything rare and special about all this, still it's most delightful. After all, the cherry blossom blooms every year, but does anyone find it the less lovely for that?

It's also rather fun to watch how all the little lower-class girls who play outside do their best to deck themselves out as smartly as they can, and go about constantly looking at their own clothes and comparing them with others', absolutely bursting with pride in their sweet-flag decorations, till one of the guards' children comes along and playfully tugs them off, and they dissolve in tears. And then there's the delightful custom of finely wrapping a spray of purple melia flowers around purple paper, or a sweet-flag leaf around leaf-green paper, or in the case of white paper a white sweet-flag root. And the sight of a lovely long sweet-flag root enclosed with a letter gives a wonderfully elegant feel. It's also quite charming to see women huddled intimately together sharing the letters they've just received, as they discuss how to respond. Those who are involved in exchanges with a young lady or with someone in high places write particularly careful and elegant letters on this day. Indeed the whole day, down to the way the *hototogisu* gives its signature cry as it flies past in the gathering twilight, is utterly wonderful.

# RITES OF PASSAGE

## ARNOLD VAN GENNEP, 1909

*Rites of Passage* (Chicago: University of Chicago Press, 1960), 2-3, 10-11.


The life of an individual in any society is a series of passages from one age to another and from one occupation to another. Wherever there are fine distinctions among age or occupational groups, progression from one group to the next is accompanied by special acts, like those which make up apprenticeship in our trades. Among semicivilised peoples such acts are enveloped in ceremonies, since to the semicivilised mind no act is entirely free of the sacred. In such societies every change in a person's life involves actions and reactions between sacred and profane – actions and reactions to be regulated and guarded so that society as a whole will suffer no discomfort or injury. Transitions from group to group and from one social situation to the next are looked on as implicit in the very fact of existence, so that a man's life comes to be made up of a succession of stages with similar ends and beginnings: birth, social puberty, marriage, fatherhood, advancement to a higher class, occupational specialisation, and death. For every one of these events there are ceremonies whose essential purpose is to enable the individual to pass from one defined position to another which is equally well defined. Since the goal is the same, it follows of necessity that the ways of attaining it should be at least analogous, if not identical in detail (since in any case the individual involved has been modified by passing through several stages and traversing several boundaries)...

I have tried to assemble here all the ceremonial patterns which accompany a passage from one situation to another or from one cosmic or social world to another. Because of the importance of these transitions, I think it legitimate to single out *rites of passage* as a special category, which under further analysis may be subdivided into *rites of separation*, *transition rites*, and *rites of incorporation*. These three sub-categories are not developed to the same extent by all peoples or in every ceremonial pattern. Rites of separation are prominent in funeral ceremonies, rites of incorporation at marriages. Transition rites may play an important part, for instance, in pregnancy, betrothal, and initiation; or they may be reduced to a minimum in adoption, in the delivery of a second child, in remarriage, or in the passage from the second to the third age group. Thus, although a complete scheme of rites (rites of separation), liminal rites (rites of transition), and postliminal rites (rites of incorporation), in specific instances these three types are not always equally important or equally elaborated.

# DEATH FUGUE

## PAUL CELAN, 1948

*Paul Celan. Selections*, edited by Pierre Joris (Berkeley: University of California Press, 2005), 46-47. Republished with permission of Joris, Pierre (Ed.). Permission conveyed through Copyright Clearance Center, Inc.

Black milk of morning we drink you at dusktime / we drink you at noontime and dawntime we drink you at night / we drink and drink / we scoop out a grave in the sky where it's roomy to lie / There's a man in this house who cultivates snakes and who writes / who writes when it's nightfall *nach Deutschland* your golden hair / Margareta / he writes it and walks from the house and the stars all start flashing / he whistles his dogs to draw near / whistles his Jews to appear starts us scooping a grave out of sand / he commands us to play for the dance

Black milk of morning we drink you at night / we drink you at dawntime and noontime we drink you at dusktime / we drink and drink / There's a man in this house who cultivates snakes and who writes / who writes when it's nightfall *nach Deutschland* your golden hair / Margareta / your ashen hair Shulamite we scoop out a grave in the sky where it's roomy to lie / He calls jab it deep in the soil you men you other men sing and play / he tugs at the sword in his belt he swings it his eyes are blue / jab your spades deeper you men you other men play up again for the dance

Black milk of morning we drink you at night / we drink you at noontime and dawntime we drink you at dusktime / we drink and drink / there's a man in this house your golden hair Margareta / your ashen hair Shulamite he cultivates snakes

He calls play that death thing more sweetly / Death is a gang-boss / *aus Deutschland* / he calls scrape that fiddle more darkly then hover like smoke in / the air / then scoop out a grave in the clouds where it's roomy to lie

Black milk of morning we drink you at night / we drink you at noontime Death is a gang-boss *aus Deutschland* / we drink you at dusktime and dawntime we drink and drink / Death is a gang-boss *aus Deutschland* his eye is blue / he hits you with leaden bullets his aim is true / there's a man in this house your golden hair Margareta / he sets his dogs on our trail he gives us a grave in the sky / he cultivates snakes and he dreams Death is a gang-boss *aus* / *Deutschland* / your golden hair Margareta / your ashen hair Shulamite

# COUNT THE ALMONDS

## PAUL CELAN, 1952



Count the almonds
count what was bitter and kept you awake,
count me in with them:

I searched for your eye which opened
when nobody saw you
I spun that mysterious thread
down which the dew that you dreamed
slithered into a pitcher
kept from harm by a word found in nobody's heart

There you first came into a name that was yours,
sure of foot you advanced on yourself,
the clappers swung free in your silence's belltower,
whatever you heard took a hold of you
whatever what was dead laid its hands on you too,
and threefold you moved through the evening.

Make me bitter.
Count me in with the almonds.

# THE REAL EXPERIMENT

## ALLAN KAPROW, 1983

Allan Kaprow, "The Real Experiment" (1983) in *Essays on the Blurring of Art and Life*, edited by Jeff Kelley (Berkeley: University of California Press, 2003), 201-204.

*Guide: "There are no pictures here."*
*"I see", said the blind man.*

Western art actually has two avant-garde histories: one of artlike art and the other of lifelike art. They've been lumped together as parts of a succession of movements fervently committed to innovation, but they represent fundamentally contrasting philosophies of reality.

A supposed conflict between art and life has been a theme in Western art at least since ancient Rome, resolved, if at all, in the dialectics of the artlike artwork – as, for example, in Robert Rauschenberg's statement: "Painting is related to art and life. Neither can be made. (I try to act in that gap between the two.)"

Simplistically put, artlike art holds that art is separate from life and everything else, whereas lifelike art holds that art is connected to life and everything else. In other words, there is art at the service of art and art at the service of life. The maker of artlike art tends to be a specialist; the maker of lifelike art, a generalist.

The usual questions of subject matter and style become relevant once you accept certain cultural givens, like the specialist notion of "art", the subnotions of "poetry" and "music", and the notions of "exhibit", "audience", "creativity" and "aesthetic value". These are normally taken for granted. But Western culture appears to be changing so markedly that these givens are at best uncertain. What if they weren't "givens"? What if I had only a vague idea about "art" but didn't know the conventions that told me when I was in its presence or was making it? What if I were digging a hole – would that be art? What if I didn't know about audiences and publicity? What if I were to go shopping? Would that not be art? What if I didn't realise that art happened at certain times and in certain places? What if I were to lie awake imagining things in bed at 4:00? Would that be the wrong place and the wrong time for art? What if I were to think art was just paying attention? What if I were to forget to think about art constantly? Could I still make, do, engage in art? Would I be doing something else? Would that be okay?

Of the two, artlike art and lifelike art, avant-garde artlike art occupies the attention of the majority of artists and the public. It is usually seen as serious and as a part of the mainstream Western art-historical tradition, in which mind is separate from body, individual is separate from people, civilisation is separate from nature, and each art is separate from the other. Despite the occasional socio-cultural and spiritual interpretations of this art, artists in this tradition have tended to see their work as engaged in a professional dialogue, one art gesture responding to a previous one, and so forth.

Avant-garde artlike art is supported, tardily but steadily, by high culture's institutions, the galleries, museums, concert halls, theatres, schools, government agencies, and professional journals. These share the same separating point of view about art and life: that art could vanquish life's problems as long as it was far enough away from life so as not to be confused by it and sucked back into its mire. These institutions need artists whose work is artlike.

Avant-garde artlike art basically believes in (or does not eliminate) the continuity of the traditionally separate genres of visual art, music, dance, literature, theatre, and so forth. The combinations of these genres that are commonplace in dance, film, and particularly opera are hierarchic arrangements, with one of the genres (dance, say, or music) presiding over the others and all the genres identifiably distinct, though interrelated. Either singly, or in satellite order, they need, and get the support of, galleries, museums, concert halls, theatres, schools, government agencies, and professional journals. Hands in gloves.

There is no essential difference between a Jean-Baptiste-Siméon Chardin painting hung in a museum and a Frank Stella painting hung in a museum. Similarly, there is no essential difference between the music of Mozart in a concert hall and the music of Karlheinz Stockhausen in a concert hall. Museum and concert hall embed the works equally in late Western cultural history. Every time you walk into a museum or concert hall, it instantly triggers references to that history, and if you don't know much about it, you will miss of the meaning of the art. Call the museums, concert halls, theatres, journals, and so forth frames of mind. These frames of mind are what give the Chardin, Stella, Mozart, and Stockhausen their meaning. That is what tradition is, and it is the real content of the works. In fact, museums, concert halls, and theaters needn't have a thing in them; they are still the signs for art. Like the dog in Ivan Pavlov's conditioned-reflex experiment, we spontaneously salivate a million artworks when they are even mentioned.

Avant-garde lifelike art, in contrast, concerns an intermittent minority (Futurists, Dadas, Gutai, Happeners, Fluxartists, Earthworkers, Body artists, Provos, postal artists, noise musicians, performance poets, shamanistic artists, Conceptualists). Avant-garde lifelike art is not nearly as serious as avant-garde artlike art. Often it is quite humorous. It isn't very interested in the great Western tradition, either, since it tends to mix things up: body with mind, individual with people in general, civilisation with nature, and so on. Thus it mixes up the traditional art genres or avoids them entirely – for example, a mechanical fiddle playing around the clock to a cow in a barnyard. Or going to the laundromat. Despite formalist and idealist interpretations of art, lifelike art makers' principal dialogue is not with art but with everything else, one event suggesting another. If you don't know much about life, you'll miss much of the meaning of the lifelike art that's born of it. Indeed, it's never certain if an artist who creates avant-garde lifelike art is an artist.

For these reasons, avant-garde lifelike art has never fit into traditional arts institutions, even when they offered their support. These institutions "frame" lifelike art right out of life into art (more or less ineptly, at that). "Look," I remember a critic exclaiming once as we walked by a vacant lot full of scattered rags and boxes, "how that extends the gestural painting of the fifties!" He wanted to cart the whole mess to a museum. But life bracketed by the physical and cultural frames of art quickly becomes trivialised life at the service of high art's presumed greater value. The critic wanted everyone to see the garbage as he did, through art history; not as urban dirt, not as a playground for kids and a home for rats, not as rags blowing about in the wind, boxes rotting in the rain. Avant-garde lifelike art does very well in such real-life circumstances. It is not a "thing" like a piece of music or a sculpture that is put into a special art container or setting. It is inseparable from real life.

The root message of all artlike art is separateness and specialness; and the corresponding one of all lifelike art is connectedness and wide-angle awareness. Artlike art's message is appropriately conveyed by the separate, bound "work"; the message of lifelike art is appropriately conveyed by a process of events that has no definite outline. For each kind of art, the conveyance itself is the message, regardless of the details. Artlike art sends its message on a one-way street: from the artist to us. Lifelike art's message is sent on a feedback loop: from the artist to us (including machines, animals, nature) and around again to the artist. You can't "talk back" to, and thus change, an artlike artwork; but "conversation" is the very means of lifelike art, which is always changing.

# THE INTERPRETATION OF A DREAM

## STEPHAN WEST, 1985

"The Intrepretation of a Dream: The Sources, Evaluation, and Influence of the *Dongjing Meng Hua Lu*" in *T'oung-pao* 71, no. 1 (1985): 63-108; excerpt 66-70. Extended glossary and notes have been omitted.


The Dream of Hua was created in a period of Chinese history when nostalgia for the material comfort and urban joys of Kaifeng hung like mist in the air... From this background of melancholic *Heimweh* came many important works...These sentiments seem to have been shared by many writers of the age, but find no better expression than in the preface to *Dongjing meng Hua lu*, written by Meng Yuanlao in 1148:

I followed my father on his official travels north and south. In the year *guiwei* of the Chongning [reign period, 1103], we arrived at the capital city and sited our residence in the western part of the prefecture, on the south side of the westerly road that lines the Jinliang Bridge. By and by I grew up beneath the hub of the [imperial] chariot. Peace stretched on day after day; people were many and all things were in abundance. Youths with trailing locks practiced naught but drumming and dancing, the aged with white speckled [hair] recognised neither shield nor spear. Season and festival followed one upon the other, each with its own sights to enjoy. Lamplit nights there were and moonlit eves, periods of snow and times of blossoming, beseeching skills and climbing heights, training reservoirs and gardens to roam in.

Raise the eyes and there were green bowers and painted chambers, embroidered gates and pearly shades. Decorated chariots vied to park in the Heavenly Avenue and bejeweled horses competed to spur through the Imperial Street. Gold and kingfisher dazzled the eye, silky cloth and silken gauze let float their perfumes. New sounds and sly giggles were found in the willowy lanes and flowered paths, pipes were fingered and strings were harmonised in the tea districts and wine wards.

The eight wilds strived to assembled [in Bianlang], the myriad states were all in communication [with the capital]. Gathered together were the valued and the rare from the four seas – all found their way to market for trade. Assembled were the rare flavours of the whole world – all were in the kitchens [of Bianliang]. The radiance of flowers filled the roads – what limit to spring excursions? Pipes and drums sounded in the empty air – night feasts in how many households? As for skills and crafts – they startled a person's eyes and ears; as for the waste and extravagance – they prolonged a person's spirit.

To look upon the Heavenly countenance [of the emperor] there were the events of Prime Eve and the training reservoir, the Suburban Sacrifice and the

Ancestral Rites of the First [Quarter]. Time after time we observed imperial princess being handed down in marriage or august princes receiving their consorts. As for refurbishing and new construction, there was the raising of the Bright Hall; as for casting and moulding, there was the creation of the Great Cauldrons.

As for observing the registery of the sing-song girls, when the official duties of the sub-functionaries of [Kaifeng] Superior Prefecture were finished, then they returned to feast in the Inner Councils. As for looking at changes and transformations, there was the calling out of names of recommended scholars and the changing and bestowing [of rank] for the promotion of military men [because of their talent].

For tens of years I thoroughly enjoyed [the sights] and roamed often [through the city], yet never did I know enough. Then one morning came the fires of war and in the next year, year *bingwu* of the Jingkang [reign period, 1126, I] went out of the capital and came south to this haven on the left (i.e. eastern) side of the Jiang. My emotions despondent and fallen, by and by the sun set into the mulberry and the elm [as I passed into the dusk of my life].

Silently remembering those years, of the style and sophistication of the things that belonged to each season, of the gentleness and comeliness of human feelings - these became naught to me but disconsolance and vexation. In recent times, when meeting with kith and kin, as the discussion turned back to olden times, the younger-born constantly fancied what was never so. I feared that, as time went by, those who would discuss the customs and traditions [from the capital] would lack all hard fact - and this was truly lamentable. [I] have carefully abridged my records and compiled them in sequence to make this collection. I would hope that, as soon as one opened a chapter, one could see the flourishing of that time.

The Ancient One had a dream of roaming in the land of Hua Xu, and the pleasure of it knew no bounds. Now, I push my thoughts back and turn my head [to the present] in disappointment - is this not awakening from the dream of Hua Xu? I have entitled [this work] *A Record of the Dream of Hua Xu.* But from all that widespread bustle in the capital, of those places I myself never ventured but only heard of from others, there cannot but be omissions. If an old, virtuous man of my home village should be met who could supplement or add to this record and thus bring it to fullness and completeness - would that not be great fortune?

That the language of this record is coarse and vulgar and that it is not adorned by literary style is that [I] wanted everyone, high or low, to know about it. Reader, please take careful note of this!

# THE EARLY CONFUCIAN DISCOURSE ON FAMILY RITES

PATRICIA BUCKLEY EBREY, 1991

*Confucianism and Family Rituals in Imperial China: A Social History of Writing About Rites* (Princeton: Princeton University Press, 1991), 14-15, 16-21. 

*When the rituals of funerals and sacrifices are made clear, the common people will be filial.*

Ta Tail li-chi[1]

The oldest of the texts that mediates the performance of family rituals in imperial China were written during the Chou and early Han. These texts reflected and helped create early Chinese society and cultures. In the early Chou ancestral rites were central features of political rule. In the late Chou critics of Confucians charged them with performing rituals in an exaggeratedly grave or bookish manner to gain attention. In the Han reputations for filial piety were often based on nearly suicidal mortification during mourning for parents. Family rituals clearly tapped into deeply felt emotions connected with life, death, and the survivors' relations with the dead, and were often used for ends beyond the immediate ones of bringing in brides and disposing of or honoring the dead.

Yet the early Confucian discourse on family rituals cannot be understood solely in terms of the social and emotional realities of ritual. The discourse was powerfully conditioned by the basic philosophical premises of Confucianism. Ritual *(li)* became a central concept in Confucian thinking about human nature, ethics, social harmony, cultural identity, and the relationship between the human world and the sphere labelled heaven. The *Li-Chi* [Records of ritual] asserts that all moral and social order is attained through ritual, that without ritual no virtues can be perfected, that observing ritual keeps the powerful from arrogance and the humble from exceeding their station, and that a society in which rituals are observed will be a secure and tranquil one.[2] In passages of these sorts the term *li* was used to encompass the observable actions that constitute rites, ceremonies, manners, and deportment – actions that bind men to each other and link them to numinous realms. *Li* was also culture; Chinese *li* distinguished Chinese from other ethnic groups, each of which had its own *li*.

The great bulk of early Confucian writing on ritual concerns the rituals of the rules and those closest to him, his family, nobles, and highest officials. Domestic family rituals of ordinary people or even officials were, by contrast, treated as relatively marginal in early theorising on ritual. Yet classical Confucian texts provided many basic premises for Confucian discussions of family rituals over the next two thousand years. This chapter, accordingly, concentrates on the formulation of these basic premises...

**Confucius and the Concept of *Li***

When later writers used the term *li*, they generally assumed that their readers understood what *li* was and what made it powerful and desirable. The *Analects* of Confucius provided much of the basis for this common ground. In the *Analects* Confucius seldom spoke of specific rituals but did repeatedly refer to the general category of *li*. Despite his great admiration for the early Chou leaders and respect for texts like the *Book of Poetry* and *Book of Documents*, Confucius did not put particular emphasis on communication with ancestors; his concerns were more with human virtue and good government.

Sacrificial rituals remained important, but because proper performance of such rituals, especially by rulers, was one of the most effective means of attaining orderly society and cultivating morality among its members. Thus for Confucius the rituals themselves brought results, rather than the ancestors.[3]

Confucius sometimes tended toward a cosmic view of ritual, attributing great power, even "magic" in Fingarette's [American philosopher and scholar of Confucius, 1921-2018] sense, to proper performance of *li*. When the disciple Yen Hui asked about true goodness (*jen*), Confucius replied, "Restraining oneself and returning to *li* is true goodness. The whole world would respond to the true goodness of one who could for one day restrain himself and return to *li*"...Yen Hui said, "I beg to ask the detailed steps of how to do this." The Master said, "Look at nothing that is contrary to *li*; listened to nothing that is contrary to *li*; speak of nothing that is contrary to *li*; make no movement that is contrary to *li*."

In the first part of this exchange, *li* could be taken to mean propriety or correct behaviour in a moral sense, and its power is described as so great that even one day's mastery of it would produce remarkable results. The second part of this exchange shows that *li* was at the same time seen as conformity to an established or external code of behaviour regulating every moment, glance, and word.[4]

Confucius validated the idea that preserving a traditional feature of a rite was good in itself, even if it seemed to have no clear moral meaning. When in monthly ceremonies of the Dukes of Lu, Confucius disagreed; he said Tzu Kung loved the sheep and therefore wanted to spare it, whereas he had similar feelings toward the rite itself.[5] The aesthetic dimensions of *li* also appealed to Confucius. He was moved by the beauty of well-choreographed ceremonies combining instrumental music, song, and dance. He once described a court dance as at once perfect beauty and perfect goodness.[6]



Although Confucius spoke of conformity to *li*, he expected it to be tempered by reason and custom. Not every detail had to be exactly as in the prescriptions: "The Master said, 'The hemp cap is the *li*, but now a silk one is worn, which is economical, so I follow the common practice. Bowing at the base of the steps is the *li*, but now it is the practice to bow after ascending the steps, which is arrogant. Even though I am opposing the common practice, I follow bowing at the base'."[7]...

Confucius also argued that true emotion must lie behind ritual performance, providing ample textual authority for an inner-oriented approach to ritual: "*Li* performed without reverence, the forms of mourning observed without grief, how can I bear to look on these things."[8]

Inward virtues were not all that mattered, however; they needed the discipline of conformity to *li* to be truly effective: "Respect without *li* is tiresome; caution without *li* is timidity; boldness without *li* is insubordination; straight-forwardness without *li* is rudeness."[9] Likewise filial piety was not merely an attitude but a pattern of behaviour. It required that "when alive parents should be served according to *li* and when dead they should be buried according to *li* and sacrificed to according to *li*."[10] Confucius, however, does not seem to have fully explored the implications of seeing moral feelings as deeper than ritual. He did not tell his disciples to scrutinise any discrepancies between their feelings and conventional forms, apparently expecting true inner feelings to be largely congruent with the established form of ritual behaviour.

Confucius saw ritual not only in terms of the personal actions of the ruler but also as part of the way the ruler dealt with his subjects. "If the people are led by virtue and regulated by *li*, they will have a sense of shame and behave properly."[11] From other passages in the *Analects* it seems Confucius thought that rulers could rule through ritual by the power of their example and the forms of interaction they initiated.[12] The *Analects* does not discuss teaching the common people ritual. Confucius' ideas about *li* were inseparable from his ideas about human nature, ethics, and the ideal social order. *Li* was desirable because it brought people to recognise and fulfil their responsibilities toward others. Confucius assumed that everyone recognised the universal necessity of loyalty to lords, filial piety to parents, and love and compassion for children and subordinates. He also assumed that all would share his joy and awe at the prospect of a society in which friction was absent because everyone had a role to serve and served it well, that is, where hierarchical differentiation resulted in harmonious coordination. To a very large extent Confucians in later generations did make these assumptions. Nevertheless, Confucius' references to *li* are brief, and possible contradictions are not explored. Later scholars could not turn to the *Analects* to discover unambiguous answers to such questions as who had the authority to decide what constituted *li* or how to govern through *li*.

### The Ritual Classics

A key element in the Confucian discourse on ritual was a focus on texts as the repository of correct knowledge about rituals. How to perform a ritual and what each step meant were secrets known only to gods or priests, but a part of human culture accessible to those who studied the texts of the sages. During the Han period, surviving text on ritual came to be transmitted as three separate classics, the *Chou-li* [Ritual of Chou], *Li-chi* [Records of ritual], and *I-li* [Etiquette and ritual]. The *Chou-li* has little to do with family rites, dealing rather with the administrative structure said to

1 "Sheng-te", 66: 279.

2 Outside the Confucian discourse these claims were not always accepted. Within Taoist philosophy in particular there was a strong distrust for ritual as well as from the imposition of conventional social roles and restraints on behaviour in general.

3 Schwartz, *World of Thought*, 49-50, suggests that this attitude may already have been present in the early Chou before Confucius. Bilsky, *State Religion*, 124-30, 162-82, attributes the decline in the importance of ancestral rites to the weakness of the royal court and the rising importance of rites to territorial deities as the religious basis of rule.

4 Chapter 10 of the *Analects* give many examples of *li* treated as an external or objective code of behaviour. The man who has mastered *li*, for instance, "When saluting his colleagues he moves his hands to the right or left as needed, while keeping his robe even in front and behind. He quickly advances with dignity", *Lun-yü*, 10.3, 10: 1b; Waley, *Analects*, 146.

5 *Lun-yü*, 3.17, 3:10a; Waley, *Analects*, 98.

6 *Lun-yü*, 3.25, 3:15b, Waley, *Analects*, 99. On the aesthetics of ritual see Eno, "Masters of the Dance", esp. 144-46, 150-51.

7 *Lun-yü*, 9.3,9: 1b; Waley, *Analects*, 138.

8 *Lun-yü*, 3.26, 3:15b; Waley, *Analects*, 101.

9 *Lun-yü*, 8.2, 8:1b; Waley, *Analects*, 132.

10 *Lun-yü*, 2.5, 2:2b; Waley, *Analects*, 89.

characterise the early Chou government. The other two texts, however, became the authoritative written sources on cappings, weddings, funerals, and ancestral rites. In later centuries scholars who wished to analyse or formulate these domestic ancestor-oriented rites invariably drew from these texts, directly or indirectly.

The *I-li* as it survives today preserves fragments of late Chou liturgies. For capping, marriage, and funeral rites, only the version for ordinary officers (*shih*) survive. For sacrifices there is also a version for ministers and great officers (*ch'ing-ta-fu*). From other early references it is clear that in Chou times there were liturgies for at least four grades: the king, feudal lords, ministers and great officers, and ordinary officers. There do not seem to have been any Chou texts that prescribed family rites for commoners.[13]

In Han times there were two versions of what is now the *I-li*, the "new text" and "old text". The "new text" was reconstructed from the oral recitation of Kao T'ang during the major effort to recover the classics after the destruction of them during Ch'in times (256-206 B.C.). The "old text" of the *I-li* was a version discovered in the 2. Century BCE in ancient (seal) script and divided into 56 sections. After this discovery ritual scholars continued to teach the "new text" version (two of them Tai Te and Tai Sheng, arranging the text in different order). In the Later Han, Cheng Hsüan (127-200), the greatest classical scholar of the Han, compared the new and old text versions of the *I-li* and produced a version based on the 17-section "new text" but drawing on the "old text" for notes.[14]

This *I-li* as arranged and annotated by Chen Hsüan became the canonical liturgy for family rituals and the basis for all later imperial or private liturgies. The proper sequence of the steps to be followed and the names of each step were thus largely set by the Han. For the four family rites, these steps were as follows:

11 *Lun-yü*, 2.3, 2:1b; Waley, *Analects*, 88.

12 E.g., *Lun-yü*, 2.20, 2:6b-7a:8-2-. 8:1b; 11.25, 11:10a-11a; 12.2, 12:1b; 13.4, 13:3a; Waley, *Analects*, 92, 132, 159-61, 162, 172.

13 The *Li Chi* contains the famous statement that "The rites do not go down to the commoners", but in context this statement meant that the daily behaviour of commoners was not regulated by the same code as that of the nobility and officers. It did not mean that commoners had no rituals of did not perform weddings and funerals. See *Li Chi*, "Ch'ü-li a", 3:6; Legge, *Book of Rites*, 1:90.

14 *Shih-chi* 121:3126; *Han-shu* 30:1710; Steele, *The I-li*, xvi-xvii; *Ssu-k'u ch'üan-shu tsung-mu* 20:158-59.

**Capping**

Divining for the day
Inviting guests
Selecting a sponsor by divination and inviting him
Informing those concerned of the hour of the ceremony
Welcoming the sponsor
The first capping
The second capping
The third capping
Pledging the initiate
Presenting him to his mother
Conferring an adult name on him
Entertaining the sponsor
Presenting the initiant to the relatives
Presenting him to social and political superiors
Rewarding the sponsor and assistants

**Weddings**

Sending the betrothal gifts
Asking the girl's name
Sending news of the favourable divination
Sending the wedding gifts
Asking the time of the ceremony
Escorting the bride in person
The shared meal and wine
The bride and groom left alone in the chamber
The bride meeting her parents-in-law the next day

**Funerals**

Calling back the soul
Plugging the teeth open and propping the feet
Curtaining off the hall
Sending announcements of the death
Taking up places for wailing
Receiving condolences and contributions of grave clothes
Washing the body
Putting food and valuables into the mouth
Putting on grave clothes
Setting up the libation stand and inscribed banner
The preliminary laying out
Receiving gifts
The final laying out
The encoffining
Putting on mourning garments on the 3. day
Wailing in the morning and evening
Divining for the grave site
Divining for the date of the burial

Taking the coffin out of the hole and presenting it to the ancestors
The farewell libation
Reading the list of contributions and gifts
The procession
The burial
Returning to wail
The sacrifice of repose
Placing the tablet in the ancestral hall
The first sacrifice of good fortune after one year
The second sacrifice of good fortune after two years

**Sacrifices**

Divining for the day
Divining for the impersonator of the dead
Informing the impersonator and the guests
Inspecting the animals and utensils
Preparing and arranging the food
The impersonator enters and eats
The presiding man exchanges toasts with the impersonator, then offers wine to the liturgist and assistant
The presiding woman does the same
The presiding woman gives the presiding man a cup of wine, and he does the same for her
Further exchanging of cups of wine with guests, relatives, and the principal heir
General drinking
The impersonator leaves
The feast

# THE WHEEL OF TIME: SAND MANDALA

BARRY BRYANT, 1992

*The Wheel of Time, Sand Mandala: Visual Scripture of Tibetan Buddhism* (San Francisco: Harper, 1992), 21-25. 

The Tibetan word for Mandala is *kyilkhor*, which means "centre and surrounding environment". The mandala of a tantric deity includes the deity and his palace, which is also a representation of the mind of the deity. Based on symbols familiar to the people of India during the Buddha's lifetime, each mandala is a pictorial manifestation of a tantra. It may be "read" and studied as a text, memorised for visualisation during meditation, and interpreted.

The most commonly known mandalas are depicted in two-dimensional form, showing a floor plan – like a blueprint – of the three dimensional palace of the deity, including the architectural design and the many decorative details. Every component is a symbol representing an aspect of the teaching.

The purpose of a mandala is to acquaint the student with the tantra and the deity and to allow the student to "enter into the mandala", that is, to enter into the state of being in which the deity dwells.

The texts state that a mandala can be drawn, painted, made of particles, or constructed by meditative concentration. A two-dimensional mandala may be made of powdered and coloured rice or flowers, particles of stone or jewels, or coloured sand. There are also three-dimensional mandalas constructed out of wood, metal, or other solid materials...

**The Kalachakra Tantra**

Kalachakra (in Tibetan *Du kyi khorlo*) is a Sanskrit word that can be translated literally as "wheel of time"...The Kalachakra Sand mandala is a visual representation of the entire Kalachakra Tantra. It is a two-dimensional representation of the five-storey palace of the Kalachakra deity, in which a total of 722 deities reside, with Kalachakra and his consort Vishvamata united in an embrace of perpetual bliss at the very centre...

Those who participate in making the sand mandala place themselves within the realm of the deity. While we tend to see the mandala as a work of art in the process of creation, the monks who do this work are not creating, but reconstructing a representation of something that already exists. By doing so, they are perfecting and attaining the awakened state of mind. Rather than the emphasis being placed on creating something of material value, the monks are engaging in a process that benefits them and will also serve to benefit others.

### A Teaching for our Time

One of the important features of the Kalachakra Tantra is that it is given for a community. The Buddha offered it for an entire country, the mythical kingdom of Shambala, so historically the initiation has been given to larger groups. The Dalai Lama has remarked that in earlier times communities were separated by valleys, rivers, mountains, or oceans, whereas today, with instant communication and transportation, our community includes the entire planet. This is another reason why he feels Kalachakra is a teaching of our time.

Although it is particularly useful for subduing crisis or warfare (both internal and worldwide), the Dalai Lama makes it clear that the Kalachakra Tantra alone is not enough to achieve world peace. We need world leaders in economics, religion, sociology, politics, and, perhaps most importantly, the physical sciences to work together, sharing their different traditions in order to find innovative solutions to the problems ahead of us. He states further that this cooperation must be motivated by a true sense of universal responsibility to all fellow human beings, which, as an expression of the union of wisdom and compassion, is itself the very essence of Kalachakra.

# THE KINGDOMS OF EDWARD HICKS

CAROLYN J. WEEKLEY, 1999

*The Kingdoms of Edward Hicks* (Williamsburg: Colonial Williamsburg Foundation, 1999), 90-94, 123, 130. Reprinted with the permission of The Colonial Williamsburg Foundation from *The Kingdoms of Edward Hicks* by Carolyn J. Weekley.

The Kingdom pictures have been interpreted as aesthetic expressions of Quaker quietism, as testimonies on peaceful coexistence, and, more recently, as Edward [Hicks'] efforts to satisfy critics of his easel art. But why did Hicks select the Peaceable Kingdom theme in Isaiah? Why not Noah's Ark, of which only one version by Edward [Hicks]...survives? Why not another biblical subject – Daniel in the Lions' Den, for example? Isaiah's prophecy was not only a central and concise statement that embodied key Quaker beliefs, including the issues of inward and outward religious life. It was also a part of the common metaphorical language of the Quaker ministry that often alluded to man's animal propensities and natures. Such meanings are not stressed in the story of Noah's Ark or some other popular as well as illustrative biblical teachings. Other reasons may have influenced Edward [Hicks'] decision to depict the Isaiah prophecy. He cleverly selected a subject that was acceptable to Friends and reinforced the timely messages of his and Elias [Hicks'] ministries. By doing so, he could pursue his art, which admittedly he loved.

The irony is that by creating a pictorial format in easel painting that satisfied – or at least quelled – the concern of his critics, Edward [Hicks] elevated himself to something beyond a tradesman who produced largely utilitarian work. He would never be a "fine arts" painter, but he could have achieved that rank had the circumstances of his life been different, since his talent far exceeded the limitations he imposed on it by adhering to the Quaker way of life. His choice, although self-imposed, was shaped significantly by peer pressure that epitomised the prevailing conservatism and rural nature of his Bucks County world.

The composition and rendering of the group of *Peaceable Kingdoms* Edward [Hicks] painted after the Cleveland picture are significantly more sophisticated... It has been assumed that after Edward [Hicks] began the Kingdom pictures, he continued to paint them at regular intervals. This assumption probably is not true of Edward [Hicks'] earliest efforts. What had begun as a way to express his religious convictions and legitimise his easel work had not yet become a genre through which the artist depicted his perception of growing dissension within the Society of Friends. Three or perhaps four years may have elapsed before Edward [Hicks] began to create the surviving Kingdoms that followed the Cleveland picture.

Scholars have also assumed that the compositions of the Kingdoms evolved chronologically; once Edward [Hicks] changed a picture or major element, he usually did not return to it. While generally true, there were occasional overlaps between the various types. With the exception of the 13 paintings comprising the first Kingdom group, a reconsideration of the dates for many of the extant Kingdom pictures is necessary. The 13 paintings discussed here...were created after the Cleveland *Peaceable Kingdom*. All but one retain their original borders. Five were titled either by the artist or later scholars as "the peaceable kingdom of the branch." Eight have rhymed borders that paraphrase the Isaiah prophecy. Edward [Hicks] signed five of the paintings, one of which was dated 1826. Hicks probably painted the 13 between 1822 and 1829-1830, so this group overlaps another type of Kingdom. Edward [Hicks] rarely signed or dated Kingdom pictures...further complicating the assignment of dates...

Edward [Hicks] ultimately arrived at a formula that seemed to fulfil his goals. Six of the surviving Kingdoms..., three of which may be the most sophisticated he ever painted..., illustrate this point. The most impressive pictures are those at the Folk Art Center and a nearly identical version owned by the Worcester Art Museum. All feature large, seated, centrally placed lions. The gazes of the seated lions and the powerful, outstretched leopards in these paintings are intense, riveting, and magnetic. Neither at peace nor angry, they exude energy and appear ill at ease and somewhat startled. Their poses suggest a tenuous peace, a delicate balance of difficult and unresolved issues. The bear and wolf, also carnivorous beasts, are complaisant in comparison...

Many consider the *Peaceable Kingdoms* of Edward [Hicks'] middle years the most captivating and striking of the genre because of the stories they relate, their successful compositions, and the fine quality of their painting. The artist may have borrowed elements from other sources and combined them in various ways, but a single source for the *Peaceable Kingdoms* of this group does not exist. They are Edward [Hicks'] compositions.

# EXPECTATIONS OF RECIPROCITY

MARIA HEIM, 2004

*Theories of the Gift in South Asia. Hindu, Buddhist, and Jain Reflections on Dāna* (New York: Routledge, 2004), 33-41.


When Marcel Mauss framed his discussion of gift giving as a set of obligations to give, to receive, and to reciprocate, he was giving voice to a long tradition in European thought that identifies social solidarity and integration in terms of reciprocity. Given this emphasis on mutuality, it is somewhat surprising that Mauss does not mention the Stoic Seneca's *De Beneficiis*, since Seneca's philosophy of the gift has been so influential in European thought and shares much with Mauss on the social value of mutual exchange (see Goux 2002; Davis 2000:8). For Seneca, as with Mauss, the gift is to be given freely and yet it bears obligations for the recipient: "the giving of a benefit is a social act, it wins the goodwill of someone, it lays someone under obligation" (Basore 1958:321). These obligations work as social glue that binds human beings to one another. Seneca inveighs against nothing so much as ingratitude, for the ingrate fails to realise how mutual exchange is the condition of security and fellowship: "there is nothing that so effectually disrupts and destroys the harmony of the human race as this vice"...Giving and gratitude create the bonds of fellowship cementing harmonious human relations and security through mutual aid and acknowledgement. Mauss is perhaps not as quick as Seneca to identify gift exchange as the key to human *survival*, but still for him mutual gift exchange, as practiced in premodern or clan-based societies much less driven by mores of *Homo Economicus* than modern capitalist societies, is the key to human solidarity. The gift is a moral relation, and Mauss' essay, like Seneca's, has moral implications: Mauss calls for us to return to archaic society, to "social security" and "the solicitude arising from reciprocity and co-operation" (Mauss 1990:69). This is not to suggest that he recognised no tensions in the gift, and that these tensions never cause a breach in the social fabric. The gift courts violence, debt, competition and agonistic conflict. However, apart from excessive gifts such as potlatch, the gift, for Mauss as with Seneca, is the bedrock of human moral relations, and the study of gift circulation is the study of social interconnectedness.

Against this perspective on the gift as a mechanism of social solidarity through mutual exchange, South Asian theories of *dāna* offer a sharp contrast. *Dāna*, according to all formal discussion on it, is not obligated in any way. It does not evoke return from the recipient, and is not premised on a notion of reciprocity and

1 DK, 4.

2 See Gouldner 1960; Michaels 1997; Parry 1986, 1994; Raheja 1988; Trautmann 1981; Vatuk and Vatuk 1971. As some of these authors note, there are other kinds of gift giving in South Asia besides *dāna* that may include reciprocity and obligation.

interdependence. As the Dharmaśhāstra author Lakṣmīdhara bluntly states: "reciprocal gifts are not part of dharma."[1] Moreover, *dāna* does not and should not inspire gratitude from the recipient. Mauss himself was not unaware of these features of *dāna* ideology, and acknowledges, in a footnote, the lack of obligations of return in gifts given to brahmans (Mauss 1990:146-7). Indologists and others have puzzled over the significance of this denial in *dāna* theory of the otherwise apparently ubiquitous principle of reciprocity, both in terms of what it suggests about Indian thought as well as what this large-scale exception might mean for Mauss' general conclusions.[2]

One view of the Indian denial of reciprocity is that while *dāna* theory denies earthly reciprocity it, like the sacrificial cult it replaced, yields religious merit and reward in the afterlife (Trautmann 1981:279-82). *Dāna* is to be given not for earthly recompense from the recipient, but for spiritual merit, wherein one is repaid in the next life for religious gifts given in this life. One gives with an eye fixed not on the recipient's gratitude and counter-gift, but on one's next life where one reaps the rewards of merit. In this view, *dāna* may be an instrument of social life that arranges certain forms of human relationships, but its social dimension is a byproduct rather than a central feature of the gift.

# THE DESIGN CONCEPT [FOR THE RESTORATION OF THE GROPIUS BAU, 1978-1981]

JENS-OLE REY, 2012

*Bauen zwischen autonomer Gestaltung und Denkmalschutzvorgaben: Der Architekt Winnetou Kampmann* (Marburg: Tectum Verlag, 2012), 262-265.

Together with the responsible persons, Kampmann and Weström decided to undertake the sculptural completion of the stucco surfaces and paintings, but to render ornamental surfaces in clearly lighter colours and simplified forms. In large parts, the restoration of the decor fragments was limited to the extant remnants of the surfaces…“The observer will still be able to see that the arcades of the Grand Atrium are only restored in individual sections of the ceilings, mainly on the ground floor, while in the atrium itself only the dome and the area above the first floor on the east side of the atrium façade have been reconstructed.”[1] Extensive plastering has been undertaken in original techniques, stucco elements have been reconstructed in accordance with the salvaged sections. Here – as in many other rooms of the buildings – the architects have restored surviving original surfaces through retouching and filling in missing sections. In some sections, they attempted to restore what had been lost, but always in a recognisable way or in modern, sanitised forms. The decision was made to give visual priority to the recognisably historical material over the new work that lies next to it and to emphasise it through simple forms. As a result, the extant material is underscored and, furthermore, given new “voice” through the repairs, completions and complementary interventions. Changes to the floor plan were permitted only in sections that were already destroyed, for example on the north side.

Kampmann and Weström handled the façade entirely differently… Here, they aimed for the complete reconstruction of the historical condition as required by the Antiquities and Monuments Office, although with the simplification of small details for economic reasons. Nevertheless, Kampmann and Weström later claimed, not without pride, that “even if they looked through binoculars, modern observers wouldn’t be able to tell which parts of the building are from 1880 and which parts from 1980."[2] The architects opted for a wide range of individual measures, taking into account the degree of destruction or the aesthetic value of certain elements. Structurally, this range stretches from small-scale repairs to the existing building, the strengthening or support of the original construction through to the restoration of the volume of the building or the replacement of missing structural elements. Accordingly, the brick – in this case old bricks – represents the smallest modular unit, to be found in the small-scale repairs to the original building as well as in the large-scale structural repairs. Inside, measures range from the reconstruction of decorative plaster bands on the pillars in the atrium to the restoration of plaster surfaces and the corresponding remodelling of missing balustrades in the atrium. Kampmann and Westström have been guided by very different considerations in the restoration process, giving special consideration to each individual case. Their principal concern was to do justice to function: a museum building must be able to function as such. "An observer of the building can see that, despite any fragmentariness in a number of areas, wherever possible, the future function of the building was given primary consideration, even if in a small number of cases this led to a clash with the principles of heritage preservation", Winnetou Kampmann later wrote.[3] So right from the start, Kampmann had the needs of future exhibitions in mind. The architectural shell and its contents are inextricably connected...

It almost seems as if he and his partner were trying to use this dialogue between old and new to open up a new perspective for an audience already schooled and sensitised by museum experiences, a perspective that has its point of departure in the darkest parts of German history, made visible in an architectural memento. Yet surmounting that history does not set a pedagogical tone, much rather it presents visitors with a dignified setting in which to experience the art of Berlin. The Gropius Bau thus does not simply reflect the multifaceted history of the city of Berlin, nor simply the conflict of vying forces in public spaces, but also a shift in the understanding of heritage preservation.

1 Winnetou Kampmann and Ute Westström, "Rekonstruktion im Außenbereich – Die Terrakottagesimse" in *Martin-Gropius-Bau, die Geschichte seiner Wiederherstellung*, edited by Kampmann and Westström (Munich: Prestel, 1999), 70.

2 Ibid.

3 Winnetou Kampmann, "Wiederaufbau des ehemaligen Kunstgewerbemuseums" in *Baukultur*, no. 5 (1981): 27-31; 28.

# THE CHANGING LANDSCAPE OF CHINA'S CONSUMERISM

ALISON HULME, 2014

*The Changing Landscape of China's Consumerism* (Oxford: Chandos Publishing, 2014), 136-139.


For Confucians, it is everyday life that matters, both as a source of wisdom and as an object to be improved or at least constantly harmonised in the ceaseless reconfiguration of people, animals, things, and over all circumstances in which we find ourselves. One's most mundane actions, responses, and habits are indicative of one's personal development. They are exercises. As a matter of fact, the good life is a matter of continuous exercise. And life, at least the good life, is always a *social* kind of living. Since everyday life requires constant and regular consumption of things, how we consume is an integral part of the exercise of life. What and how we eat, how we dress, what sort of things we acquire, and how we acquire them are all indispensable in the process of our personal cultivation. It is here that *li*, the customs of self and interpersonal behaviour come into the picture. While often translated as "rituals" or "ceremonies", *li* also entails informal actions or gestures of etiquette, decorum, and courtesy which are thoughtful, but in the case of the most advanced individuals also spontaneous, responses to unique circumstances arising in reciprocal relations between two or more persons. They are not necessarily pre-ordained, though in the course of history many precisely laid-down rituals, ceremonies, and rules of etiquette have been formed and consolidated under the authority of tradition. But tradition according to Confucianism is not a fixed entity and must adapt itself, however resistantly, to the continuous changes taking place in the physical and cultural environment, and this applies as well to even the most seemingly anchored kinds of *li*.

The Confucian emphasis on *li* is immediately relevant to the question of consumption, for acts on this basis would constitute the only instances in which potentially immoderate expenditures could be seen as justifiable. Respect and deference toward others as well as toward the natural forces (energies in the world and in our bodies as Confucians believed) are often displayed through lavish gifts, delicious food, exquisite clothing, and other costly means. This was duly noted and criticized by Mo Di as we shall see in the next section. *The Book of Rites* contains many intricate descriptions of what things, food items, clothing, etc. are required for certain rituals, sacrifices, and ceremonies: "Whatever heaven produces, whatever earth developes in its growth; – all were then exhibited in the greatest abundance",[1] as the book says about sacrifices.[2] In some cases, these can seem excessive. Those of us who have been guests in China, or, for that matter, in any of the other East Asian countries, have had the often unconscionable experience of being served delicacies during a single meal in more quantities than the diners could possibly have devoured in several days, and felt the embarrassment of receiving presents vastly disproportionate to the ones we brought along ourselves. These are instances of traditional customs that are originally Confucian, of "appropriate" ways to receive and treat honoured guests, especially those "from distant quarters", as Confucius himself indicates in the very first analect attributed to him. "Propriety", it says in the *Book of Rites*, "is seen in humbling one's self and giving honour to others." It therefore comes as no surprise that relative to Western countries, a large proportion of luxury items are bought as gifts in contemporary China: "Gifts for government officials, gifts for lovers, gifts for clients".[3] Now as before, however, there is an unquestionable emphasis on reciprocity:

> In the highest antiquity they [sages] prized (simply conferring) good; in the time next to this, giving and repaying the thing attended to. And what the rules of propriety value is that reciprocity. If I give a gift and nothing comes in return, that is contrary to propriety; if the thing comes to me, and I give nothing in return, that also is contrary to propriety.[4, 5]

Certainly, it is expected that gifts will be reciprocated in one way or another. Perhaps this aspect has been overly formalised throughout the ages in Chinese culture so that a presenter of a gift will now expect some concrete favours in return. But gifts are still to a large extent a sign of good will and sincere intentions, and, from a Confucian point of view, they ought not to revolve merely around the display of external goods. The section on sacrifices quoted above from the *Book of Rites* continues: "Everything was there from without, and internally there was the utmost effort of the will: – such was the spirit in sacrificing".[6]

As Chapter 10 in the *Analects*[7] reveals, Confucius himself placed considerable emphasis on proper attire depending on circumstances (e.g., 10.6) and seems even to have been some kind of gourmand, as he "would not eat food that was improperly prepared, or that was lacking the appropriate condiments and sauces" (10.8). But he would never be immoderate, nor eat more than his fill (10.8), and be quite willing to make changes to certain formal rituals should they traditionally require items that had become expensive (9.3). "In observing ritual propriety", in any case, "it is better to be modest than extravagant" (3.4). Some occasions, moreover, may in fact call for more modesty in terms of diet or clothing, such as periods of purification during which "he would invariably wear a spirit coat made of plain cloth" and "invariably simplify his diet" (10.7) and "in the presence of someone in mourning" when he "would not eat his usual portions" (7.9).

*Li* are traditionally formed guidelines as to how we should act in our particular roles, relations, and circumstances. Their gradual adoption is a learning process that should teach us how to act reciprocally, respectfully, and responsibly toward others. While certainly entailing cultivation of one's person, such learning is not aim directed in a simple sense as the relations and all that they engender are changing with time along with all those involved. Thus, the configuration of these relations as informed by *li* is in a continuous process of re-evaluation. Roger T. Ames speaks of *li* as "achieved propriety in one's roles and relations", thus emphasising that *li* are first and foremost enacted in the dynamic context of social relations, beginning in the family.[8] While there is certainly a blurry frame within which my enactment of *li* is expected to take place in each of my roles, I nevertheless have considerable scope to creatively personalise that enactment in each case.[9] The description of Confucius' own comportment betrays both the extensive scope of *li* according to his embodiment of these customs in real life and his creative personalisation of them. As noted in the *Analects*,[10] *li* applies to a way of life carefully choreographed down to appropriate facial expressions and physical gestures, a world in which a life is a performance requiring enormous attention to detail. Importantly, this *li*-constituted performance begins from the insight that personal refinement is only possible through the discipline provided by formalised roles and behaviours.

*Li*, then, are both the means and end of life as a work of art in constant progress. As discipline and training they constitute the means, and as the end, perhaps, they are exemplified by the life of Confucius himself as recorded in the *Analects*. His behaviour, however, is not presented as laying down universal rules to be imitated. It is, on the contrary, highly personalised as manifesting the particular character traits of Confucius himself, and therefore a mode of action ultimately inimitable by others but certainly inspirational to them. Every action enjoys its particularity as an action performed by that particular person in that particular circumstance and her particular phase of life.[11]

Hence the level of consumption is in all cases dependent on, and thus secondary to, the appropriate action as guided by *li*: "Virtue is the root; wealth is the branches", as the *Book of Rites* states quite clearly (*Li Chi*, 1967 [Da xue §26]).[12] The point, in other words, is not material goods and their acquisition and consumption, but propriety.

1 Ji tong in *Li Chi: Book of Rites*, translated by James Legge, two vols. (New York: University Books, 1967), §4.

2 See Liu Jialin 2000: 153, Huang Yong 2003:76, and the list of newspapers and magazines carrying advertising provided by Wang Jian 2000: 24-5.

3 April Rabkin, "Scenes From the Chinese Consumerist Revolution", *The Cut*, 16.8.2012, https://www.thecut.com/2012/08/scenes-from-the-chinese-consumerist-revolution.html.

4 Qu li in *Li Chi*, §6.

5 See Dal Lago 2000 and Hestler 2005.

6 Ji tong in *Li Chi*, §4.

7 Confucius, *The Analects*, translated by David Hinton (Washington: Counterpoint, 1998).

8 Roger T. Ames, *Confucian Role Ethics: A Vocabulary* (Hong Kong: The Chinese University Press, 2011), 109.

9 Cf. Ames, *Confucian Role Ethics*.

10 Confucius, *The Analects*, 52.

11 Geir Sigurosson, "Li, Ritual and Pedagogy: A Cross-cultural Exploration", *Sophia* 51, no. 2 (2012): 227-42.

12 Da xue in *Li Chi*, §26.

# THE GEO-CULTURAL CONDITIONS OF KINTSUGI

GUY KEULEMANS, 2016

"The Geo-cultural Conditions of Kintsugi" in *The Journal of Modern Craft* 9, no. 1 (2016): 15-34; excerpt 16-17. Reprinted by permission of the publisher (Taylor & Francis Ltd, http://www.tandfonline.com).

*Kintsugi* repair is a traditional craft technique for repairing broken ceramics using *urushi*, a plant-based adhesive lacquer resin, decorated with gold or silver. It has developed since the time of the Azuchi-Momoyama period in the late 16th Century.[1] While there is evidence of *urushi* based repairs dating from this time (and also further back), the earliest notable works of *kintsugi* date from the first half of the 17th Century, the early Edo period; Seppo by Hon'ami Koetsu is an example. *Kintsugi's* aesthetic appeal results from its unique use of gold or silver dressing over *urushi* lacquer in a way that embellishes the appearance of the original ceramic object...It is identified as a uniquely Japanese technique. Its products are highly esteemed and used in culturally significant practices, such as the tea ceremony.[2] As a repair craft, it responds to the principle of *mottainai*, a Japanese concept for the regret experienced from waste.[3] However, *kintsugi* is also a *transformative* repair craft.[4] It uses precious metals to draw attention to the object and transform the object's appearance, in contrast to other forms of repair that attempt to hide a history of damage – for example, in the case of using transparent or invisible glues...[5]

A key aspect of transformative repair practices is that a material record of an object's damage and subsequent repair is overtly sensible. Sealed cracks are, for example, visible and may be felt underneath the fingers when held. This positions *kintsugi* as material craft that has capacities to *affect*; to engage with the senses and potentialise *perceptions* of damage and repair. For Deleuze and Guattari, the affects of such things as cracks do not operate in isolation, but have relations, and work in sensory compounds.[6] A repaired crack can trigger and link to many things, not least perceptions of threat, urgency, catastrophe, risk, but also care, amelioration or hope. These compounds of sensation modulate human behaviour as a micropolitical consequence – consequences at the level of the individual. Deleuze and Guattari contend that affects are mediated by materiality, and furthermore extend outwards into fields that have *macropolitical* effects at the level of society and culture.[7]

1 Steven Weintraub, Sadae Y. Walters, and Kanya Tsujimoto, "Urushi and Conservation: The Use of Japanese Lacquer in the Restoration of Japanese Art", *Ars Orientalis* 11 (1979): 54.

2 Christy Bartlett, "A Tearoom View of Mended Ceramics" in *Flickwerk: The Aesthetics of Mended Japanese Ceramics* (Ithaca: Herbert F Johnson Museum of Art and Münster: Museum für Lackkunst, 2008), 12.

3 Kintsugisouke, "When Mending Becomes an Art (Japanese Urushi Art)", video, 8.12.2009, https://www.youtube.com/watch?v=k3mZgs0vkDYThegoldmendingtechniquesofurushilacquerartistRyugaku-Miyahara.

4 Charly Iten, "Ceramics Mended with Lacquer–Fundamental Aesthetic Principles, Techniques and Artistic Concepts" in *Flickwerk*, 18.

5 There are other historical ceramic repair techniques that also alter appearance: the ancient techniques of metal stapling that developed in China and subsequently spread to Europe are notable (Albert, 2012: 2-3). In Japan, however, *kintsugi* became more widely adopted.

6 Gilles Deleuze and Félix Guattari, *What is Philosophy?* (New York: Columbia University Press, 1994), 168.

7 Gilles Deleuze and Félix Guattari, *A Thousand Plateaus: Capitalism and Schizophrenia* (Minneapolis: University of Minnesota Press, 1987), 208-16.

# ZHEN JI: ORIGINAL

BYUNG-CHUL HAN, 2017

*Shanzai: Deconstruction in Chinese*, translated by Philippa Hurd (Boston: The MIT Press, 2017), 10-16. 

In classical Chinese the original is called *zhen ji* (真跡). Literally this means the "authentic trace". This is a particular trace, as it does not follow a teleological path. And there is no promise inherent in it. It is associated neither with anything enigmatic nor kerygmatic. Moreover, it does not condense into a clear, monomorphic presence. Rather, it deconstructs the idea of any such original that embodies an unmistakable, immutable, centred presence and identity.[1] Processuality and differentiality give the trace a deconstructive, centrifugal force. The trace does not tolerate any completed centred work of art that might possess a final form and avoid any change. Its *difference* to itself does not allow the artwork to come to standstill whereby it could achieve its final shape. Thus the trace always lets the artwork *differ from itself*. The Chinese notion of the original as trace (*ji*, 跡) contains the structure of the Freudian "memory-trace" that is subject to continual rearrangement and transcription. The Chinese idea of the original is determined not by a unique act of creation, but by unending process, not by definitive identity but by constant change. Indeed, change does not take place within the *soul* of an artistic subjectivity. The trace effaces the artistic subjectivity, replacing it with a process that allows no essentialist positing.

The Far East is not familiar with such pre-deconstructive factors as original, origin, or identity. Rather, Far Eastern thought *begins with* deconstruction. Being as a fundamental concept of Western thought is something that resembles only itself, and that tolerates no reproduction outside itself. Plato's banishment of mimeses is a direct result of this conception of Being. According to Plato the beautiful or the good is something immutable that resembles only itself. It is monomorphic (*monoeides*). Thus it allows no variation. In every reproduction, this notion of Being sees something demonic that destroys original identity and purity. The notion of the original is already outlined in the Platonic Idea. *A lack of Being* is inherent in every image. By contrast, the basic figure in Chinese thought is not the monomorphic, unique *Being* but the multiform, multilayered *process*.

A Chinese masterpiece never remains the same itself. The more it is admired, the more its appearance changes. It is regularly overwritten by connoisseurs and collectors. They inscribe themselves into the work by means of inscriptions and seals. In this way inscriptions are layered upon the work like memory-traces in the psychic apparatus. The work itself is subject to continual change and permanent transcription. It is not *static*. Rather, *it is fluid*. The trace makes it fluid. The trace is opposed to presence. The work empties itself out to become a generative, communicative locus of inscriptions.[2] The more famous a work is, the more inscriptions it has. It presents itself as a palimpsest.

Not just individual works but an artist's entire oeuvre is subject to transformation as well. The oeuvre changes constantly. It shrinks and grows. New pictures suddenly turn up to fill it, and pictures that were once ascribed to a master's oeuvre disappear. For example, the oeuvre of the famous master Dong Yuan looks different in the Ming dynasty from how it looked during the Song dynasty, with even forgeries or replicas defining a master's image. A temporal inversion occurs. The subsequent or retrospective defines the origin. Thus the inversion deconstructs it. The oeuvre is a large lacuna or construction site that is always filling up with new contents and new pictures. We might also say: *the greater a master, the emptier his oeuvre*. He is a signifier without identity, who is always being loaded with new significance. The origin turns out to be a *retrospective construction*.[3]

Adorno too sees the artwork not as a static, fixed, immutable construction, but as something spiritual and alive that is able to change. For example, he writes about Wagner: "But what has changed about Wagner...is not merely his impact on others, but his work itself, in itself...As spiritual entities, works of art are not complete in themselves. They create a magnetic field of all possible intentions and forces, of inner tendencies and countervailing ones...Objectively, new layers are constantly detaching themselves, emerging from within; others grow irrelevant and die off. One relates to a work of art not merely, as is often said, by adapting it to fit a new situation, but rather by deciphering within it things to which one has a historically different reaction.[4] Here the artwork is presented like a living creature that grows, sheds its skin, and transforms itself. However, the change is founded not in the *external* "situation" but in the *inner essence* that lies at the heart of the work. Adorno explicitly distances himself from the kind of change in the *self* that is due to a situation. In addition, according to Adorno, the artwork is a changing or shape-shifting body (*Wandlungsleib*) that is, however, not *subjected* to change, but

1 Derrida too calls this *différance* that resists any mark of presence and identity the "trace" (see *Margins of Philosophy*, translated by Alan Bass [Chicago: University of Chicago Press, 1982], 18). His concept of the trace also lacks any teleological, theological notion of the "trail", which as an "almost imperceptible promise" announces "that we would be set free into the open, now dark and perplexing, now again lightning-sharp like a sudden insight." *On the Way to Language*, translated by Peter D. Hertz (New York: Harper & Row, 1971), 41.

2 Not just the history of its reception but other factors as well are implicated in the constant alteration of the original: changes in format as a result of new mountings, cropping because of material damage, aesthetic or even commercial considerations, retouchings or retrospectively added signatures all have an impact on the work's form over time. With regard to a Chinese picture in extreme cases the metaphor of a ship holds true, a ship that returns to its home port for the first time in generations after all its parts have been gradually replaced en route in the course of repairs. Is this the same ship to any extent? The crew is different, the inhabitants of the home city are different, and there are no blueprints that could provide information as to whether at least the original shape of the ship has remained the same while its parts have been replaced. (Christian Unverzagt, *Der Wandlungsleib des Don Yuan: Die Geschichte eines malerischen OEuvres* [Stuttgart: Franz Steiner Verlag, 2007], 184).

3 Even the claim to truth, which is alien to the Chinese, cannot clearly establish a master's oeuvre. Wilhelm Valentiner's 1921 catalogue of Rembrandt's work contains 711 paintings. In 1935 Bredius listed 630 works as being by the artist's own hand. Thirty years later in 1968 Horst Gerson identified only 420 pictures as being authentic. The Rembrandt corpus of the Rembrandt Project, which claims to eliminate from his oeuvre paintings by Rembrandt's colleagues as well, lists approximately 300 works. Even the meticulous stylistic analysis of so-called connoisseurs or experts is not free from arbitrariness.

changes *itself* from within. The *inner* richness and *inner depth* of the work make it living and adaptable. It is characterised by inexhaustible *fullness* and unfathomable *depth*. They *inspire* it to become a living organism. Its richness develops independent of the situation. By contrast, the Chinese artwork is in itself *empty* and *flat*. It is without soul and truth. The desubstantialising emptiness opens it up for inscriptions and transcriptions. Thus even the oeuvre of a Chinese master is capable of transformation, as it is in itself *empty*. It is not the inwardness of the essence but the outwardness of the tradition or the situation that drives change onward.

Not only a master's style, but his subject matter, too, changes all the time. Each era visualises the masters differently. For example, it is quite possible for the master's true originals to be removed from his oeuvre, while forgeries that suit contemporary taste are included, thus making an impact on art history. In this case, the forgeries have more art-historical value than true originals. Indeed, they are more original than the originals. The aesthetic preferences of an era, the prevailing contemporary tastes influence a master's oeuvre. Pictures treating subjects that are not fashionable are forgotten, while pictures of preferred subjects proliferate. For example, if an era is characterised by a love of folklore, pictures with folkloric motifs turn up more frequently in Dong Yuan's oeuvre. The quiet transformations of his oeuvre follow the various requirements of the time. In the Ming dynasty, for instance, when merchants played an important role in art as patrons, a new motif suddenly appeared in Dong Yuan's pictures: that of the dealer.[5] Forgeries and replicas are constantly transforming oeuvres.

In ancient Chinese artistic practice, learning takes place specifically through copying.[6] Moreover, copying is considered a sign of respect toward the master. One studies, praises, and admires a work by copying it. Copying is the same as praising. Indeed, this practice is not unknown in European art. Gauguin's copy of a work by Manet is a declaration of love. Van Gogh's imitations of Hiroshige are expressions of admiration. It is well known that Cézanne often visited the Louvre to copy the Old Masters. Earlier Delacroix had regretted the fact that the practice of copying, which he considered to be an essential, inexhaustible source of knowledge for Old Masters such as Raphael, Dürer, or Rubens, was being increasingly neglected. The cult of originality relegates this practice, which is essential to the creative process, to the background. In reality, creation is not a sudden *event*, but a slow *process*, one that demands a long and intense engagement with *what has been*, in order to *create* from it. In this sense, creation is primarily the act of creating. The construct of the original spirits away what has been, the prior entity from which it is *created*.

4 Theodor W. Adorno, "Wagner's Relevance for Today", in *Essays on Music*, edited by Richard Leppert, translated by Susan H. Gillespie (Berkley: University of California Press), 586-587.

5 See Theodor W. Adorno, "Classicism, Romanticism, new Music", in *Sound Figures*, translated by Rodney Livingstone (Stanford: Stanford University Press, 1999), 108.

6 See Wen Fong, "The problem of Forgeries in Chinese Painting", *Artibus Asiae* 25 (1962): 100: "The fact is that the age-honoured tradition of learning the art of painting through copying in China made every Chinese painter a potential forger, and it is well known that some of the greatest Chinese painters and connoisseurs were, or were said to be, master 'forgers.' According to Chao His-ku (early thirteenth century), Mi Fu made a habit of taking advantage of his preeminence as a connoisseur by substituting important masterpieces, which were bought to him for 'authentication,' with exact copies."

# SONIC BLOSSOM

2013 / 2020

Chair, music stand, costume, spontaneous song

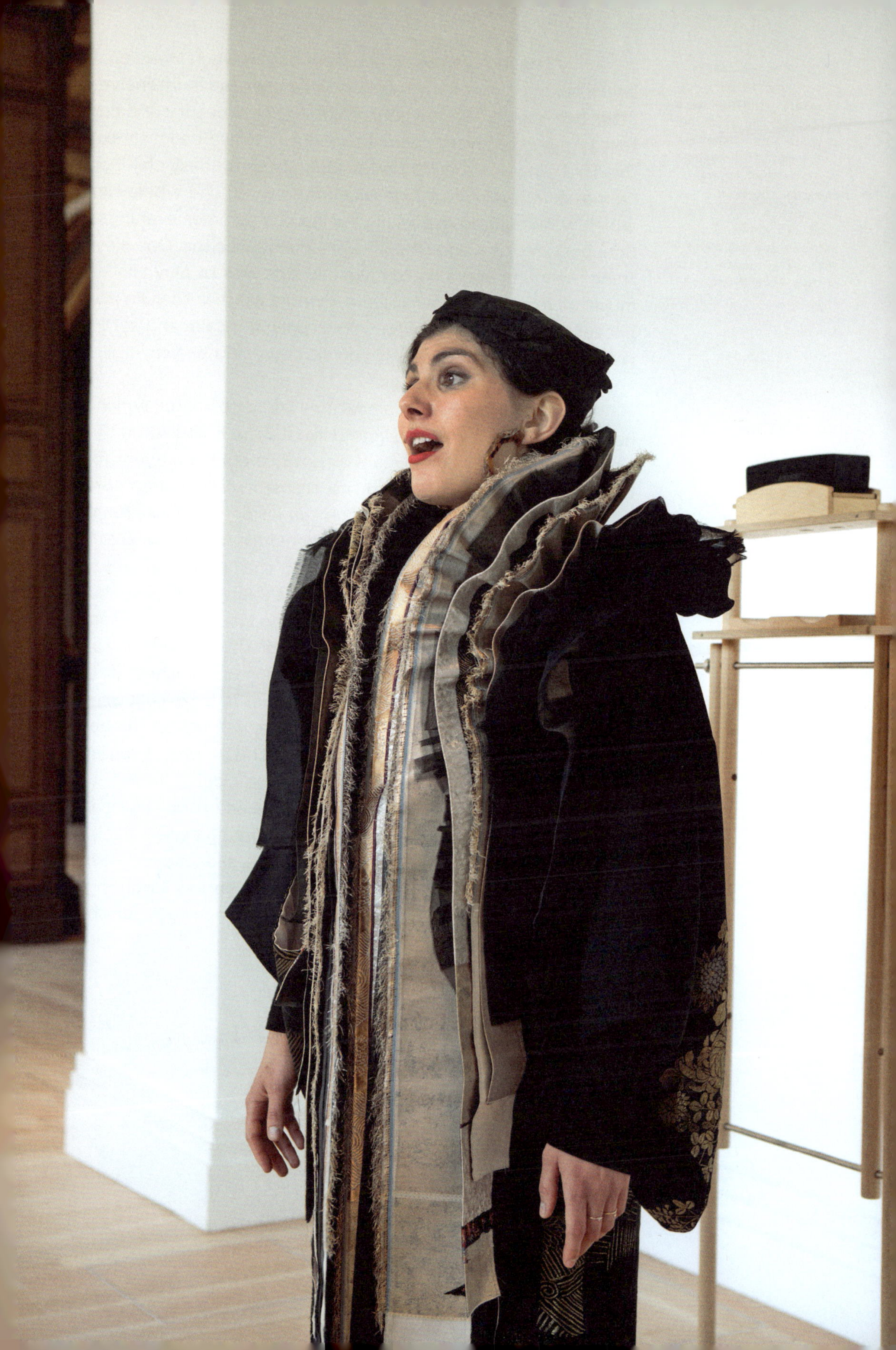

*Sonic Blossom* posits music, and in particular, singing, as a gift that can lift the spirits and inspire a deep emotional response in both the listener and the singer. As such, it appeals to the audiences' visceral reactions and proposes a form of intimate listenership in the art institution's galleries.

"The idea for *Sonic Blossom* began when I was back in Taipei taking care of my mother while she was in intensive care after her open-heart surgery. To bring some beauty and comfort into the recovery room, I thought it would be lovely to play for her Franz Schubert's Lieder. One of my fondest childhood memories is listening to classical music with the whole family, which we would do especially during hot summer evenings. Schubert, Mozart and Chopin were our favourites. One clever thing my mum would do to calm the kids was to play the music at a relatively low volume. I would ask her to turn it up because I couldn't hear. She would reply in a calm and soft voice: "Adi, (my nick name), if you sit down and be very still, you'll hear Schubert's songs."

The singers wear a costume to perform, for which I have collaborated with designers like Kelima K and Akira Isogawa. I would bring Kelima K an antique obi from Kyoto for her to create what she called the 'transformation cloak'. She often placed a small note sewn on the inside lining just for the singers to see. It says: 'This cloak transforms the / wearer into a wondrous / being, bestowed with the / power to give the gift of music. / Sound waves travel the / labyrinth of folds creating / a magical experience, / blessing the giver and / recipient.' I realised how important the role of the costume is to the singers when once someone had to perform without it, because repairs were needed. They were just in their regular black formal attire instead. They said they felt naked and powerless when giving the gift of song and this is when I realised the power of the mythical 'transformation cloak'.

I often think of *Sonic Blossom* as an exotic flower that blossoms every five years. During the blooming period, each sentient being encounters it with joy, hope, sadness and desperation. The flower then goes into its dormant period, savouring and reflecting on each encounter while getting ready for the next blooming season."

LEE MINGWEI

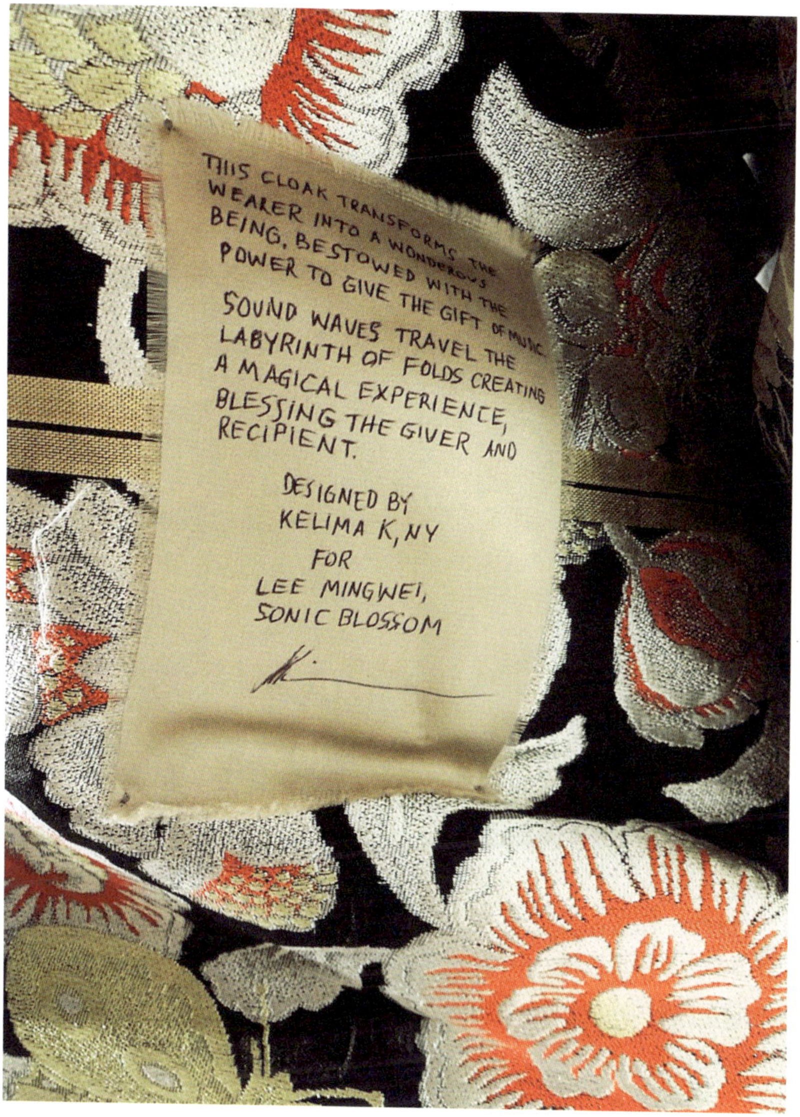


Designer Kelima K's antique obi costume for *Sonic Blossom* includes a hand-sewn message on the inside lining. It is placed just for the singers to see.

"I sat down and thought I knew what was going to happen. But when she started singing I was so moved, I immediately started to cry and cried throughout the whole song. I worked as a classical violinist for almost two decades, performing and also listening to countless concerts in the world's most renowned concert halls. In all these years I was never as touched by music as I was when I received the gift of a song in Lee Mingwei's *Sonic Blossom*. Some of the singers were still students, yet all of them embodied what is so essential for making music and, possibly, for life in general: the grace and courage of going into relationship with one another and the practice of giving a gift to another. I was lucky and received a second song during another iteration of *Sonic Blossom* during my stay in Singapore, and then another one at the Centre Pompidou in Paris. Each time I was moved to tears. The acts of giving and receiving belong together; they cannot exist without each other. Sonic Blossom therefore does not present or perform. It unfolds as a precious invitation, which engages the visitors fully."

AYUMI PAUL

Encountered *Sonic Blossom* at the National Gallery Singapore in 2018, and at the Centre Pompidou, Paris, 2018

"When I received the gift of Schubert's *Nacht und Träume,* eye contact with the singer from across the room felt intimate, commanding and compelling. Hushed comments about Lee's transformation cloak and the singer's resemblance to a woman in the surrounding portraits by the likes of Velázquez, Poussin and van Dyck distracted my thoughts. An extraordinary voice filled the room. This complex and complementary context allowed *Sonic Blossom* to unfold in a way that will never be replicated, transforming forever my experience of the Cleveland Museum of Art with all its history, new-found meanings and human emotion. I stayed for hours and watched exchanges between the singers, sitters and observers grow and recede again with every performance. It stirred memories and intense emotions, and I wanted to share it over and over again."

JAMIE HARDIS

Received a Schubert Lied in 2019 at Cleveland Museum of Art

"As a singer, your daily life is to 'give' in front of an audience, but *Sonic Blossom* is one of the purest experiences I have had in my life as a singer. We sing as little children, so it gives a strong connection to your inner source of creative energy. To be honest, I did not expect the emotional blast that hit me by being part of this work; a firework of emotions. I thought I would be in control of the moment, but the first rehearsal showed me, refreshingly, the absolute opposite. A person was sitting just five meters from me, smiling with every muscle of their face and their eyes. It brought me to tears. There is an exchange that connects both sides; the first sound creates a bridge and emotions start to change sides. You feel a transformation; the ego switches off. That's what it means to become a medium. For the length of just one Schubert lied you are out of this world. From then on, I have sung and performed in a new, refreshed way. I grew as a human, as well as an artist."

SARAH KEHDER

Singer for *Sonic Blossom* at Städel Museum, Frankfurt in 2017, Centre Pompidou, Paris in 2018 and at the Gropius Bau in 2020

"I have performed *Sonic Blossom* in many museums. I have been granted different experiences every single time. One thing has never changed: to give and receive the gift at the same time. I see myself as a part of the art and this empowers me to host every guest I encounter. When I am singing the song to the guest, I receive the energy back from them. I embrace this energy as a gift as well. The connection between the two of us makes each gift so unique and special. After the song, I receive smiles, tears, hugs, sighs and sometimes also have a short dialogue with visitors if they would like to share their life stories or offer wishes. All of their reactions touch my heart and motivate me to open my heart to offer a sincere gift. I remember one lady who received the gift and later wrote a letter to the museum, sharing that her husband has been fighting cancer for years. That day she was feeling so hopeless and asked if life could give her a sign of hope. That same day, she cried during the performance, believing that the gift was a sign, a sign of hope. All of those special moments will stay in my heart and keep reminding me of *Sonic Blossom*'s beauty."

BEIBEI GUAN

Singer for *Sonic Blossom* at Museum of Fine Arts, Boston in 2015, the Metropolitan Museum of Arts, New York in 2015, the Centre Pompidou, Paris in 2018 and the Isabella Stewart Gardner Museum, Boston in 2019

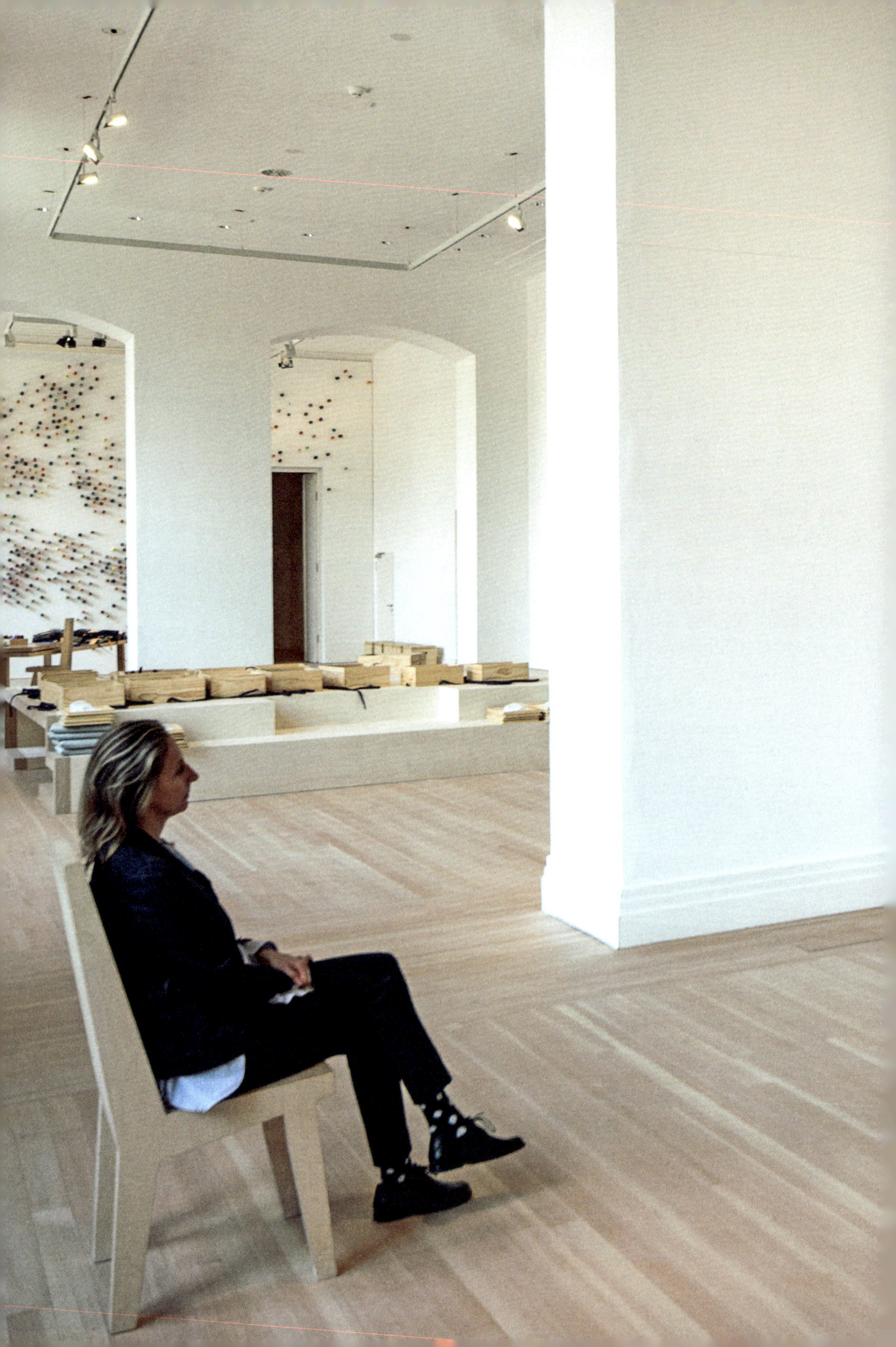

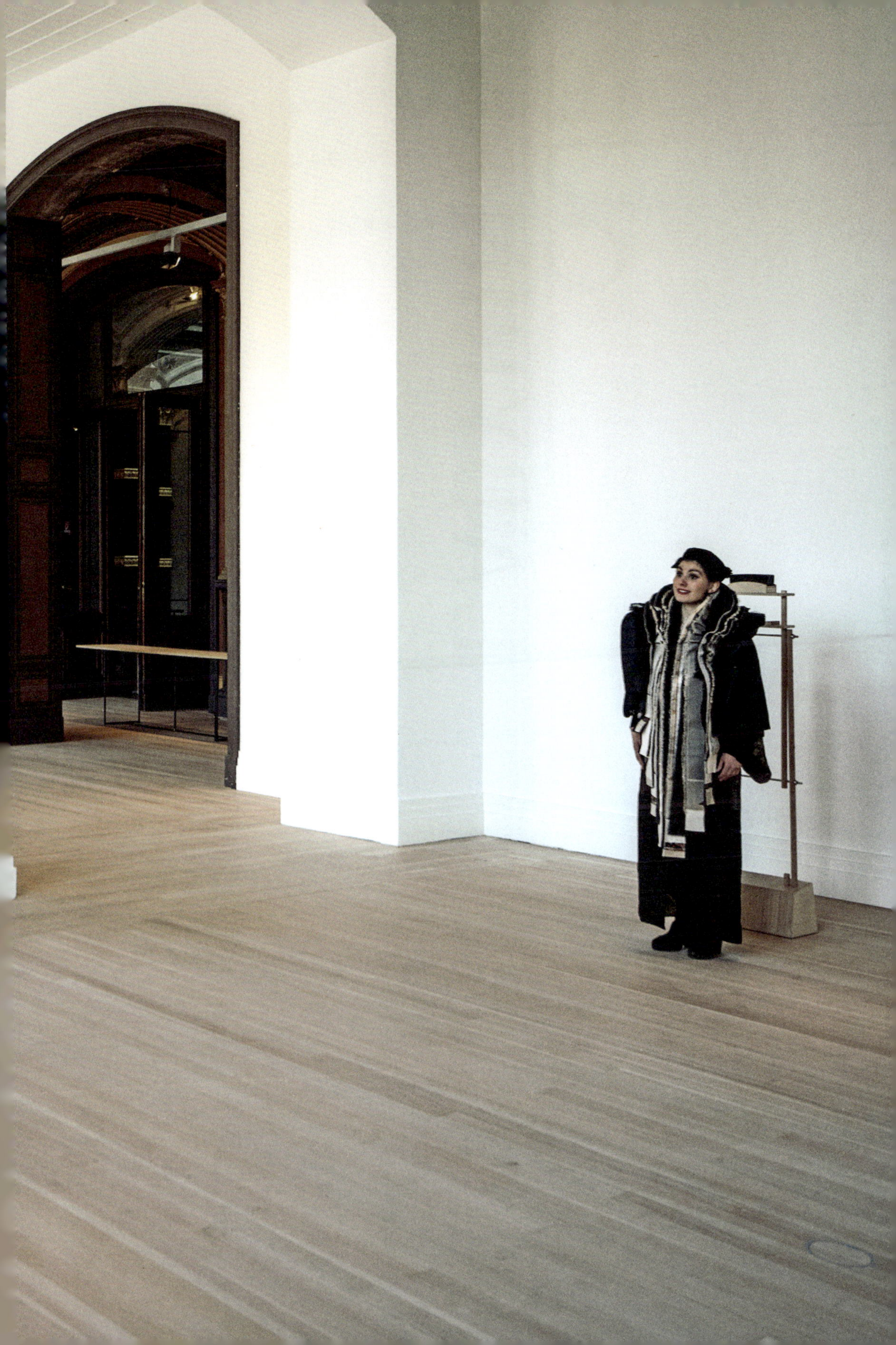

# OUR LABYRINTH

2015 / 2020

Rice, broom, costume, ankle bells, folded paper, wooden box, dance floor, dance

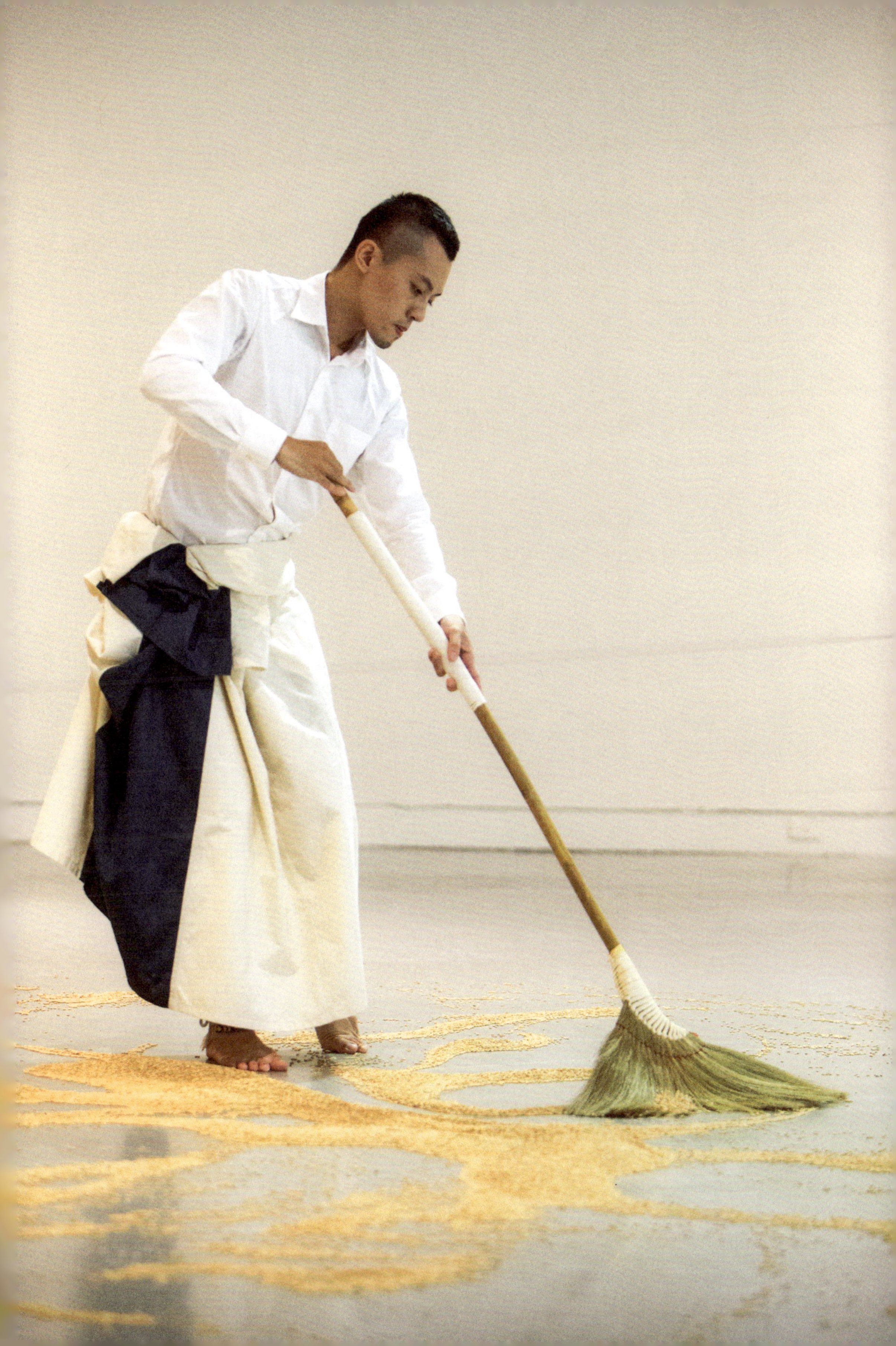

This geometric drawing derives from a book owned by Lee Mingwei of Japanese dance patterns. They mark the path that a kabuki performer – a major form of classical Japanese dance drama – will dance or walk according to the role they play. The red marks signify the duration and degree of one's turn, dip and extension of limbs. Considering these drawings as both sublime and enigmatic, Lee Mingwei sees the connection between *Our Labyrinth* and the kabuki dancers' paths.

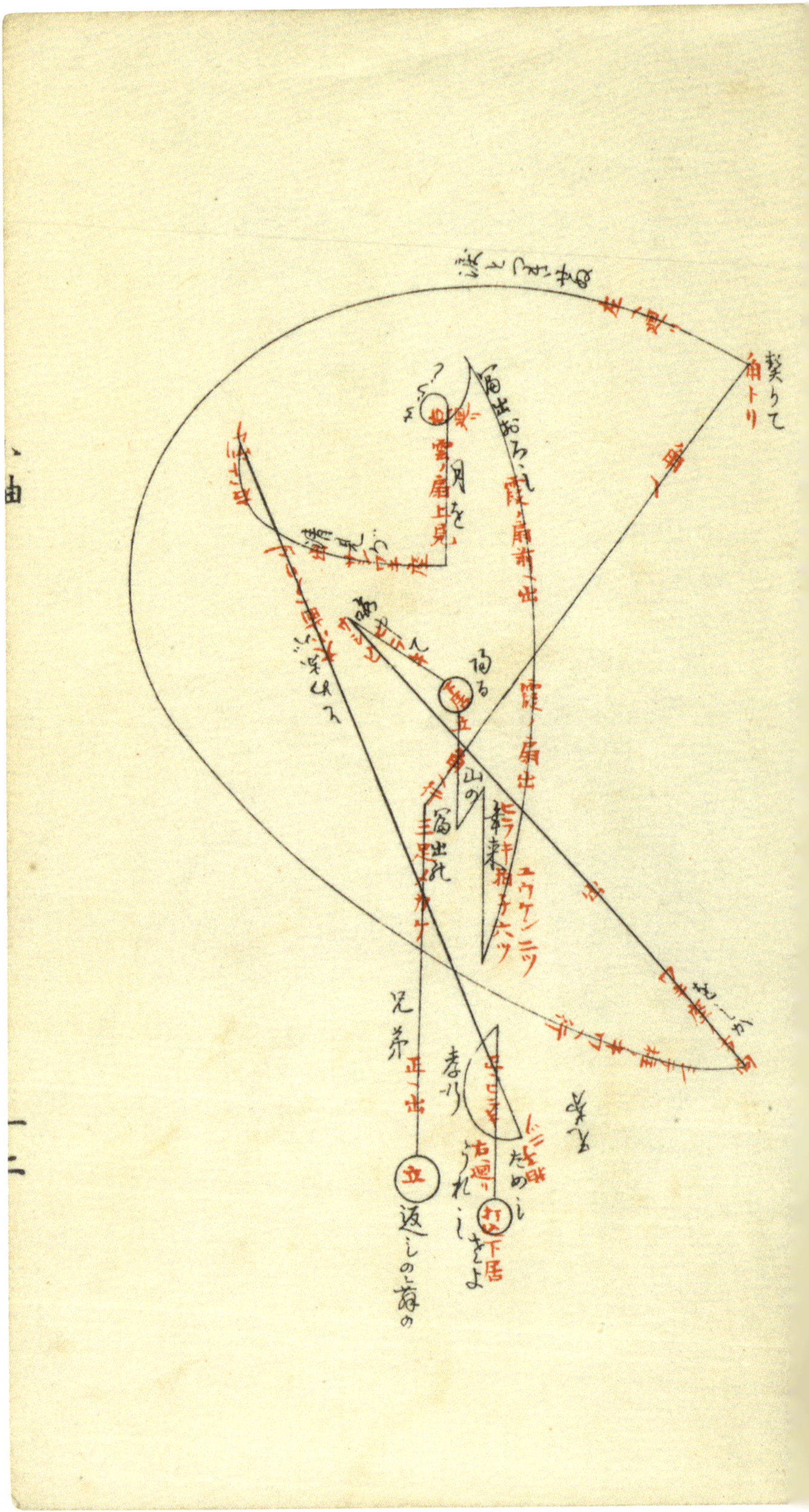

“In 2014 I visited Myanmar and went to various ancient temples in the countryside. There are little huts far from the temple where visitors can remove their shoes and walk barefoot. I was impressed by the path leading to the temple and noticed there were always volunteers continuously cleaning the path throughout the day. I thought this was a physical and spiritual gift from the volunteers to the visitors and was thoroughly inspired by this solemn activity of brushing the path ever so gently, collecting the leaves with such grace and loving care.

To make *Our Labyrinth*, firstly I laid out the path for the dancer, almost as a direct iteration of what I saw in Myanmar. Originally I also wanted the work to have a sound component, with the dancer carrying a birdcage containing a canary. Quickly I realised this would be too controlling, removing the dancer's freedom and breathing space. Instead, I used the subtle sound of ankle bells, which reminded me of the sound of crackling ice as the dancer moved slowly across the floor. I invited the dancers to do two things: to move very slowly – almost like morning fog drifting over a marshland – and to listen to the rice with their heart, not by thinking or planning their next move. The rice guides them through the dance. It was during one rehearsal that I watched two dancers moving together around the same pile of rice. I was completely mesmerised by this unexpected duet and it gave me the idea that this project could be done with two people, instead of just one lone dancer. They might collide slowly as if they were galaxies in the celestial sky, slowly evolving and engaging with each other and then separating when time comes. It would be quite magical.”

LEE MINGWEI

*Our Labyrinth* asks dancers not to think but to feel in order to create meditative patterns upon the floor, using simply a broom and rice.

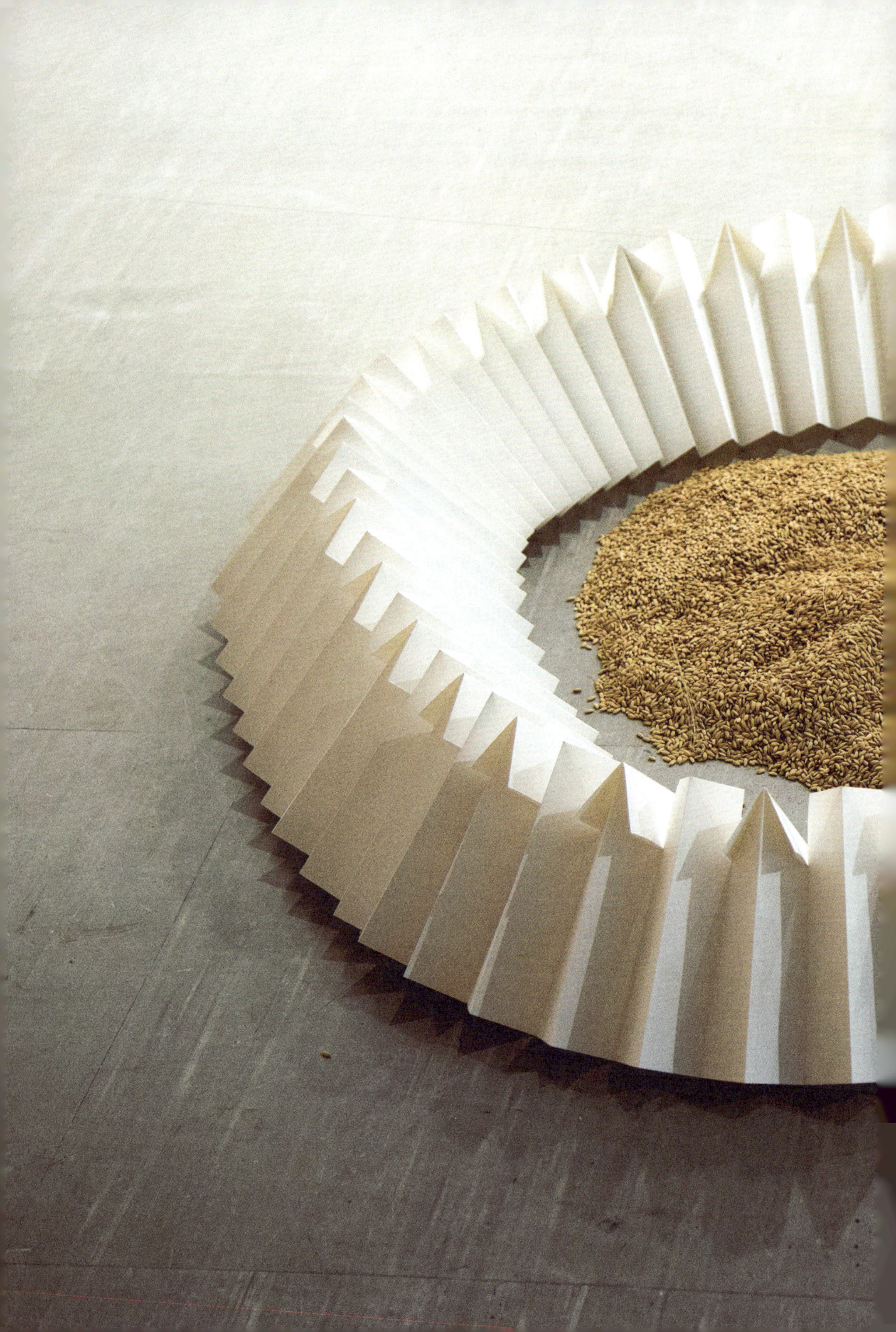

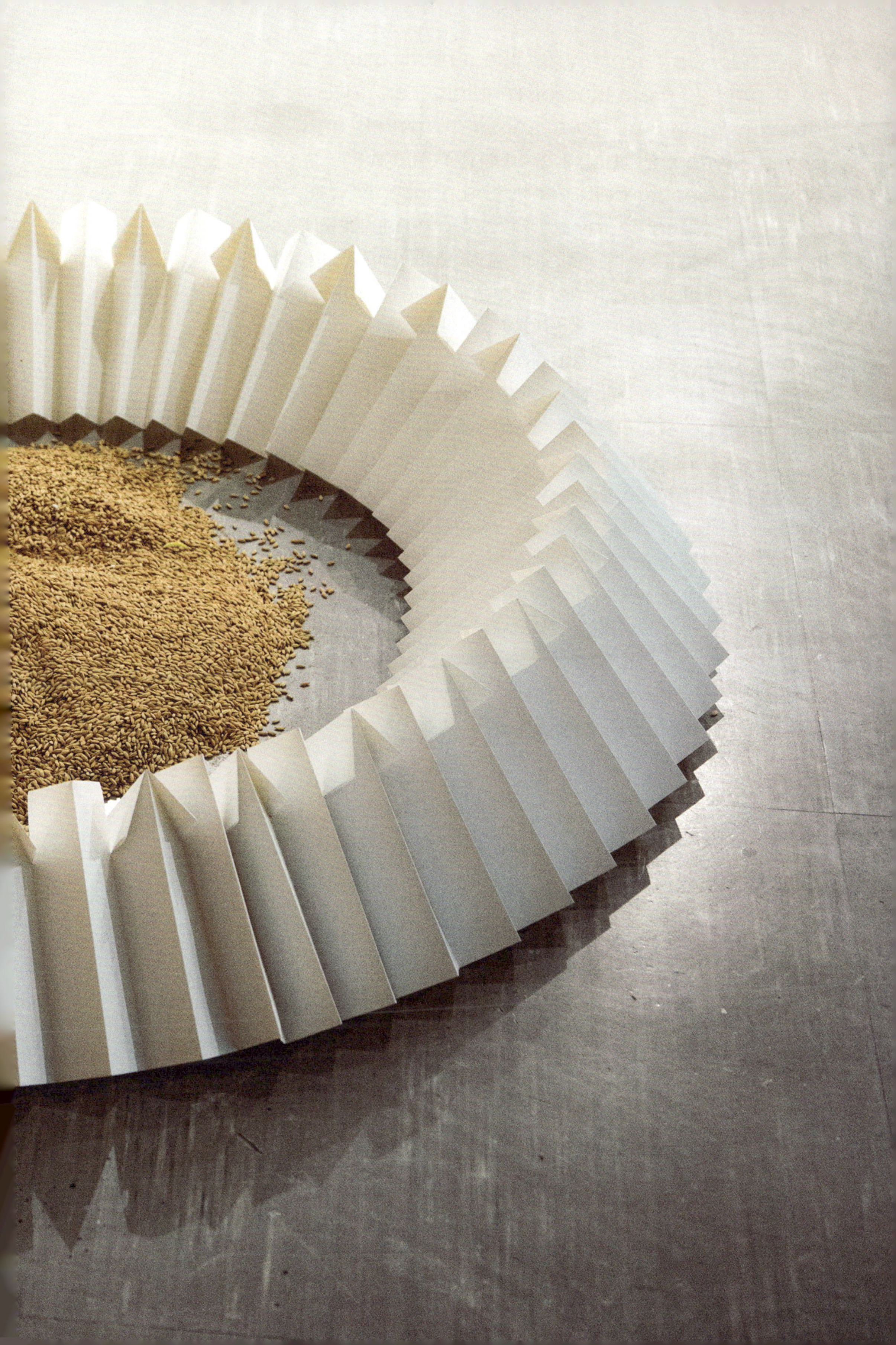

"*Our Labyrinth* was like a meditation for me. It offered me a kind of medicine, an antidote for my lack of awareness of myself and others. Sweeping the rice on the floor was not like sweeping dust from the house; it was more like sweeping my ego from my personality. I was initially confused when Mingwei taught us about 'building connection and communication with the rice; let it show you the way'. I wondered, how can I communicate with rice? If I pushed myself, it felt so hard and in the end I feel like giving up and just surrendering myself to it. I never thought that 'letting go' would make it easier. I started to sweep without thinking and the most funny moment I've ever had was realising I made a pattern shaped like a penis. I shared this experience with Mingwei and we all laughed about it! I didn't realise that rice could reveal the subconscious. I felt like the rice was an amazing choreographer leading me to dance through the broom – showing me how to 'let go'."

DESI ARDY

Dancer in *Our Labyrinth* at Museum MACAN in Jakarta, 2018

"As a dancer, this work appears to me as an ever-renewed path led by the dialogue between the rice and the performer. It requires a peaceful state of mind so the body becomes able to express what comes from listening to the rice and to the surroundings. One step after another, it's a careful walk through the unknown. Performing *Our Labyrinth* gives a feeling of being hosted by the space itself: the building, the audience, the country; a sense of profound respect arises from this. As there is seldom a direct interaction with the audience in *Our Labyrinth,* the act of giving and receiving in this work is subtle yet substantial. By interacting with the rice, the dancer exchanges a flow of information, which he then offers to the audience through dance and patterns created on the floor. A friend of mine wrote after seeing the performance that the work is a gift of meditation and mindfulness. To me, this work is an invitation, both for the dancer and the audience, to welcome life with peace and an open heart."

JEAN-GABRIEL MANOLIS

Dancer in *Our Labyrinth* at Centre Pompidou, Paris in 2017, Museum MACAN, Jakarta in 2018, and at the Gropius Bau in 2020

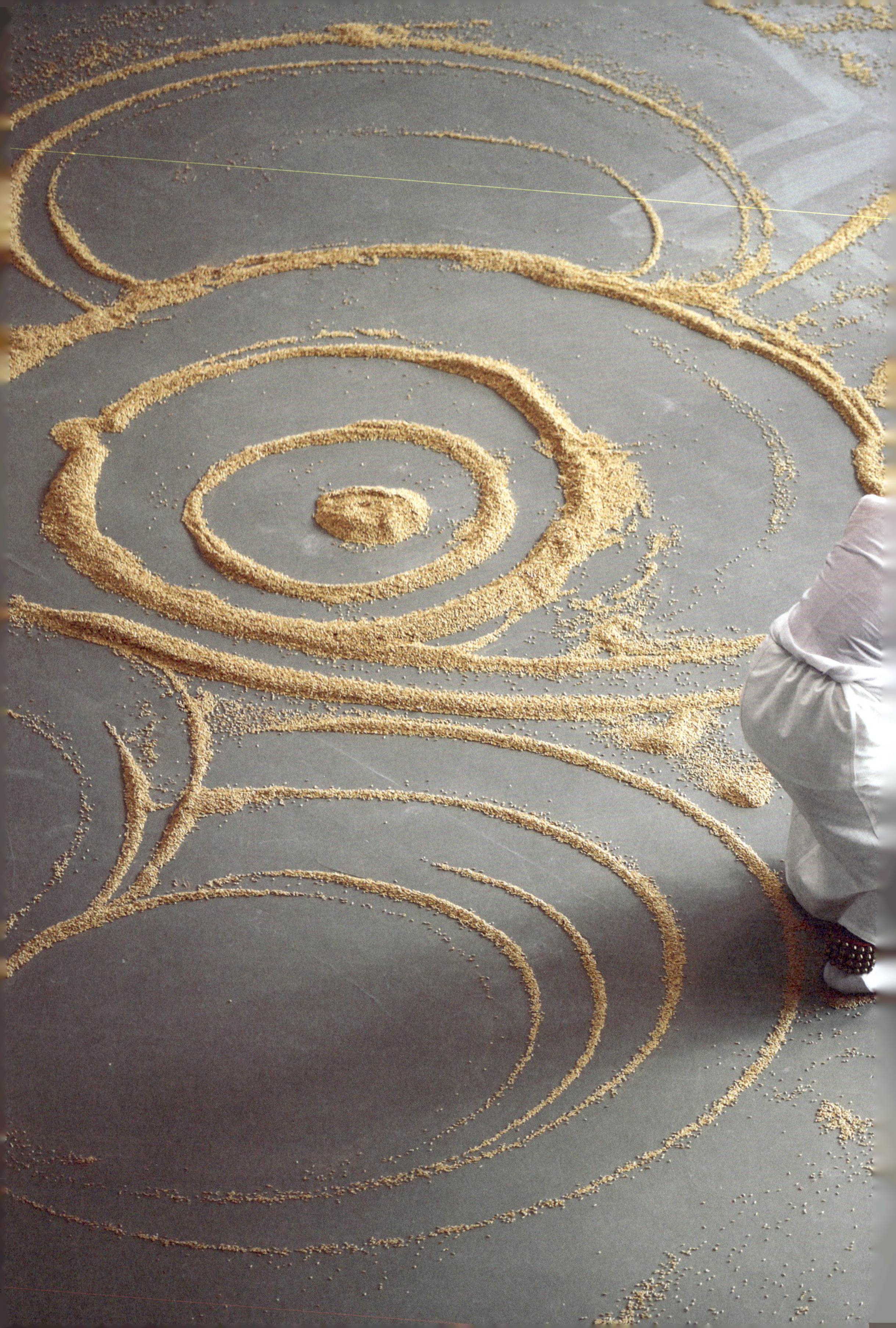

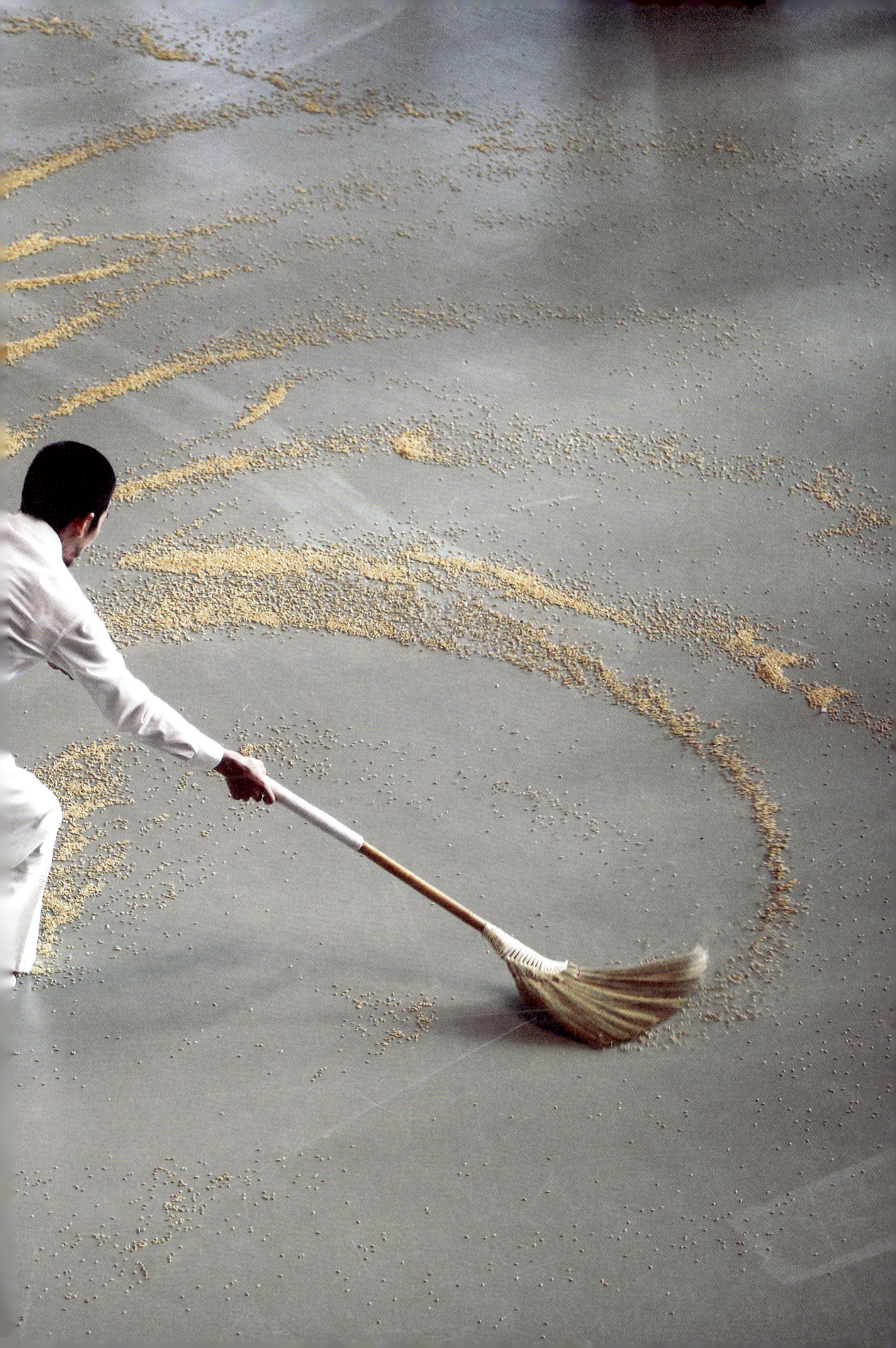

# OUR PEACEABLE KINGDOM

2020

27 framed paintings, easels

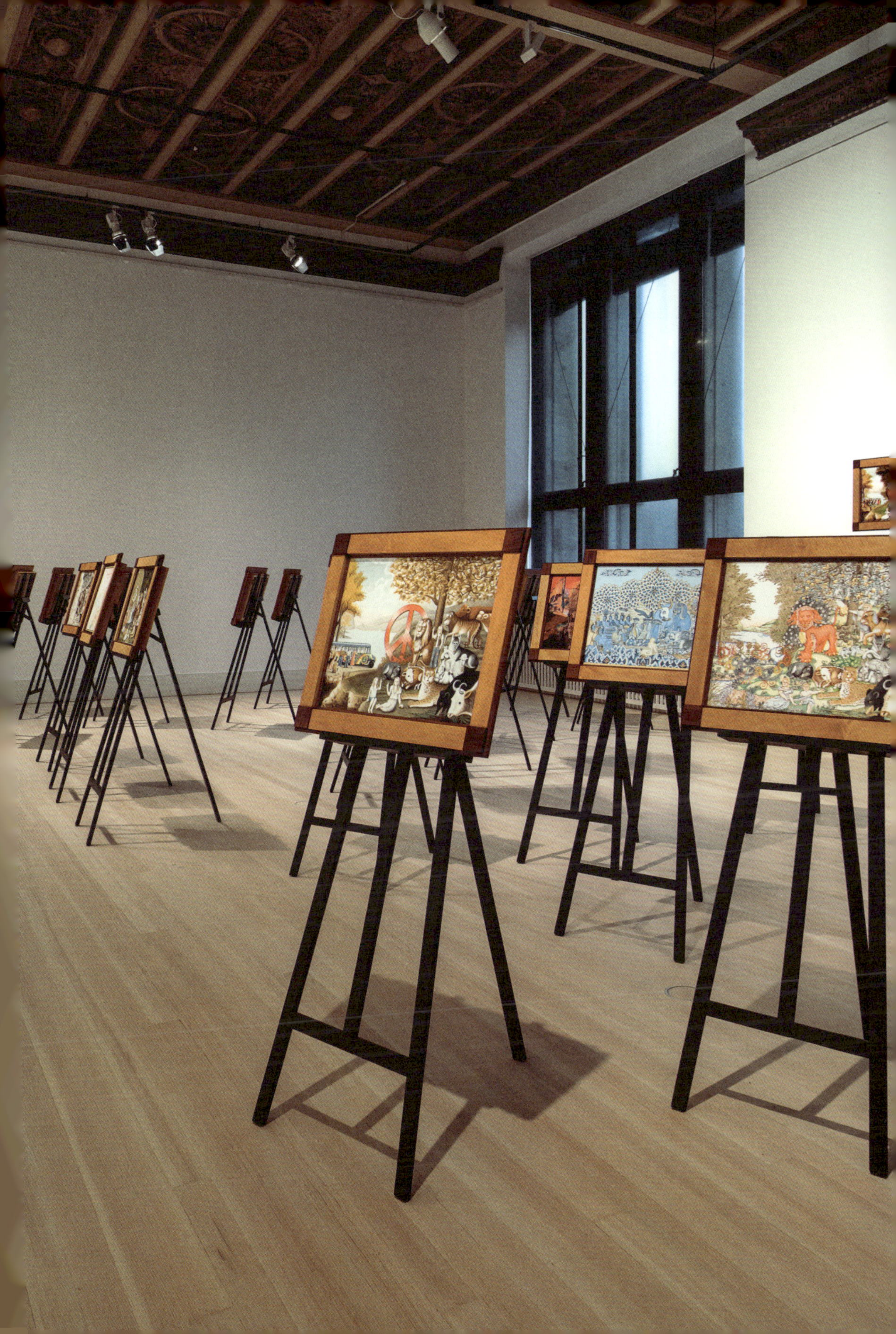

*Our Peaceable Kingdom* is Lee Mingwei's most recent artwork, created for his exhibition at the Gropius Bau. The installation is comprised of 27 different artists' paintings, which reflect on the idea of peace as posited by the artist Edward Hicks. The works are displayed alongside an Edward Hicks *Peaceable Kingdom* original from the Worcester Art Museum, Massachusetts.

"I saw a catalogue about the work of Edward Hicks in Pegasus Books, a landmark bookstore in Berkeley, California, during a time when I was fascinated by Quaker philosophy. Edward Hicks was an American folk artist and Quaker minister. What caught my attention was his image of wild animals with whom children peacefully coexisted. I thought this portrait of peace painted through the eyes of a Quaker was brave, original and beautiful. Hicks' naive style of painting too reminded me of Henri Rousseau's work, which I admire.

Initially, I invited a group of eleven artists to copy *Peaceable Kingdom*, c. 1833, a relatively small painting of 44 x 60 cm. For the second round, each of these eleven artists recommended another two artists to copy from *their* painting. Essentially, this process produces a family tree of copies with multiple descendants. I wanted to experience each individual artist's interpretations of peace. To copy a work of art has a long history and different meanings in Western and Asian art practices. In the exhibition at Gropius Bau, the original Hicks painting is the centrepiece, with the first- and second-generation copies radiating outward.

Germany is at the centre of Modern European history, and for 28 years the Berlin Wall blocked the front door of the Gropius Bau building, which sat in West Berlin. As such, this museum is the most appropriate venue in which to present Edward Hicks' vision of peace alongside the views of more contemporary artists."

LEE MINGWEI

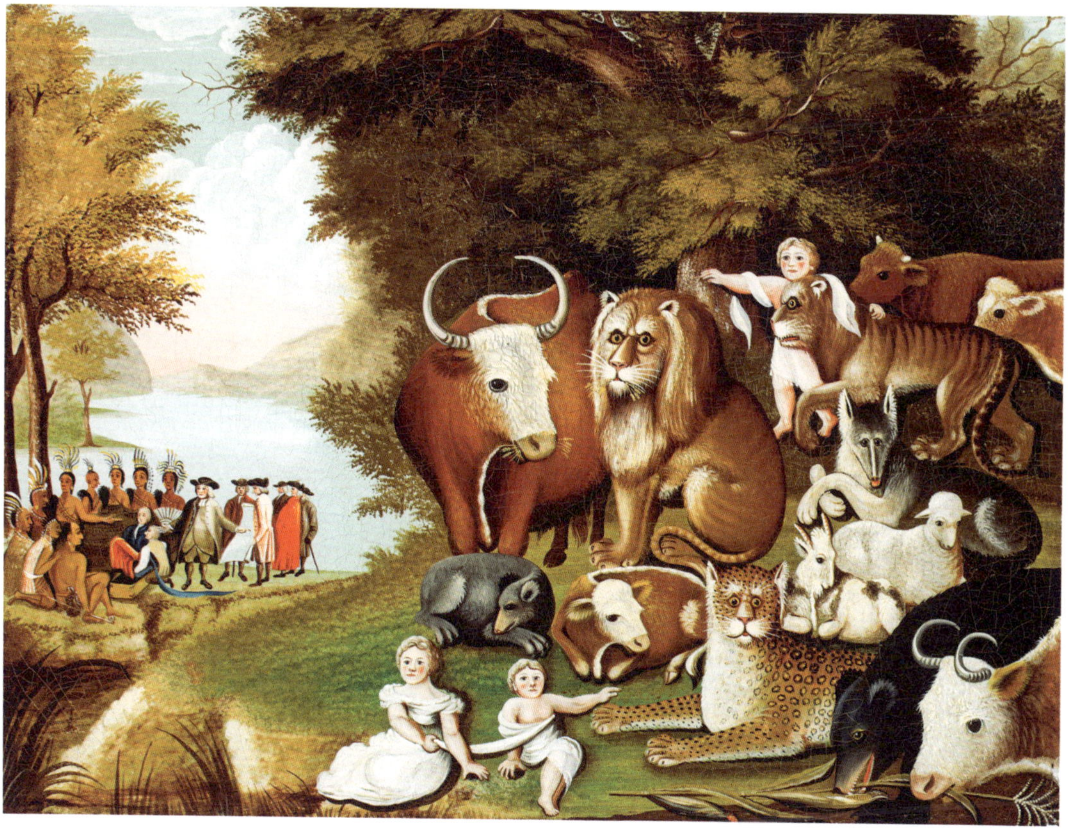

Quaker minister Edward Hicks obsessively rendered scenes from the Bible and Pennsylvanian Quaker history, as part of which he repeatedly painted Isaiah's peace prophecy. His prolific series *Peaceable Kingdom* comprises numerous versions produced between 1820 and 1849, 62 of which still exist today in public and private collections.

Of the eleven artists initially invited to respond to Edward Hicks' *Peaceable Kingdom*, c. 1833, each invited a further two artists to copy from their interpretation, of whom 16 accepted. This equals 27 artworks in total that comprise Lee Mingwei's installation *Our Peaceable Kingdom*.

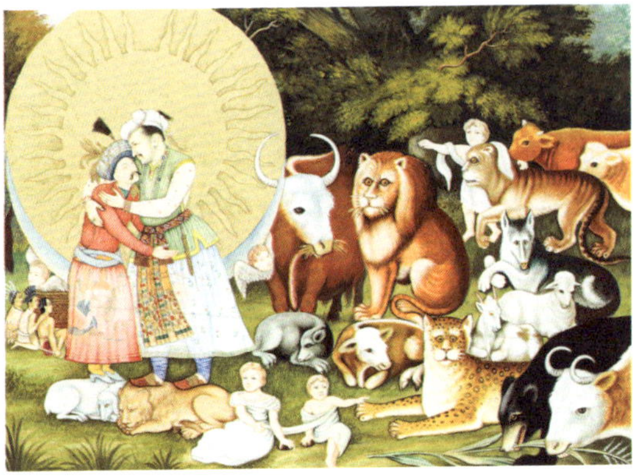

KHADIM ALI

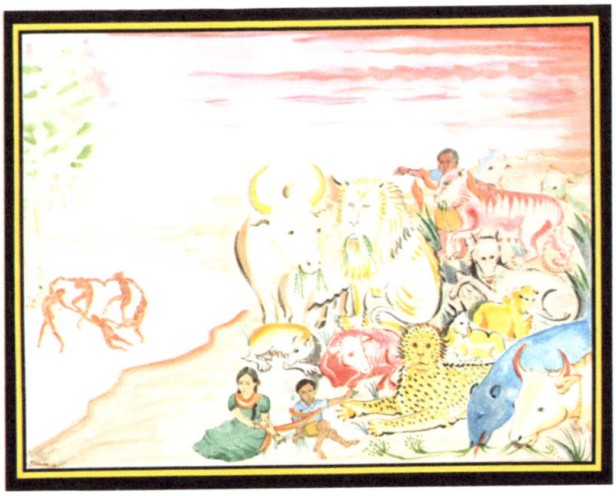

N.S. HARSHA

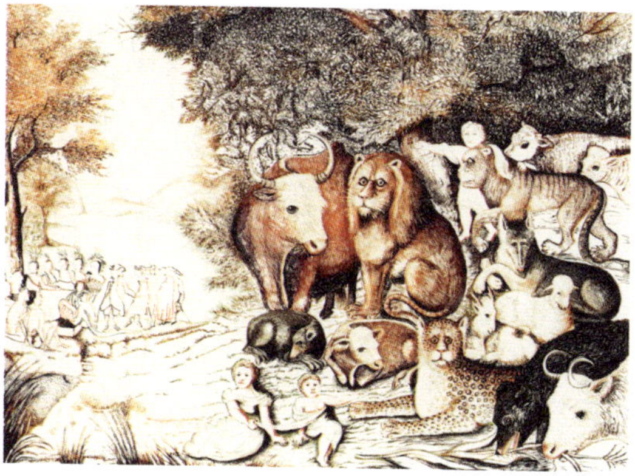

AMBREEN BUTT

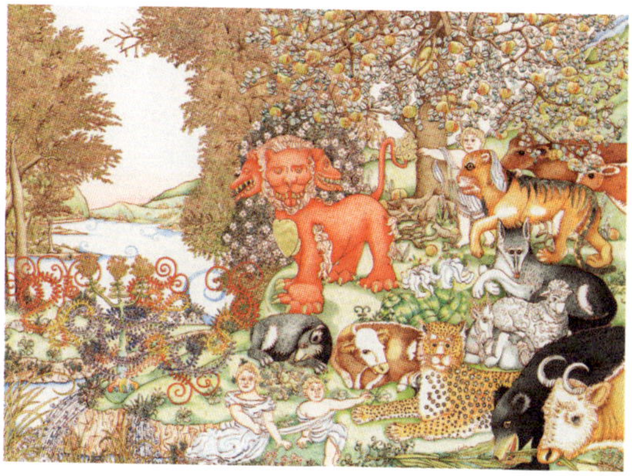

MICHAEL EADE

It felt so appropriate to me to re-examine Hicks' legacy message of peace between all creatures. I immediately removed the vignette depicting William Penn's treaty with the Native Americans, feeling the history and what happened to those people was just too politically incorrect for the painting's message. Instead, as a gay man, I had the perfect form from my own paintings to fill in the compositional gap - my Rainbow Plant. This appears in many of my landscapes and intentionally grows with the colours of the international gay pride flag, symbolising equality.

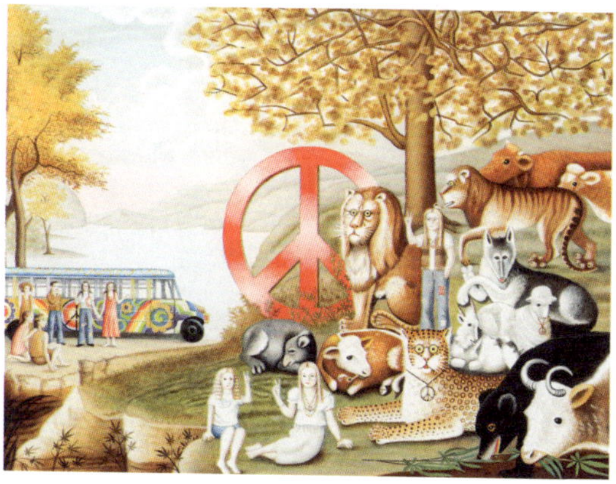

AMY HILL

The counterculture of the 1960s was a big influence on me, especially its attitude towards war. Peace is not a tangible thing, but the hippies made it visual with the peace sign and the victory hand. I associate even their lifestyle with war protest, their clothing style and attitude towards drugs and sex. In my take on the Edward Hicks' painting, where he already creates a happy universe of animals and people, I turn them, too, into hippies.

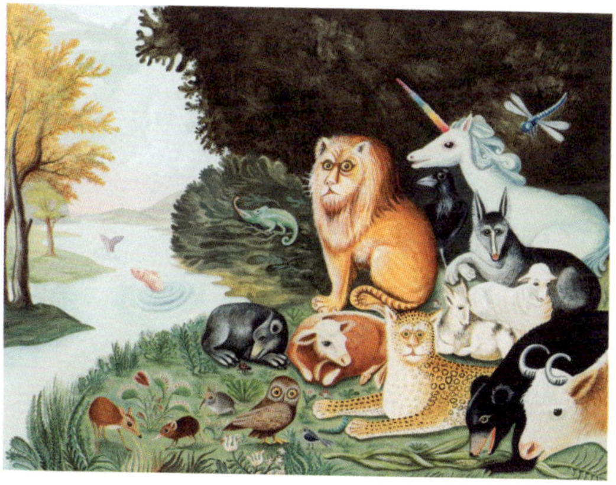

ANDREA DEZSÖ

My *Peaceable Kingdom* is my vision of a world where freedom, peace, friendship, beauty, joy and the imagination thrive. Here, among plants, water, sky and earth live a community of wild, domestic, real and imaginary animals; birds, fish and insects in perfect harmony. I replaced some of Hicks' farm animals with beings that are especially dear to me: a raven, a songbird, a Jackson chameleon, a dragonfly, an owl, an inchworm, a rainbow unicorn, a fish, a ladybug, a pair of deer mice and an elephant shrew. A benign Venus flytrap and a few well-intentioned *Amanita muscaria* mushrooms complete my "peaceable kingdom".

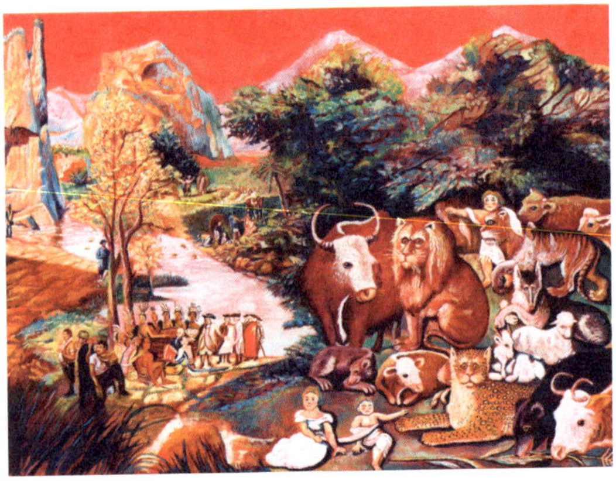

ZICO ALBAIQUNI

I kept Hicks' original images on the right and expanded the painting to the left, to represent how the Quran is read from right to left, connecting my painting with my prayers. I took imagery from Raden Saleh's *A Landscape in the Dutch East Indies*, 1857, and S. Sudjojono's *Alangkah Indahnya Tanah Airku (How Beautiful My Motherland Is)*, 1983. He was the pioneer of Indonesian modern art and one of the intellectuals who fought colonialism through art during the Indonesian National Revolution (1945-1949). I have connected our shared history of war, conflict, and violence, extending Hicks' prayer into universal language and desire towards a peaceful world.

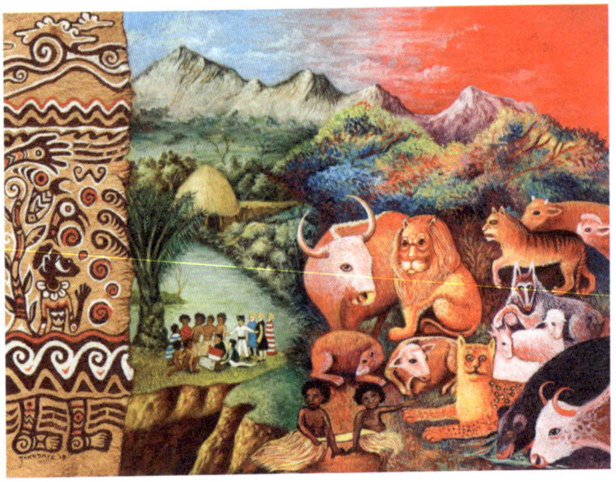

IGNASIUS DICKY TAKNDARE

My homeland, Papua, is one of the most conflicted places in the world because of the "golden mountain", a gold mine. I caught a fiery anger through Zico's selection of colours. I changed the community group under the tree to a group of indigenous Papuans, Indonesians and Americans, also changing the tree to a sago tree, a symbol of Papua. Instead of canvas, I used a traditional sheet of bark, which conveys stories to the next generation of our society. There is a narrative of universal balance in which humans and other creatures live in harmony.

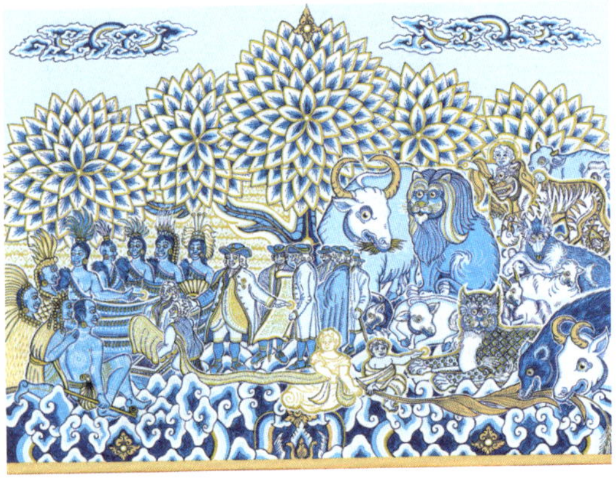

RADI ARWINDA

I felt disturbed the first time I saw the red colour of *Peaceable Kingdom* by Zico. Honestly, his painting resonated with anger, with an energy opposite to the word "peace". My painting is another opposite and also a balancer of Zico's *Peaceable Kingdom*. I use a blue tone colour to symbolise the process of relieving angry energy, changing it with peaceful energy. Above all, I think we must help each other: to make peace with the past, to be thankful for today and to reach a better future.

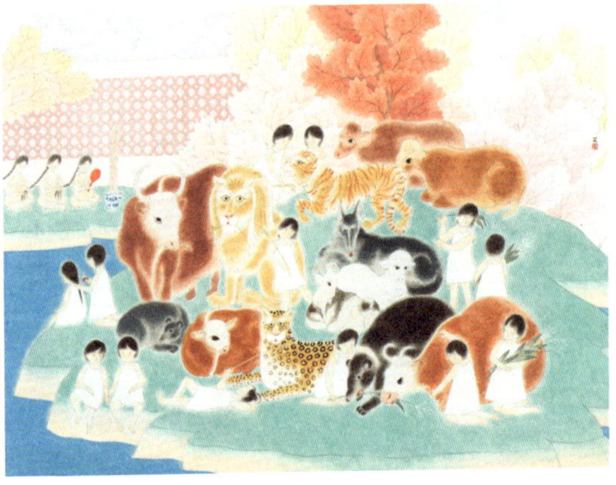

YEH TSAI-WEI

I was drawn to Hicks' depiction of animals, their stiff pose and clumsy, endearing appearance. From the outset, I decided that I would follow the original form of his animals. Seemingly kind and lovely girls play between animals, feeding the animals grass, gentle and strong. Dressed in the same garments and hairstyle, they dissipate each other's characteristics. In the distance, the pregnant women braid each other's hair. As long as everyone is the same, this is a *Peaceable Kingdom*: a small and beautiful garden, exquisite and fragile, only existing in the hypocrisy of an ideal.

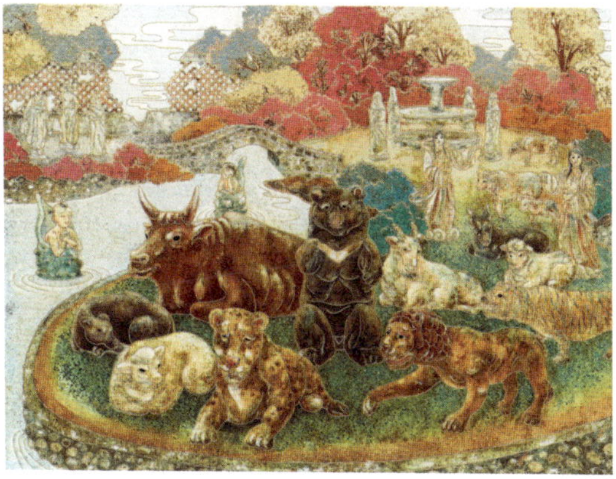

YUYU CHEN

My copy is a depiction of a park of homogenised women with captive animals. The women appear like hostages, operating like a factory. Understanding the depressing role of women in society, I decided to emulate and extend the species, with contradictory animals existing in my interpretation, perishing according to nature, and humans creating symbolic animal sculptures, placing them within the park. The designs of the animal sculptures are based on sculptures created by various old masters in Taiwan. In deliberately using rusting pigments and oil paint to recreate the deserted park and peace as folklore, this is my interpretation of *Our Peaceable Kingdom*.

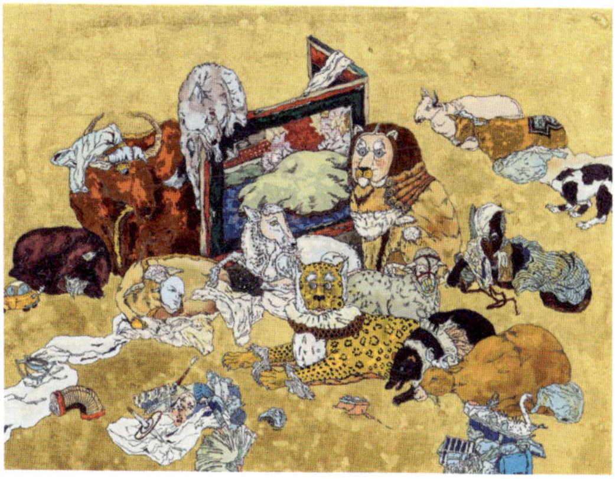

HSIAO PEI-I

My depiction of *Peaceable Kingdom* is such: animals occupying various levels of the food chain, tamed and kept together. They wear wigs and "cones of shame", play toys with the vacant stare of a doll, eat pet food and play their roles. Beautiful and pleasant: a paradise on earth. This morbid garden with a banner of peace deprives animals of their hunter instincts and obscures the reality of killing in the food chain. Conflict within harmony in fact encompasses the rules of relative perpetuity and cycle. Perhaps the greed from human expectations is the source of true conflict.

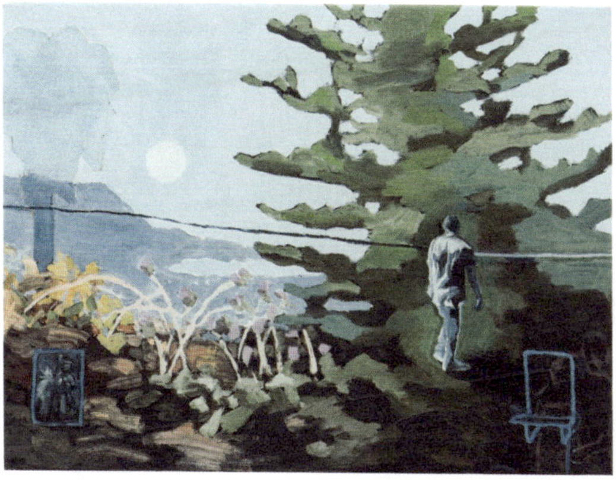

CLAUDIA BRAND

For me, to be at peace is to be content. It is sometimes only presented in fleeting moments. I store years' worth of printed photographs. For this painting I pulled out pairings, thematically, emotionally or by chance. One chance pairing I pulled is mirrored in the painting's bottom corners: the Hindu god Aiyanar on an elephant and a silhouette of the wooden ledge that seats a painting of the Madonna and Child. Drawing pairings in this way allows me to find balance in these otherwise widely differing parts of my life. The process in itself gave me a great deal of peace.

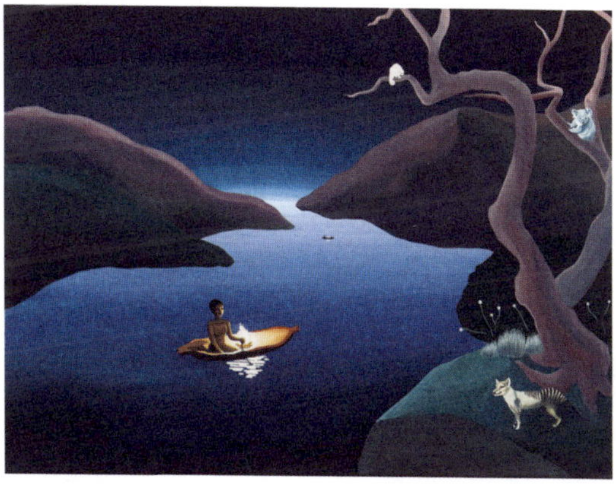

THEA PERKINS

Growing up I was always struck by etchings of aboriginal women night-fishing along the East Coast of Australia, pre-colonisation. It so perfectly encapsulates the notion of *Peaceable Kingdom*. I was taken by the possibilities of the low light of Claudia's painting, which inspired a night scene, as well as the disparate, collaged elements. Like Hicks' scene, it is imaginative in its elements, with the extinct Tasmanian thylacine and Sydney red gum, which defy a possible place. Unlike Hicks' peaceful commerce, my vision of peace is aboriginal society pre-contact, with gender parity and sustainable land-management practices that safeguarded the country since time immemorial.

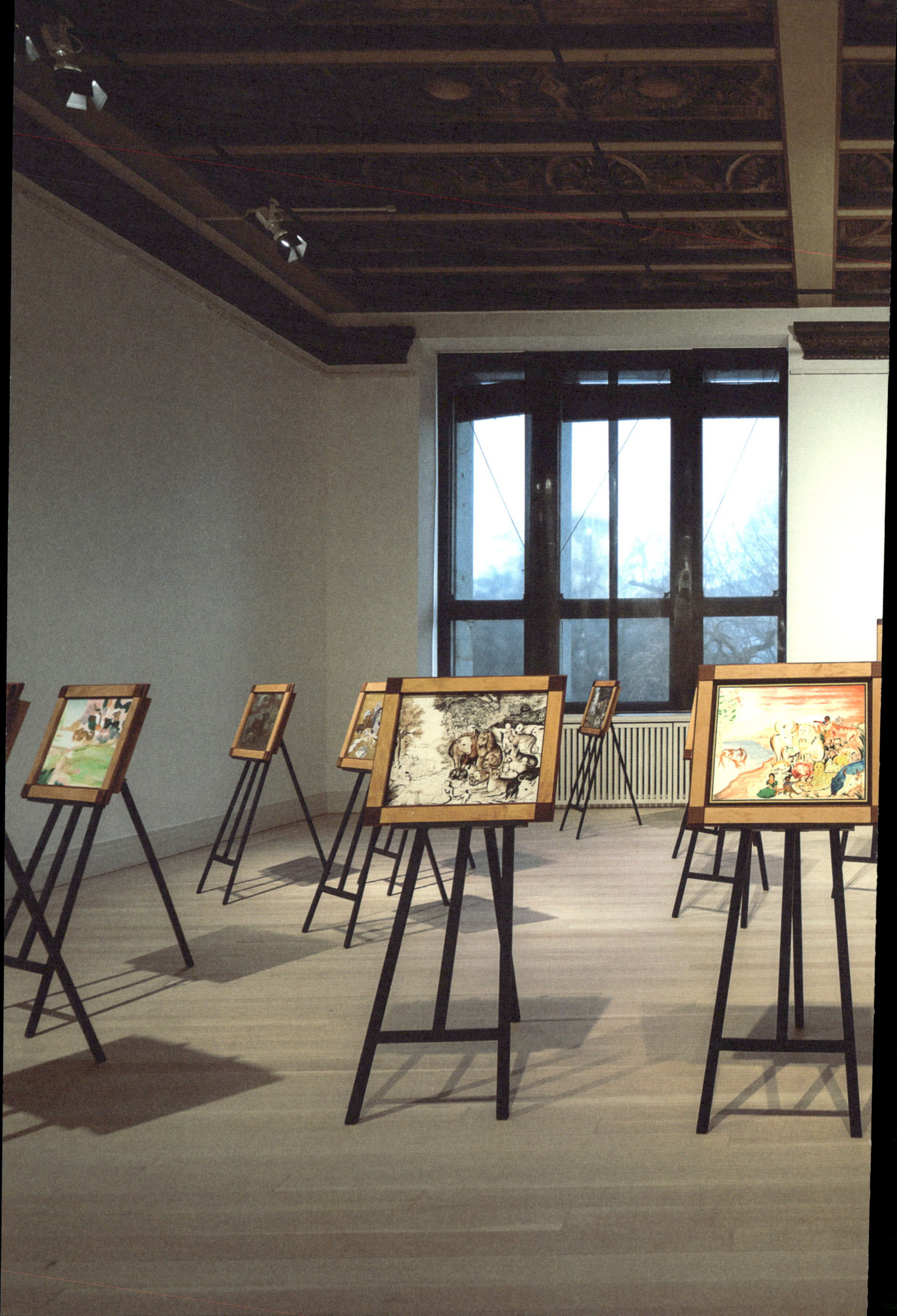

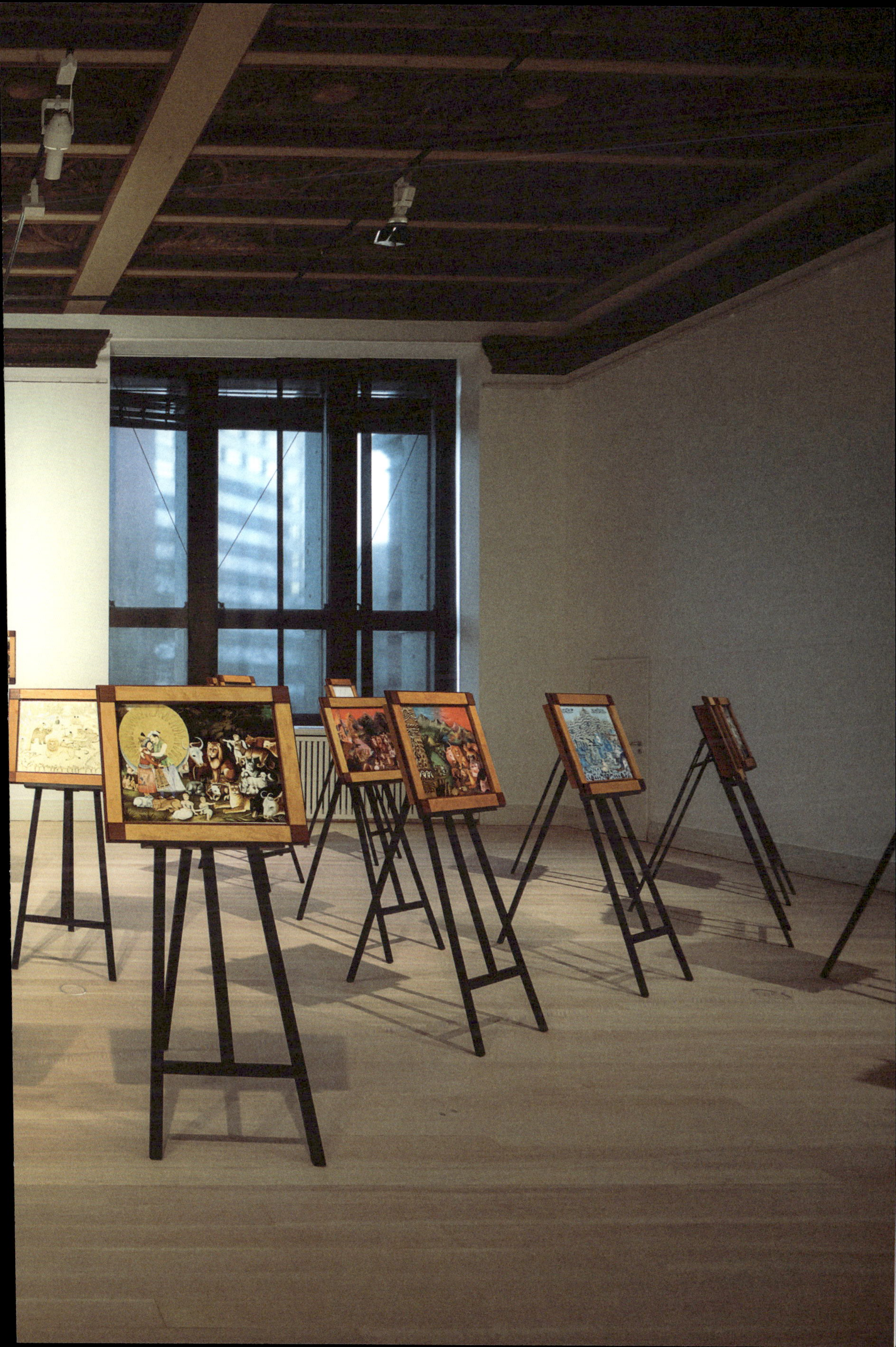

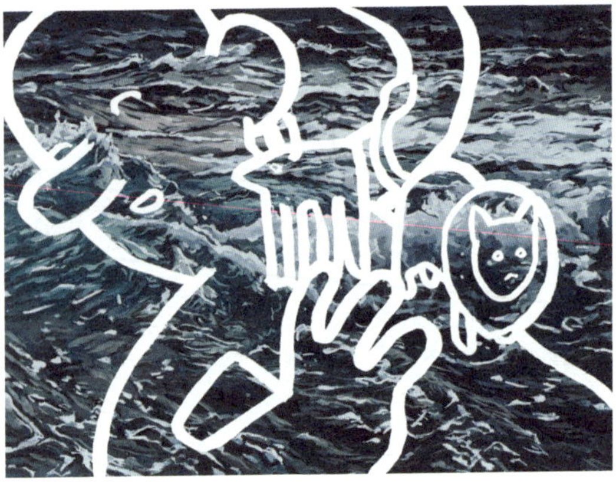

ABDUL ABDULLAH

The ocean or sea stands as a universally applicable metaphor for a boundary – an obstacle between where you are and where you wish to be. In my interpretation of peace I looked to those rare moments of personal respite, when a thought or resurfaced memory affords the subject a brief experience of calm joy. In this work the figure lies on a plane in tangent to the dangerous and horizon-less ocean. The figure appears at rest, with the buffalo and lion from *Peaceable Kingdom* returning as toys on their chest. When I think of peace I think of a happy memory from my childhood.

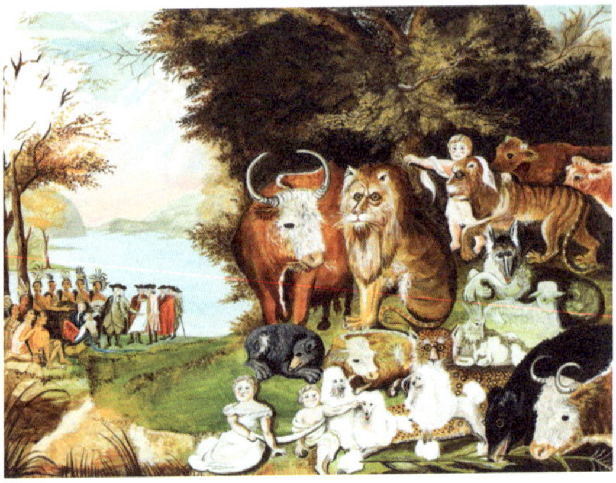

FABIEN LERAT

The white men in Hicks' painting seem to bear gifts, but as we know now, those presents carried sicknesses that the indigenous people had never known. Reproducing is such an investment. You want to copy exactly, but obviously you can't. I started from the most complicated element of each section, finally deciding to leave some space unfinished – like the beginning is always coming. I realised that in Hicks' work, the group on the left is only men. In my version, a child's hand reaches out to three French poodles, a nod to the artists of General Idea, who represented themselves in certain works as poodles.

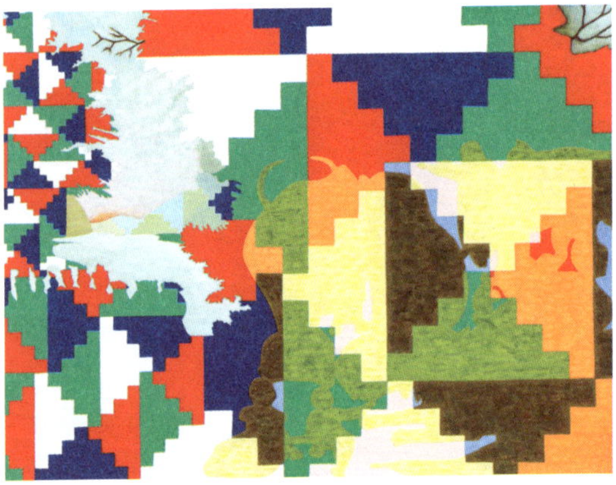

MARIE LEPETIT

I have used the ziggurat, a staircase and symmetrical form originally supporting a Mesopotamian temple. Its memory survived thanks to the biblical account of the Tower of Babel, inspired by the ziggurat of Babylon. The ziggurat is also an abstract, repetitive form with the contrasting colours of General Idea. The space of the painting is the same world with its landscape and characters. Naturalistic colours distinguish the group of animals in the foreground from the rest. And the ziggurats are the link with different scales. Making peace without taking into consideration the people you are facing is vain. Making peace without knowing the other is utopian.

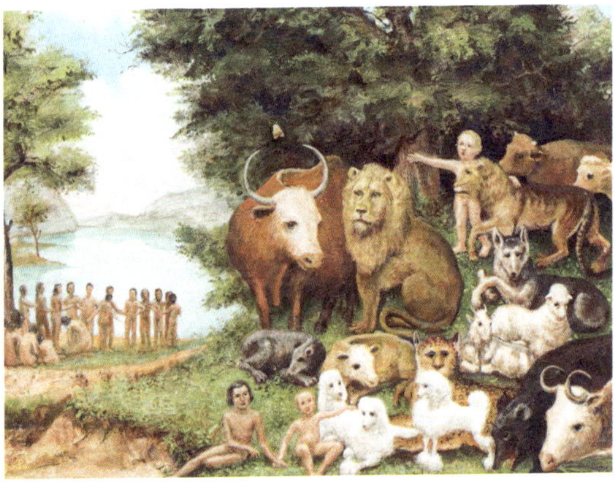

SIMON PASIEKA

This painting is the first one I have completed since the death of my wife Kazuyo this summer. She was a singer from Yokohama and for 20 years we lived together here in Paris. In recent months, I've been thinking a lot about a peaceful life. I tried to feel the desire for this scenery. The colour is thick, with many earth tones but also cobalt blue, violet and green. On the four edges I have slightly enhanced the colour, as if they had been less bleached by the sunlight. Painting this tidy world for a few weeks in September and October was a salutary experience.

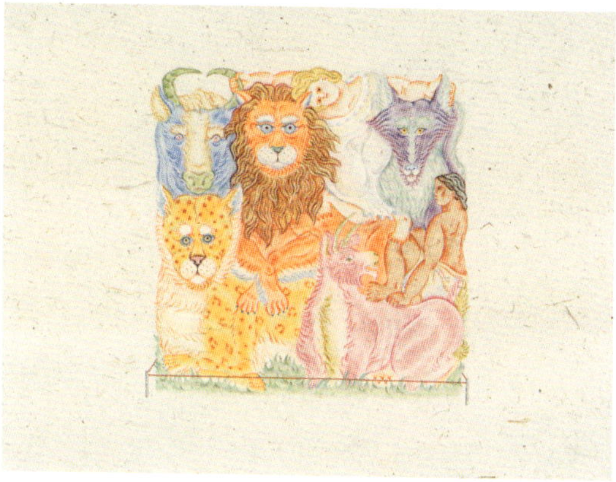

YEN YU-TING

I choose to work with fine brushwork and ink to reinterpret *Peaceable Kingdom*. In the painting, the wedged, moulded mass of animals and a red line acts as a clue to uncover the indescribable discomfort and anxiety I felt when I first saw *Peaceable Kingdom*, in hopes of contemplating questions such as: is peace within a red line truly peace? Is freedom within a red line truly freedom? And with that, further reflecting on Taiwan's circumstances.

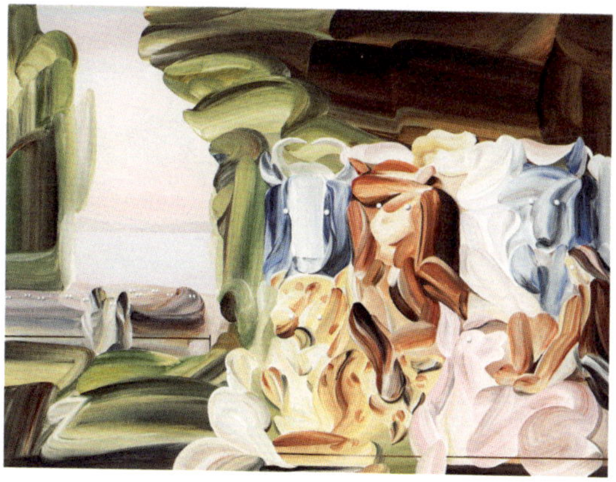

HUANG KO-WEI

I was instantly concerned with the dynamics between the group of animals in the foreground and the characters in the background in Hicks' painting. Brushstrokes have always been a focus of mine. I am constantly thinking about the semantic gap between translations, often intuitively recording images in sketches through strokes. I treat them as subjects, rewriting this. The process of translation highlights some features, but loses others. In extreme proximity, people and animals fundamentally have identical eyes, each staring into the foreground. How one simplifies an image and reconstructs it with imagining is my basis in the broad proposition of peace.

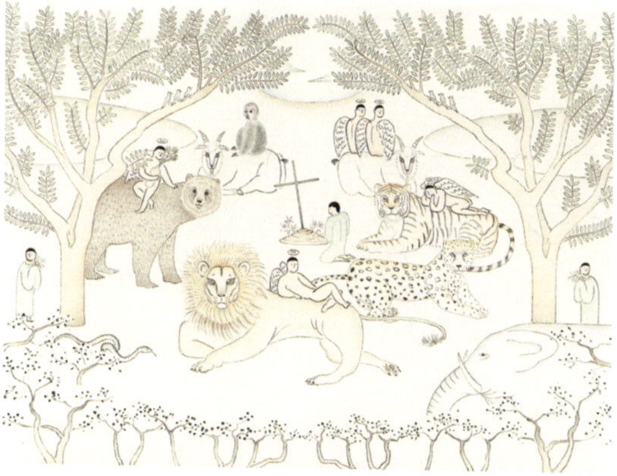

JIAN YI-HONG

My reinterpretation imagines a group of animals resting on crowded land after hostile combat. There is a tomb with a cross in the middle of the composition, like the inheritance of this inter-animal war. After the war, the animals have returned to rest on the land, with humans bringing flowers to pay their respects. On the left of the composition, an angel seated on a bear carries daisies as a symbol of peace, while the elephant in the foreground, hidden in the groves, brings harmony. After conflict, only memory can return us to tranquillity.

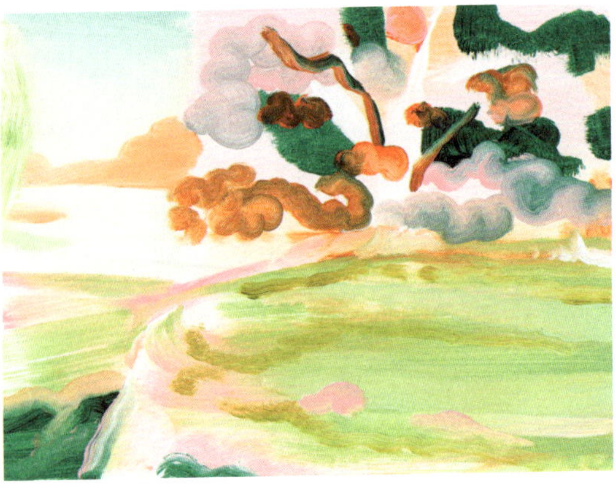

PHILIPP KREMER

I am not able to create an ideal image of peace in my mind. Realistically, animals would always eat each other, and between humans there would always be disagreement, argumentation and struggle to find the right way. I also can't agree to the symbol of a peace treaty, they have too often been part of a greater scheme to repress. Peace can only be the result of a yet unknown process that lies in the future. So I wanted to make the painting with a lot of joy, but remain in the world of fantasy, inviting the viewer to imagine peaceful activity.

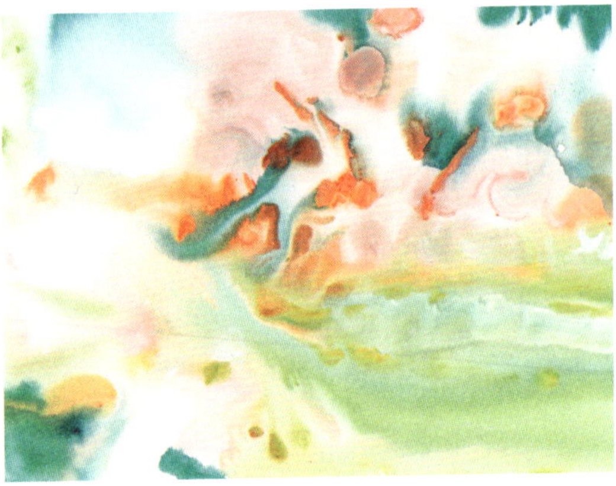

RAN ZHANG

Peace is a cultivated notion, a behaviour, and either derives from social agreement or personal internal disposition. From the Western view, peace has always been held as the highest value of humanity, based on the absence of all disagreement. In the Eastern culture, the concept of peace was a tool, a method, not a pursuit but a collective concept. Looking at both cases, as said by R.J. Rummel, "peace is meaningful only within a framework, a particular perception of reality and by its relationship to ideas or assumptions about that reality."

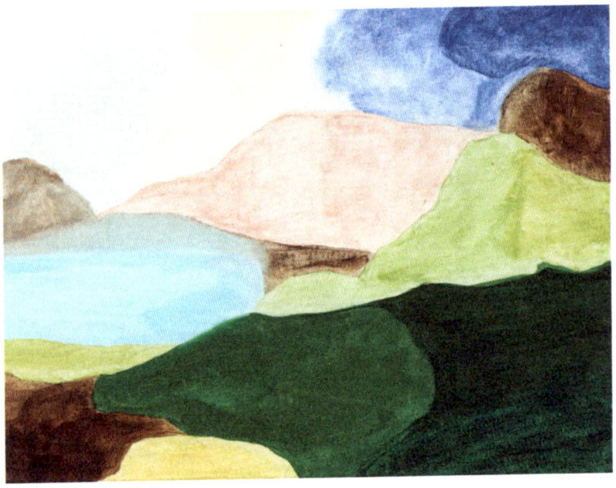

JAN SEBASTIAN KOCH

I do not think that a kingdom can be peaceful. And even democracy does not seem to make it. Peace can only be found in each human – those who work for it. Those people could be able to share it.

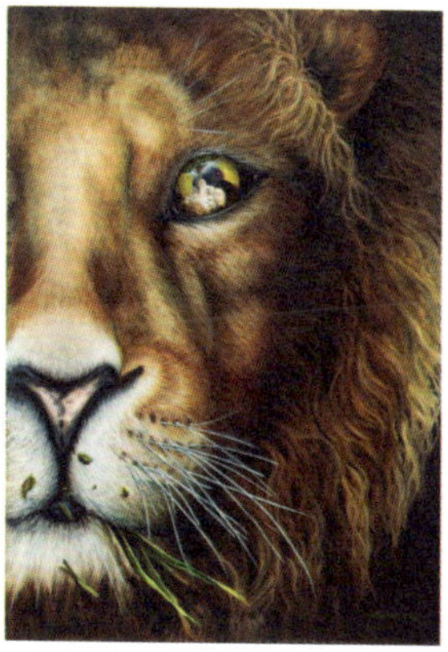

SANDY WONG SHIN

Eyes are the windows to the soul. Through the eyes, we see things. This is an important way to understand the world. They say that "seeing is believing", and so we see history and understand history. I would like to imagine a "peaceable kingdom" outside of mankind, an alternative species, like through the eyes of a lion. You can see a lion grazing and chewing grass, it looks up and sees a girl and lioness embracing, a wolf and lamb resting on the grass on the hillside in the distance.

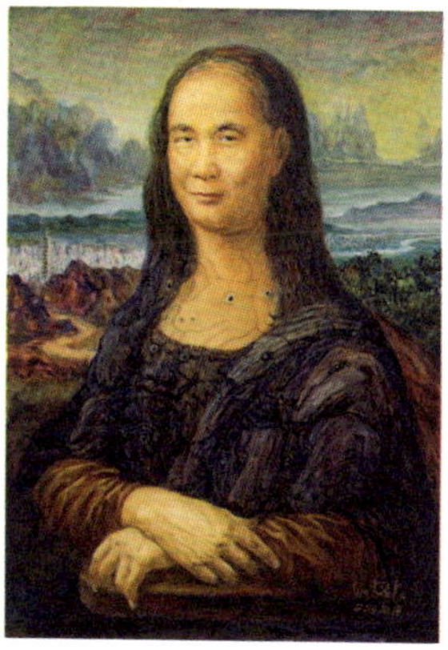

WU TA-KUANG

*Mona Lisa* is an unparalleled historical masterpiece by Leonardo da Vinci, also seen as an eternal work symbolic of a community transcending time and space. I have intentionally included a breadth of animals, with the twelve bronze animal heads of the *Yuanmingyuan* or Garden of Perfect Brightness, in kinship and an integration of East and West, of life's link in the tunnel of time. Furthermore, I have included the landmark Taipei 101 in the east (on the left) and Mount Guanyin and the Tamsui River in the west (on the right), suggesting all countries being at one.

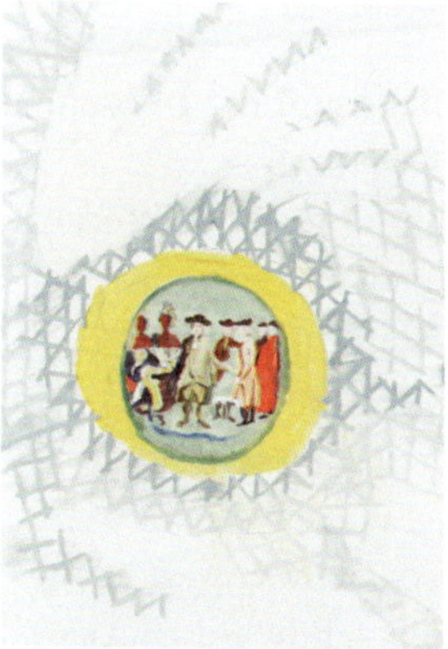

JENG JUNDIAN

Sharbat Gula, the young Afghan woman with lake-green eyes whose picture appeared on the cover of National Geographic in 1985, became known to the world over night. I can relate to these experiences of war, growing up at a time when nationalist troops in Kinmen and communist troops in Xiamen were still exchanging mortar and bombs. The world is not perfect; our lives are not perfect; and so we pray. Humanity faces unceasing challenges to its survival. But peace is a common aspiration and a core value in our lives.

# LEE MINGWEI'S VISION OF PEACE FOR CONTEMPORARY TIMES

CLARE MOLLOY

*Our human minds, being of different calibre and disposition, need different approaches to peace and happiness.*

His Holiness, 14. Dalai Lama of Tibet, 2004[1]

*Ye are called to peace...So live in the peaceable kingdom of Christ Jesus.*

George Fox, Quakers founder, 1658[2]

One of Lee Mingwei's principle concerns is examining models of peace for contemporary times. The new commission for the Gropius Bau, *Our Peaceable Kingdom*, 2020, brings together a polyphony of paintings and writings on peace. The installation comprises 27 different artists' reflections on the theme via their interpretations of a painting from the *Peaceable Kingdom* series by Pennsylvania-born Quaker minister Edward Hicks (1780-1849), displayed alongside an original. The installation is indicative of Lee's vision of peace as predicated upon celebrating and honouring difference. This essay traces the genesis of *Our Peaceable Kingdom*, considers how the Quaker view of peace influenced Lee and examines the additions and omissions that respond to and question Hicks' *Peaceable Kingdom* composition.

**Lee Mingwei, Edward Hicks and the Influence of Quakerism on *Our Peaceable Kingdom***

Lee's nuanced understanding of how different systems of thought approach peace is informed by his contact with Chan Buddhism, Catholicism and Confucianism. Yet, it is the Quaker faith tradition that provides the starting point for *Our Peaceable Kingdom*. In the summer of 2019, Lee invited eleven artists to paint an interpretation of the *Peaceable Kingdom* by one of the US' most celebrated folk artists, Edward Hicks. Like Lee, Hicks was an artist and a man of faith, whose beliefs and artistic practice centred on striving towards understanding models of peace.

Formally known as the Religious Society of Friends, Quakers are a faith group that emerged from 17th-Century Protestantism. Formed in opposition to the warmongering and hypocrisy of both Protestant and Catholic denominations during the English Civil War (1642-1651), the Quaker movement aimed to align with the simplicity and authenticity of the early Christian church. Quakers were truly countercultural; they opposed the need for hierarchical clerical structures and the notion that believers should follow a fixed creed. Instead, their faith was – and remains – guided by three testaments: the pursuit of peace, tolerance of difference and the principle of the *inner light*, meaning that the divine dwells in everyone.

The combination of these core beliefs underpins Quakers' commitment to pacifism and anti-war protests, and in 1947, the Quakers became the first religious organisation to be awarded the Nobel Peace Prize. For Lee, who was moved away from Taiwan to the Dominican Republic and then the US by his family when he was twelve, so as to avoid military conscription under the Kuomintang government, it is understandable that the movement's commitment to peace-making found resonance with his own direct experience of pacifism. Lee's encounter with Hicks' iconic work has become a generative point of departure, so many years after he first saw a reproduction of it in a Californian bookshop.

### Contextualising the Motifs of Edward Hicks' *Peaceable Kingdom*

Quakers do not swear oaths and their refusal to pledge allegiance to the Anglican Church of England led to their persecution and incarceration. In search of religious freedom one of the foremost Quakers, William Penn (1644-1718), leveraged Charles II for land in the British Colonies in lieu of debts that the Crown owed his father, Admiral William Penn. Seeing this as an opportunity to deal with the "Quaker problem", the king granted the request and insisted that the colony be named Pennsylvania in honour of the admiral. William Penn travelled to the new colony and famously established what he called the "holy experiment", a jurisdiction characterised by equality.

One of the enduring images of Penn's rule is the way that he negotiated with the First Nations people, the Lenape. The 1682 Treaty of Shackamaxon, in accordance with Quaker principles, was not a sworn oath.[3] Instead the oral tradition records that Penn purchased lands from the Lenape, with the Lenape retaining the rights to fish, hunt and gather across Pennsylvania. This approach of establishing friendship, of negotiating a mutually beneficial arrangement stood in stark contrast to the violent approach that English colonists adopted in almost all other cases – massacring Native American peoples and claiming their land by force.[4]

Hicks was enraptured by the story of William Penn and "The Great Treaty". For him it was indicative of the Quaker ideals of peace, pacifism and tolerance in action. A committed Quaker, Hicks was both a minister and an artist. As preaching is not a paying profession in Quakerism, he relied on his training as a sign painter and earned a living painting coaches and signage. Even though painting was not highly thought of within the "plain" aesthetic of the Quaker tradition,[5] Hicks resolved the contradiction by

1 His Holiness, 14. Dalai Lama of Tibet, "A Human Approach to Word Peace", 2004, https://www.dalailama.com/messages/world-peace/a-human-approach-to-world-peace.

2 George Amos, ed., "Ye Are Called to Peace, An Epistle by George Fox, 1658" in *The Works of George Fox*, 1990 reprint of 1831 edition, vol. 1, *The Journal*, (State College: George Fox Foundation, 1990), 387-389.

3 Andrew Newman, "The Most Valuable Record" in *On Records: Delware Indians, Colonists, and the Media of History and Memory* (Nebraska: University of Nebraska, 2012), 95-132.

4 Roxanne Dunbar-Oritz, "Culture of Conquest" in *An Indigenous Peoples' History of the United States* (Boston: Beacon Press 2014), 32-44.

rendering scenes from Pennsylvanian Quaker history and the Bible. He returned repeatedly to depicting a prophecy of peace from the Book of Isaiah:

The wolf shall dwell with the lamb, and the leopard shall lie down with the young goat, and the calf and the lion and the fattened calf together; and a little child shall lead them. The cow and the bear shall graze; their young shall lie down together; and the lion shall eat straw like the ox.[6]

A fantastical image, Hicks certainly would have read the passage as being a metaphor for humans needing to restrain their animal instincts in order for peace to flourish. Why Hicks obsessively returned to painting Isaiah's peace prophecy is partly explained by the major Quaker schism that he lived through. In 1827 his cousin, Elias Hicks, was responsible for a disagreement that split the group into the Orthodox and the Hicksite factions, a fraught time for the peace-seeking organisation.[7] *Peaceable Kingdom* recalled a more harmonious time and Hicks gifted copies of the work to faithful friends between 1820 and 1849. There are many variations of this motif, and today 62 versions exist in private and public collections.

**The Genesis of *Our Peaceable Kingdom***

The *Peaceable Kingdo*m version that Lee Mingwei invited artists to copy is in the collection of the Worcester Art Museum. In a split composition, animals and children are gathered under a tree in the foreground, while in the background, the Lenape are depicted with peace pipes, sealing their friendship with Penn.

Intriguingly, Hicks copied the background scene from a Boydell-Hall engraving after a Benjamin West (1738-1820) painting.[8] The traditions that artists align themselves with, the "masters" that they learn from and the humility of making references by "copying" are gestures that fascinate Lee. In an earlier work, *Through Masters' Eyes*, 2004, Lee invited painters to copy from a 17th-Century landscape painting by Shitao, in order to reflect upon the differences in systems of thought in relation to remaking artworks. In the East Asian context, a copy can have just the same status as the original painting, whereas in Western traditions, only the source enjoys legitimacy. This is not to suggest that East Asian and Western art stand in diametric opposition to one another – the advent of printing and photography have long called into question the fetish of the original – but to underscore that Lee's approach is underpinned by a Quaker-like embracing of difference. The installation *Our Peaceable Kingdom* is a gesture of creating an exhibition-within-the-exhibition. Lee hosts other painters, their works and their visions of peace.

The first painters invited by Lee to interpret Hicks' motif include N.S. Harsha, Khadim Ali, Sandy Wong Shin, Michael Eade, Zico Albaiquni, Yeh Tsai-Wei, Claudia Brand, Fabien Lerat, Yen Yu-Ting, Philipp Kremer and Ambreen Butt. These artists have diverse practices and are based in different cities. Most of them submitted a statement on peace and their painterly process as part of the work. Eight also invited two further artists to copy from their interpretations and deliver a peace statement. In this second group are Wu Ta-Kuang, Jeng Jundian, Amy Hill, Andrea Dezsö, Ignasius Dicky Takndare, Radi Arwinda, Yuyu Chen, Hsiao Pei-I, Thea Perkins, Abdul Abdullah, Marie Lepetit, Simon Pasieka, Huang Ko-Wei, Jian Yi-Hong, Ran Zhang and Jan Sebastian Koch.

The paintings created are hybrids, at once copies and originals. There are several instances of "masters" being referenced – from Henri Matisse's *Dance I*, 1909-1910, in N.S.

Harsha's, to Leonardo Da Vinci's *Mona Lisa*, c. 1503, in Wu Ta-Kuang's painting. What I would like to analyse is the inclusion of further peace symbols, which reinterpret and channel Hicks' Quaker non-conformist conviction into other contexts.

### Peace Signs in Lee's *Our Peaceable Kingdom*

A range of internationally recognised peace signs that appear in the *Our Peaceable Kingdom* paintings include the olive branch, the victory sign, Native American peace pipes, the rainbow flag and the peace symbol. The latter is associated with 1960s counter-culturalism and Amy Hill's work in the exhibition transports Hicks' scene to the era of peace and love. In the middle of the composition stands a red peace symbol, reminiscent of art in public space. The peace symbol has its origins in peaceful protest. In 1958, Gerald Holtom was charged with creating a symbol for the Campaign for Nuclear Disarmament (CND), which was planning a four-day protest march from London to the Atomic Weapons Research Establishment in Aldermaston. The sign combines the semaphore letters for "N" and "D" surrounded by a circle, declaring support for Nuclear Disarmament – and today is a ubiquitous symbol of peace (figs. 14-15., 214).

The theme of peace as contingent on liberation is expressed in the paintings that have a feminist perspective to share, particularly Yuyu Chen and Yeh Tsai-Wei who warn against peace that is reliant upon the need to conform or that hinges on female suppression. Hsiao Pei-I is also critical of the human need to "tame" other species to ensure peace – the leopard wears a ruff and the lamb is muzzled. The need to control, dominate and make other species into playthings is starkly criticised. Yeh draws attention to the "our" in *Our Peaceable Kingdom*, petitioning for an empathetic broadening of this category to include the liberation of all species.

Queer liberation is also alluded to with the multiple rainbow references, particularly Michael Eade's rainbow plant and Andrea Dezsö's rainbow-horned unicorn. As well as poodles and ziggurats in Fabien Lerat and Marie Lepetit's paintings, which reference the Canadian conceptual art collective, General Idea. Active from 1967-1994, they were committed to questioning norms of body politics and were vocal HIV/Aids activists.

Several of the works honour the iconographies and histories of First Nation art, challenging Hicks' idealised and Eurocentric depiction of the negotiations that took place in the Delaware Valley. Ignasius Dicky Takndare works with the Papua material of khombouw bark on the surface of his painting, Thea Perkins celebrates a vision of peace that is aboriginal and matriarchal, and Radi Arwinda infuses the composition with the patterns of his community, the Sunda-Cirebon. In contrast to Arwinda's blue ornamentation, the colour of peace in Indonesia, Zico Albaiquni picks a red

5 Emma Jones Lapsansky, Anne A. Verplanck, eds., "Past Plainness to Present Simplicity: A Search for Quaker Identity" in *Quaker Aesthetics: Reflections on a Quaker Ethic in American Design and Consumption, 1720-1920* (Philadelphia: University of Pennsylvania Press, 2002), 1-14.

6 Isaiah 11: 6-8, English Standard Version of the Bible.

7 The Orthodox Quakers deeming that the Bible was the fixed word of God and the Hicksite Quakers emphasising continuous revelation, the idea that God constantly reveals wisdom to individuals.

8 Benjamin West's painting bears the regrettable title *Penn's Treaty with the Indians*, 1771.

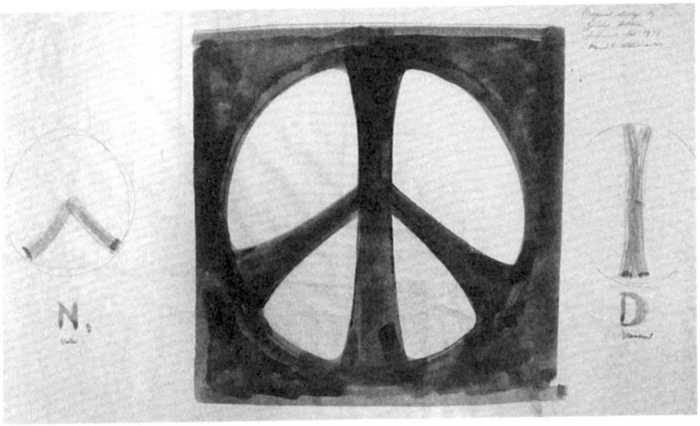

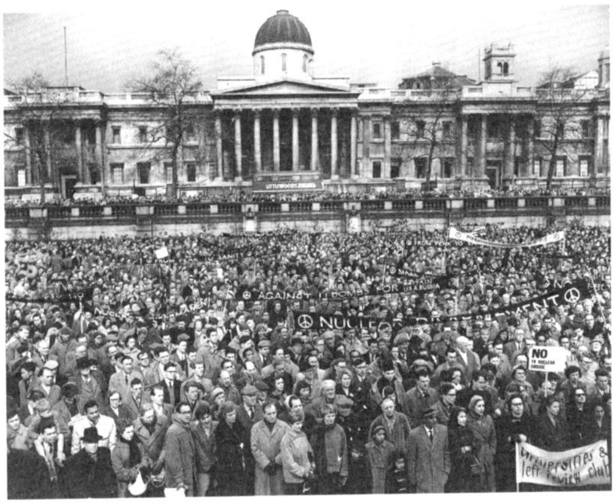

Fig. 14. Gerald Holtom's sketch of a symbol for the CND's (Campaign for Nuclear Disarmament) first major anti-nuclear march in 1958.

Fig. 15. Protestors in London's Trafalgar Square gather on Good Friday for the start of the march to Aldermaston. This is the first instance of the CND's sign being used, five hundred cardboard signs on lollipop sticks were produced for the four day march.

palette to express anger at the legacies of colonialism: slavery, the violent extraction of resources and the diseases that European settlers brought. All realities that Hicks' idealised representation fail to comprehend in the 19th Century.

### A Polyphonic Approach to Peace

Lee's understanding of peace is that it is predicated upon the healing power of transformation – peace is never "done", it exists as an ongoing process. Accordingly, *Our Peaceable Kingdom* is not yet completed. Lee will continue to invite other artists to respond to Hicks' motif, expanding this polyphonic vision of peace. Lee Mingwei's own contribution is not to create a painting, but to allow such different conceptions of peace to become part of his exhibition. *Our Peaceable Kingdom* is a powerful metaphor, for if such different conceptions can co-exist in the aesthetic sphere, perhaps this Quaker-inspired understanding of tolerating difference can be extended out into the social and political realms of our contemporary times.

# LIST OF WORKS

Cover image
GUERNICA IN SAND
2006/2015
Sand, wooden island, light
6.43 x 13 m
Installation view: *Lee Mingwei and His Relations*, Taipei Fine Arts Museum, 2015

pp. 4-5
GUERNICA IN SAND
2006/2020
Sand, wooden island, light
11 x 23 m
Installation view: Gropius Bau, Berlin, 2020

p. 15
Fig. 1. Tibetan Buddhist monk creating a Medicine Buddha Sand Mandala during a fundraising visit to the UK, Swansea, South Wales.
Fig. 2. Myanmar: Mahagandayon Monastery. Buddhist monks sweep the grounds of the Mahagandayon Monastery in Amarapura, Myanmar.

p. 16
Fig. 3. Japanese tea ceremony tea cups: repair of cracked ceramic tea cup.
Fig. 4. THE MENDING PROJECT
2009/2019
Table, chairs, threads, fabric items
Installation view: *Traversées*, Musée Sainte-Croix, Poitiers, France, 2019

pp. 21, 24-25
MONEY FOR ART
1994/2020
5 inkjet prints
Each 28 x 36 cm

p. 22
MONEY FOR ART
2006/2020
Wooden cabinet, 100-dollar notes
70 x 30 x 14 cm
Installation view: Gropius Bau, Berlin, 2020

p. 27
100 DAYS WITH LILY
1995
5 Ilfochrome silver dye bleach prints, framed
Each 166 x 115 cm

p. 29
1. Lee Mingwei's grandmother at her medical practice at Tokyo Women's Medical School [eighth from the left in the back row]
2. Lee Mingwei's grandmother with her classmates at Tokyo Women's Medical School [second from right in the back row]
3. Lee Mingwei with family, 1973

pp. 30-31
100 DAYS WITH LILY
1995
Installation view: Gropius Bau, Berlin, 2020

p. 33
THE DINING PROJECT
1997/2015
Wooden platform, tatami mats, black beans, rice, single-channel video, sound
335 x 335 x 85 cm
Installation view: *Lee Mingwei and His Relations*, Taipei Fine Arts Museum, 2015

p. 34
THE DINING PROJECT
1997/1998
Collection of Jut Art Museum (Taiwan)
Installation view: The Whitney Museum of American Art, 1998

p. 35
1. Lee Mingwei prepares a meal at The Whitney Museum of American Art, 1998
2. THE DINING PROJECT lottery cards, 1998
3. Lee Mingwei prepares a meal at The Whitney Museum of American Art, 1998
4. THE DINING PROJECT poster at Yale University, 1995

p. 37
THE DINING PROJECT
1997/2015
Wooden platform, tatami mats, black beans, rice, single-channel video, sound
335 x 335 x 85 cm
Installation view: *Lee Mingwei and His Relations*, Taipei Fine Arts Museum, 2015

pp. 38-39
THE DINING PROJECT
1997/2020
Collection of Jut Art Museum (Taiwan)
Installation view: Gropius Bau, Berlin, 2020

pp. 41, 43, 44:
THE LETTER WRITING PROJECT
1998/2020
3 wooden booths, writing paper, envelopes, pencils
Each 290 x 170 x 231 cm
Installation views: Gropius Bau, Berlin, 2020

p. 49
Fig. 5 SONIC BLOSSOM
2013/2016
Chair, music stand, costume, spontaneous song
Installation view: *Lee Mingwei and His Relations*, Auckland Art Gallery Toi o Tāmaki, 2016
Fig. 6 THE MENDING PROJECT
2009
Table, chairs, thread, fabric items
Installation view: *The Mending Project*, Lombard-Freid Projects, New York, 2009

p. 50
Fig. 7. GUERNICA IN SAND
2006/2007
Sand, wooden island, light
7.45 x 15 m
Installation view: *Lee Mingwei: Impermanence*, Chicago Cultural Center, 2007
Fig. 8. GUERNICA IN SAND
2006/2015
Sand, wooden island, light
6.43 x 13 m
Installation view: *Lee Mingwei and His Relations*, Taipei Fine Arts Museum, 2015

p. 56
Fig. 9. THE DINING PROJECT
1997/2007
Wooden platform, tatami mats, black beans, rice, single-channel video, sound
335 x 335 x 85 cm
Installation view: *Duologue*, Museum of Contemporary Art, Taipei, 2007
Fig. 10. THE DINING PROJECT
1997/1998
Wooden platform, tatami mats, black beans, rice, single-channel video, sound
335 x 335 x 85 cm

p. 60
Figs. 11. and 12. THE MENDING PROJECT
2009
Table, chairs, thread, fabric items
Installation view: *The Mending Project*, Lombard-Freid Projects, New York, 2009

p. 65
THE SLEEPING PROJECT
2000/2020
Wooden beds, nightstands, personal items
Installation view: Gropius Bau, Berlin, 2020

p. 67
1. and 2. THE SLEEPING PROJECT
2000
Wooden beds, nightstands,

personal items
Installation view: *The Sleeping Project*, Lombard Freid Fine Arts, New York, 2000

pp. 68-69, 70
THE SLEEPING PROJECT
2000/2020
Wooden beds, night stands, personal items
Installation view: Gropius Bau, Berlin, 2020

p. 73
THE LIVING ROOM
2000/2020
Furniture, private collections, plants
Collection of Jut Art Museum (Taiwan)
Installation view: Gropius Bau, Berlin, 2020

p. 75
John Singer Sargent (1856-1925)
ISABELLA STEWART GARDNER
1888
Oil on canvas
190 x 80 cm
Collection of Isabella Stewart Gardner Museum, Boston

p. 76
THE LIVING ROOM
2000
Furniture, private collections, plants
Installation view: Isabella Stewart Gardner Museum, Boston, 2000

pp. 78-81
#thecollections from Barbara Christin
Collage Book Collection from Simon Haßler
Vintage Skateboard Collection from Timo Hillbrecht
Animal Bone Collection from Petra Lehnardt-Olm
Rock Collection from Celine Loesche
Tree Decoration Collection from Katrin Mundorf
Caruso Kronenboden Collection from Karen Stuke
Polish Folk Art Collection from Urszula Usakowska-Wolff
Hat Collection from Stephan Wahner
Since 1966 - Two Lists from Thomas Oberender
23 Years of Countess Tamara from Jens Dierkes aka Countess Tamara

pp. 82-83
THE LIVING ROOM
2000/2020
Furniture, private collections, plants
Collection of Jut Art Musem (Taiwan)
Installation view: Gropius Bau, Berlin, 2020

p. 85
THE TOURIST
2001/2020
Wooden vitrine, wooden boxes, personal items, two-channel video, sound
52 min., 30 sec.
Installation view: Gropius Bau, Berlin, 2020

pp. 86-87
Jens Dierkes and Lee Mingwei during the Berlin tour of THE TOURIST
2020

p. 89
THE TOURIST
2001/2020
Wooden vitrine, wooden boxes, personal items, two-channel video, sound
52 min., 30 sec.
Installation view: Gropius Bau, Berlin, 2020

p. 91
NU WA PROJECT
2005
Bamboo, silk, cotton thread, acrylic
350 x 112 cm

p. 93
Illustration inspired by the poem *Li Sao* (Encountering Sorrow)
Illustrated by Xiao Yuncong (1596-1673)
Imprint of the Qing Dynasty (1644-1912)
22.1 x 14.8 cm

p. 95
FABRIC OF MEMORY
2006/2020
Wooden platform, wooden boxes, fabric items
485 x 485 x 65 cm
Installation view: Gropius Bau, Berlin, 2020

p. 97
Lee Mingwei and mother Lin Kuei Mei, 1969

pp. 98-102
FABRIC OF MEMORY
2006/2020
Lenders: Elena Alcaín, Hertje Brodersen, Kiran Cohen, Emanuele Crotti, Caty Forden, Barbara Gierl, Philip Goetze, Kerstin Heusinger, Amy Klement, Eva Kowalski, Koosha Moossavi, John Rivett, Jean Rivett, Freya Schwachenwald, Michael Sommer, Katja Sonnewend, Michaela Vieser, Violeta Vollmer-Dundulyte, Lisa Weber

pp. 104-105
FABRIC OF MEMORY
2006/2020
Wooden platform, wooden boxes, fabric items
485 x 485 x 65 cm
Installation view: Gropius Bau, Berlin, 2020

p. 107
GUERNICA IN SAND
2006/2015
Sand, wooden island, light
6.43 x 13 m
Installation view: *Lee Mingwei and His Relations*, Taipei Fine Arts Museum, 2015

p. 109
Gropius Bau
Ruins of the former Museum and School of Decorative Arts, 1946

pp. 110-111, 112
GUERNICA IN SAND
2006/2020
Sand, wooden island, light
11 x 23 m
Installation view: Gropius Bau, Berlin, 2020

pp. 115, 116-117
GUERNICA IN SAND
2006/2015
Sand, wooden island, light
6.43 x 13 m
Installation view: *Lee Mingwei and His Relations*, Taipei Fine Arts Museum, 2015

p. 121
Fig. 13. Pablo Picasso (1881-1973)
GUERNICA
1937
Oil painting on canvas
349 cm x 777 cm
Collection of Museo Nacional Centro de Arte Reina Sofia di Madrid

p. 127
THE MENDING PROJECT
2000/2020
Table, chairs, thread, fabric items
Collection of Rudy Tseng
Hosts: Mariángeles Aguirre, Susanne Beck-Jankowski, Monika Brückner, Maithu Bùi, Antonietta Foschini, Laula Fritz, Julia Fron, Barbara Gierl, Ariel Gout, Sven Großmann, Daniel Holznagel, Mimi Howard, Katharina Jebsen, Ivana Jecmenica, Sarah Kailuweit, Gudrun Kmoch, Eva Kowalski, Hannah Kruse, Marlise Kuert Kolb, Claire Laude, Sehnaz Layikel, Johanna Liebl, Anna Maierski,

Karin Mester, Henrike Müller, Lea Müller, Anna Neubauer, Marié Nobematsu-Le Gassic, Kristina Nowak, Elena Polzer, Carolin Rabethge, Katrin Richter, Franziska Sebode, An Seebach, Alexandra Sitaru, Katrin Sölter, Daniela Thomas, Manuela My Nghia Trinh, Katja Vaghi, Godrun von Oertzen, Lisa Weber, Anne Wesolek, Anina Wolff, Atilgan Zirek and others
Installation view: Gropius Bau, Berlin, 2020

pp. 130-131
THE MENDING PROJECT
2009/2020
Table, chairs, thread, fabric items
Collection of Rudy Tseng
Installation view: Gropius Bau, Berlin, 2020

pp. 134-135
THE MENDING PROJECT
2009/2017
Table, chairs, thread, fabric items
Installation view: *Viva Arte Viva*, 57th Biennale di Venezia - Biennale Arte, curated by Christine Macel, Venice, 2017

pp. 137, 142-143
STONE JOURNEY
2010
Glacial stones, bronze, wood
9 sets from an edition of 11
Each 10 x 50 x 15 cm
Collections of Rong-Chuan Chen, Cesar Reyes, Leo Shih, Sophia and Leon Tan, Rudy Tseng, Simon Wu
Installation view: Gropius Bau, Berlin, 2020

p. 139
Lee Mingwei collecting stones in Te Waipounamu, New Zealand's South Island, 2010

p. 179
SONIC BLOSSOM
2013/2020
Chair, music stand, costume, spontaneous song
Collection of Museum of Fine Arts, Boston
Singers: Derya Atakan, Goran Cah, Magnus Hallur Jonsson, Celina Jimenez-Haro, Sarah Kehder, Kyoungloul Kim, Alexandra Donata Koch, Julie Nemer, Birita Poulsen, Sonja Isabel Reuter, David Ristau, Alessia Schumacher, Julia Shelkovskaia
Installation view: Gropius Bau, Berlin, 2020

p. 181
Designer Kelima K's hand-sewn message inside the transformation cloak for SONIC BLOSSOM

pp. 184-185
SONIC BLOSSOM
2013/2020
Chair, music stand, costume, spontaneous song
Collection of Museum of Fine Arts, Boston
Installation view: Gropius Bau, Berlin, 2020

p. 187
OUR LABYRINTH
2015
Rice, broom, costume, ankle bells, folded paper, wooden box, dance floor, dance
Collection of Winsing Art Foundation
Installation view: *Lee Mingwei and His Relations*, Taipei Fine Arts Museum, 2015

p. 188
Kabuki dance pattern from Ikeda Seizō, *Zukai shimai kyōhon*, 1912

pp. 190-191
OUR LABYRINTH
2015/2020
Rice, broom, costume, ankle bells, folded paper, wooden box, dance floor, dance
Collection of Winsing Art Foundation
Installation view: *Lee Mingwei and His Relations*, Taipei Fine Arts Museum, 2015
Dancers at Gropius Bau, 2020: Benjamin Block, Yiyi Chen, Moonsuk Choi, Lucas Damiani Armand Ugon, Davide De Lillis, Kaveh Ghaemi, Mathis Kleinschnittger, Anja Kolmanics, Silvia Mai, Jean-Gabriel Manolis, Steffi Sembdner, Cheng-Lung Wu

pp. 194-195
OUR LABYRINTH
2015/2016
Rice, broom, costume, ankle bells, folded paper, wooden box, dance floor, dance
Collection of Winsing Art Foundation
Installation view: 11th Shanghai Biennale, Power Station of Art, Shanghai, 2016

p. 197
OUR PEACEABLE KINGDOM
2020
27 framed paintings, easels
Installation view: Gropius Bau, Berlin, 2020

p. 199
Edward Hicks (1780-1849)
THE PEACEABLE KINGDOM
c.1833
Oil on canvas
44.5 x 60.2 cm
Collection of Worcester Art Museum, Massachusetts, USA

p. 200, clockwise from top-left:
Khadim Ali (*1978, Quetta, PK, lives and works in Sydney, AU)
2019
Gouache and gold leaf on paper
40.3 x 64.7 cm

N.S. Harsha (*1969, Mysore, IN, lives and works in Mysore, IN)
2019
Watercolour and acrylic on paper
49 x 64.6 cm

p. 201, clockwise from top-left:
Ambreen Butt (*1969, Lahore, PK, lives and works in Dallas, US)
2019
Digital drawing and text printed on clay board
44 x 60 cm

Michael Eade (*1957, Portland, US, lives and works in New York, US)
2019
Egg tempera, 22-karat gold leaf, copper leaf, aluminium leaf and oil on wood panel
44 x 60 cm

Andrea Dezsö (*1968, Satz-Mare, RO, lives and works in Amherst, US)
2019
Acrylic on paper
44 x 60 cm

Amy Hill
(*1954, New York, US, lives and works in New York, US)
2019
Oil on canvas
44 x 60 cm

p. 202, clockwise from top-left:
Zico Albaiquni (*1987, Bandung,
ID, lives and works in Bandung, ID)
2019
Oil on canvas
40 x 60 cm

Ignasius Dicky Takndare (*1988, Sentani, ID, lives and works in Yogyakarta, ID)
2019
Oil and acrylic on canvas and khombouw wood bark
44 x 60 cm

Yeh Tsai-Wei (*1988, Hsinchu, TW, lives and works in Taipei, TW)
2019
Ink and gouache on paper
44 x 60 cm

Radi Arwinda (*1983, Bandung, ID, lives and works in Bandung, ID)
2019
Acrylic, ink and gel ink pen on canvas
44 x 60 cm

p. 203, clockwise from top-left:
Yuyu Chen (*1981, Taipei, TW, lives and works in Taipei, TW)
2019
Water-based metallic pigment, acrylic, gilding paint, silver foil, resin foil, copper foil, rust-effect pigment and oil on canvas
44 x 60 cm

Hsiao Pei-I (*1990, Tainan, TW, lives and works in Taipei, TW)
2019
Gold foil and acrylic on canvas
44 x 60 cm

Thea Perkins (*1992, Sydney, AU, lives and works in Sydney, AU)
2019
Acrylic on Belgian linen
44 x 60 cm

Claudia Brand (*1995, Canberra, AU, lives and works in Sydney, AU)
2019
Oil on canvas
44 x 60 cm

pp. 204-205
OUR PEACEABLE KINGDOM
2020
27 framed paintings, easels
Installation view: Gropius Bau, Berlin, 2020

p. 206, clockwise from top-left:
Abdul Abdullah (*1986, Perth, AU, lives and works in Sydney, AU)
2019
Oil on linen
44 x 60 cm

Fabien Lerat (*1960, Paris, FR, lives and works in Paris, FR)
2019
Acrylic on canvas
44 x 60 cm

Simon Pasieka (*1967, Kleve/Niederrhein, DE, lives and work in Cologne, DE and Paris, FR)
2019
Oil on canvas
44 x 60 cm

Marie Lepetit (*1959, Amiens, FR, lives and works in Paris, FR)
2019
Acrylic on canvas
44 x 60 cm

p. 207, clockwise from top-left:
Yen Yu-Ting (*1989, Taipei, TW, lives and works in Taipei, TW)
2019
Gouache on paper
44 x 60 cm

Huang Ko-Wei (*1988, Taipei, TW, lives and works in Taipei, TW)
2019
Acrylic on canvas
44 x 60 cm

Jian Yi-Hong (*1988, Yilan, TW, lives and works in Taipei und Yilan, TW)
2019
Ink and pigment on paper
44 x 60 cm

p. 208, clockwise from top-left:
Philipp Kremer (*1981, Duisburg, DE, lives and works in Berlin, DE)
2019
Acrylic on canvas
44 x 60 cm

Ran Zhang (*1981, Tianjin, CN, lives and works in Berlin, DE und Rotterdam, NL)
2019
Acrylic on canvas
44 x 60 cm

Jan Sebastian Koch (*1978, Mönchengladbach, DE, lives and works in Berlin, DE)
2019
Egg tempera on canvas
44 x 60 cm

p. 209, clockwise from left:
Sandy Wong Shin (*1963 Singapore, SG, lives and works in Singpore, SG and Taipei, TW)
2019
Oil on canvas
60 x 44 cm

Wu Ta-Kuang (*1958, Chiayi, TW, lives and works in Taipei, TW)
2019
Oil on canvas
60 x 44 cm

Jeng Jundian (*1963, Kinmen, TW, lives and works in Taipei, TW)
2019
Oil on canvas
60 x 44 cm

p. 214
Fig. 14. Gerald Holtom - Nuclear Disarmament Symbol drawing, 1958.
Fig. 15. Politics, Anti-Nuclear Protests, Trafalgar Square, London.
Anti-nuclear protesters gather in their thousands in Trafalgar Square for the start of the 50 mile protest march from London to the Atomic Weapons Research Establishment at Aldermaston in Berkshire.

Back cover
GUERNICA IN SAND
2006/2015
Sand, wooden island, light
6.43 x 13 m
Installation view: *Lee Mingwei and His Relations*, Taipei Fine Arts Museum, 2015

# IMAGE CREDITS

Cover image: photo courtesy of Taipei Fine Arts Museum
pp. 4-5: photo Laura Fiorio, courtesy of Gropius Bau
p. 15: Fig. 1. photo © Chinch Gryniewicz and courtesy of Bridgeman Images; Fig. 2. photo courtesy of Goddard_Photography/Istock.com
p. 16: Fig. 3. photo courtesy of Riya-Takahashi/Istock.com; Fig. 4. photo courtesy of the artist
pp. 21, 24-25: courtesy of the artist
p. 22: photo Laura Fiorio, courtesy of Gropius Bau
p. 27: courtesy of the artist
p. 29: all three photos courtesy of the artist
pp. 30-31: photo Laura Fiorio, courtesy of Gropius Bau
p. 33: photo courtesy of Taipei Fine Arts Museum
p. 34: photo Charly Wittock, courtesy of the artist
p. 35: photos 1-3 Charly Wittock, courtesy of the artist; photo 4 courtesy of the artist
p. 37: photo courtesy of Taipei Fine Arts Museum
pp. 38-39: photo Laura Fiorio, courtesy of Gropius Bau
pp. 41, 43, 44: photos Laura Fiorio, courtesy of Gropius Bau
p. 49: Fig. 5. photo John McIver, courtesy of Auckland Art Gallery Toi o Tāmaki; Fig. 6. photo Anita Kan, courtesy of the artist
p. 50: Fig. 7. photo Anita Kan, courtesy of the artist; Fig. 8. photo courtesy of Taipei Fine Arts Museum
p. 56: Fig. 9. courtesy of the artist; Fig. 10. photo Charly Wittock, courtesy of the artist
p. 60: Fig. 11. and 12. photos Anita Kan, courtesy of the artist
p. 65: photo Laura Fiorio, courtesy of Gropius Bau
p. 67: 1., and 2. photos Anita Kan, courtesy of the artist
pp. 68-69, 70: photo Laura Fiorio, courtesy of Gropius Bau
p. 73: photo Laura Fiorio, courtesy of Gropius Bau
p. 75: photo courtesy of the Isabella Stewart Gardner Museum, Boston, Massachusetts
p. 76: photo Anita Kan, courtesy of the artist
pp. 78-81: collection photos Laura Fiorio and image 3. on p. 78 by Nora Börding, all courtesy of Gropius Bau and the lenders
pp. 82-83: photos Laura Fiorio, all courtesy of Gropius Bau and the lenders
p. 85: photo Laura Fiorio, courtesy of Gropius Bau
p. 86: photo courtesy of the artist
p. 87: photo Jens Dierkes
p. 89: photo Laura Fiorio, courtesy of Gropius Bau
p. 91: photo courtesy of the artist
p. 93: photo courtesy of The Collection of National Palace Museum
p. 95: photo Laura Fiorio, courtesy of Gropius Bau
p. 97: photo courtesy of the artist
pp. 98-102: garment photos Laura Fiorio, all courtesy of Gropius Bau and the lenders
p. 104-105: photo Laura Fiorio, courtesy of Gropius Bau
p. 107: photo courtesy of Taipei Fine Arts Museum
p. 109: photo courtesy Ullstein Bild/Ullstein Bild via Getty Images
pp. 110-111, 112: photos Laura Fiorio, all courtesy of Gropius Bau
pp. 115, 116-117: photos courtesy of Taipei Fine Arts Museum
p. 121: Fig. 13. © Succession Picasso, by SIAE 2020; Iberfoto/Archivi Alinari
p. 127: photo Laura Fiorio, all courtesy of Gropius Bau and Rudy Tseng
p. 130-131: photo Laura Fiorio, all courtesy of Gropius Bau and Rudy Tseng
pp. 134-135: photo Anpis Wang, courtesy of the artist
p. 137: photo Laura Fiorio, courtesy of Gropius Bau and Leo Shih, Cesar Reyes, Sophia & Leon Tan, Rong-Chuan Chen, Simon Wu, Rudy Tseng
p. 139: three photos courtesy of the artist
p. 142-143: photo Laura Fiorio, courtesy of Gropius Bau and Leo Shih, Cesar Reyes, Sophia & Leon Tan, Rong-Chuan Chen, Simon Wu, Rudy Tseng
p. 179: photo Laura Fiorio, courtesy of Gropius Bau
p. 181: photo courtesy of the artist
p. 184-185: photo Laura Fiorio, courtesy of Gropius Bau
p. 187: photo courtesy of Taipei Fine Arts Museum
p. 188: photo Myriam Hofmaier, courtesy of the artist
p. 190-191: photo courtesy of Taipei Fine Arts Museum
pp. 194-195: Jay Yuan, courtesy of the artist
p. 197: photo Laura Fiorio, courtesy of Gropius Bau
p. 199: photo courtesy Bridgeman Images
pp. 200-203, 206-209: photos Chu Chi-Hung; all photos courtesy of the artist and the artists Abdul Abdullah, Zico Albaiquni, Khadim Ali, Radi Arwinda, Claudia Brand, Ambreen Butt, Yuyu Chen, Andrea Dezsö, Ignasius Dicky Takndare, Michael Eade, N.S. Harsha, Amy Hill, Jeng Jundian, Huang Ko-Wei, Philipp Kremer, Marie Lepetit, Fabien Lerat, Simon Pasieka, Hsiao Pei-I, Thea Perkins, Jan Sebastian Koch, Wu Ta-Kuang, Yeh Tsai-Wei, Sandy Wong Shin, Jian Yi-Hong, Yen Yu-Ting, Ran Zhang
pp. 204-205: photo Laura Fiorio, courtesy of Gropius Bau
p. 214: Fig. 14. The drawing is used with the permission of the Commonweal Trustees and the University of Bradford.
Fig. 15. photo courtesy of PA Images via Getty Images
Back cover: © Taipei Fine Arts Museum
Every effort has been made to trace copyright holders and to obtain their permission for the use of copyright material. The publisher apologises for any errors and will endeavour to incorporate any additional copyright information in future reprints or editions of this book.

# ACKNOWLEDGEMENTS


First and foremost we would like to express our deepest gratitude to Lee Mingwei for the inspiring exchange as well as the many gifts and rituals that he shared with us in the process leading up to and during the exhibition. Many thanks also to Daphne Chu, Sandy Wong Shin and Lin Wei-Lung from Lee Mingwei Studio.

We are very grateful to Patrick Sun, Winsing Arts Foundation, Angela Yi and Lorries Chang, Yi&C. Furniture & Projects Consulting Co. Ltd. and Grace Mei-Ching Tseng for their generous support of the catalogue. This book would not exist without the enthusiasm and vision of Rudy Tseng. We thank the Ministry of Culture, Taiwan for their support of the exhibition.

We thank all of those institutions and private collectors who lent works to this exhibition: Rong-Chuan Chen, Jut Art Museum (Taiwan), Cesar Reyes, Leo Shih, Sophia and Leon Tan, Rudy Tseng, Winsing Art Foundation, Worcester Art Museum, Simon Wu and Museum of Fine Arts, Boston as well as all lenders who wish to stay anonymous.

It has been a great pleasure to be in exchange with so many people who have experienced and taken part in Lee Mingwei's projects, we are grateful for all who contributed an eyewitness statement to this catalogue: Desi Ardy, Hubertus Breuer, Rhana Devenport, Jens Dierkes, Julie Ewington, Beibei Guan, Tim Gruchy, Jamie Hardis, Anne Hawley, Lisa Hutchinson, Sarah Kehder, Dian Ina Mahendra, Jean-Gabriel Manolis, Ayumi Paul, Cesar Reyes, Gregg Richardson, John Rivett, Leo Shih, Taro Shinoda, Michael Snelling, Sophia and Leon Tan, Rudy Tseng, Meegan Williams, Tiffany York and Ayako Yoshida.

So many people have gifted the exhibition their precious time, we would particularly like to thank all hosts, conversationalists and participants of the following projects:

*The Living Room* hosts: Barbara Christin, Jens Dierkes, Simon Haßler, Timo Hillbrecht, Petra Lehnardt-Olm, Celine Loesche, Katrin Mundorf, Thomas Oberender, Karen Stuke, Urszula Usakowska-Wolff and Stephan Wahner. Jens Dierkes also showed Lee Mingwei around his Berlin for *The Tourist* project.

*The Mending Project* hosts: Mariángeles Aguirre, Susanne Beck-Jankowski, Monika Brückner, Maithu Bùi, Antonietta Foschini, Laula Fritz, Julia Fron, Barbara Gierl, Ariel Gout, Sven Großmann, Daniel Holznagel, Mimi Howard, Katharina Jebsen, Ivana Jecmenica, Sarah Kailuweit, Gudrun Kmoch, Eva Kowalski, Hannah Kruse, Marlise Kuert Kolb, Claire Laude, Sehnaz Layikel, Johanna Liebl, Anna Maierski, Karin Mester, Henrike Müller, Lea Müller, Anna Neubauer, Marié Nobematsu-Le Gassic, Kristina Nowak, Elena Polzer, Carolin Rabethge, Katrin Richter, Franziska Sebode, An Seebach, Alexandra Sitaru, Katrin Sölter, Daniela Thomas, Manuela My Nghia Trinh, Katja Vaghi, Godrun von Oertzen, Lisa Weber, Anne Wesolek, Anina Wolff, Atilgan Zirek and others.

The lenders for *Fabric of Memory*: Elena Alcaín, Hertje Brodersen, Kiran Cohen, Emanuele Crotti, Caty Forden, Barbara Gierl, Philip Goetze, Kerstin Heusinger, Amy Klement, Eva Kowalski, Koosha Moossavi, John Rivett, Jean Rivett, Freya Schwachenwald, Michael Sommer, Katja Sonnewend, Michaela Vieser, Violeta Vollmer-Dundulyte and Lisa Weber.

We express our thanks to the 27 painters who contributed to *Our Peaceable Kingdom*: Abdul Abdullah, Zico Albaiquni, Khadim Ali, Radi Arwinda, Claudia Brand, Ambreen Butt, Yuyu Chen, Andrea Dezsö, Michael Eade, N.S. Harsha, Amy Hill, Hsiao Pei-I, Huang Ko-Wei, Jeng Jundian, Jian Yi-Hong, Jan Sebastian Koch, Philipp Kremer, Marie Lepetit, Fabien Lerat, Simon Pasieka, Thea Perkins, Ignasius Dicky Takndare, Sandy Wong Shin, Wu Ta-Kuang, Yeh Tsai-Wei, Yen Yu-Ting and Ran Zhang.

Special thanks also goes to the *Guernica in Sand* performers, John Rivett, Michael Snelling and Sandy Wong Shin.

We thank the collaborators for *Sonic Blossom*, Akira Isogawa for his custom costume design and Eric Sparks for his furniture fabrication. Many thanks also to the "Seed Performers" Sarah Kehder, Jean-Gabriel Manolis, Yiyi Chen and Cheng-Lung Wu for their contribution to *Sonic Blossom* and *Our Labyrinth*. And especially to the dancers and singers who activated *Sonic Blossom* and *Our Labyrinth* daily.

*Sonic Blossom* singers: Derya Atakan, Goran Cah, Magnus Hallur Jonsson, Celina Jimenez-Haro, Kyoungloul Kim, Alexandra Donata Koch, Julie Nemer, Birita Poulsen, Sonja Isabel Reuter, David Ristau, Alessia Schumacher and Julia Shelkovskaia.

*Our Labyrinth* dancers: Benjamin Block, Moonsuk Choi, Lucas Damiani Armand Ugon, Davide De Lillis, Kaveh Ghaemi, Mathis Kleinschnittger, Anja Kolmanics, Silvia Mai and Steffi Sembdner.

Finally our thanks to all visitors for both giving and receiving the gifts and rituals during this exhibition.

# IMPRINT

This catalogue is published on the occasion of the exhibition *Lee Mingwei: 禮 Li, Gifts and Rituals* from 27th March to 7th June 2020 at Gropius Bau, Berlin. (At the time of publication the exhibition dates were altered due to the coronavirus pandemic, with all museums in Berlin closing as a safety measure. Therefore a digital version of the show opened instead on 6th April 2020, with the show itself opening on 11th May 2020.)



CATALOGUE
*Editor* Stephanie Rosenthal
*Managing Editor* Louisa Elderton
*Assistant Editor* Clare Molloy
*Editorial Assistant* Katharina Küster
*Coordination* Lisa Tietze
*Copyeditor S Rosenthal Essay* Daniel Ehrmann
*Intern* Myriam Hofmaier
*Design and Art Direction* Julia Volkmar – Studio for Spatial & Graphic Design with Moritz Kreul
*Exhibition Photography* Laura Fiorio

EXHIBITION
*Curators* Stephanie Rosenthal with Clare Molloy
*Project Management* Lisa Tietze
*Exhibition Architecture* Simone Schmaus
*Exhibitions Fellow* Nora Bergbreiter
*Student Assistants* Sophya Kallista Frohberg, Anuschka Florine Gooß, Leonie Seitz
*Exhibition Graphic Design* Julia Volkmar – Studio for Spatial & Graphic Design
*Translation* Nikolaus G. Schneider, Erik Smith
*Conservator* Nicola Müller
*Exhibition Installation* EMArt Ruben Erber, Kruse AT
*Lighting* Marc Aldinger
*Media Equipment* visionb

ORGANISER
Berliner Festspiele / Gropius Bau
A division of Kulturveranstaltungen des Bundes in Berlin (KBB) GmbH

*Artistic Director* Dr Thomas Oberender
*Managing Director* Charlotte Sieben

GROPIUS BAU TEAM
*Director* Dr Stephanie Rosenthal
*Associate Curator, Director's Office* Dr Clara Meister
*Assistant to the Director* Susanne Goetze
*Chief Curator* Julienne Lorz
*Assistant Curator* Clare Molloy
*Assistant Curator Yayoi Kusama Exhibition* Greta Kühnast
*Curatorial Fellows* Hannah Katalin Grimmer, Katharina Küster
*Student Assistants* Jasmeen Adeoshun, Sarah Crowe
*Intern* Myriam Hofmaier

*Associate Curators* Sam Bardaouil and Till Fellrath (Art Reoriented), Natasha Ginwala
*Head of Exhibitions and Production* Simone Schmaus
*Project Management Exhibitions* Filippa Carlini, Elena Montini, Lisa Tietze, Sophie Winckler (on parental leave)
*Exhibitions Assistants* Katharina Heise, Maximilian Carlos Vietzke
*Exhibitions Fellow* Nora Bergbreiter
*Student Assistants* Anuschka Florine Gooß, Sophya Kallista Frohberg, Leonie Seitz

*Head of Communications* Annie-Claire Geisinger
*Marketing and Events* Ellen Clemens
*Marketing and Education* Katrin Mundorf
*Digital Communication and Editorial* Natalie Schütze
*Press Fellow* Anne-Kathrin Biegler
*Student Assistants* Nora Diepenbrock, Luis Kürschner, Lynh Nguyen
*Editor at Large* Robert Maharajh

*Curators of Education* Jenny Sréter, Julia Moritz
*Student Assistant* Miriam Ewering

*Head of Technical Office* Bert Schülke
*Deputy Head of Technical Office* Dan Leopold
*Assistants to Technical Office* Johanna Greinert (on parental leave), Liubov Oleksiienko
*Technical Office Exhibitions* André Merfort
*Technical Office Events* Thomas Wittmütz
*Technical Office Electrical Engineering* Michael Wolff
*Technical Office Building* André Klose, Thorsten Seehawer

*Head of Finance and Partnerships* Eva Winkeler
*Finance and Commerce* Carlos Rodríguez Artavia
*Ticket Office* Peter Decker
*Third-Party Funding* Wiebke Koch

Gropius Bau is supported by

Die Beauftragte der Bundesregierung für Kultur und Medien

The exhibition is made possible by

文化部 MINISTRY OF CULTURE, TAIWAN

# LEE MINGWEI

# 禮 LI

# GIFTS & RITUALS

ED. STEPHANIE ROSENTHAL

Berliner Festspiele
GROPIUS BAU

SilvanaEditoriale

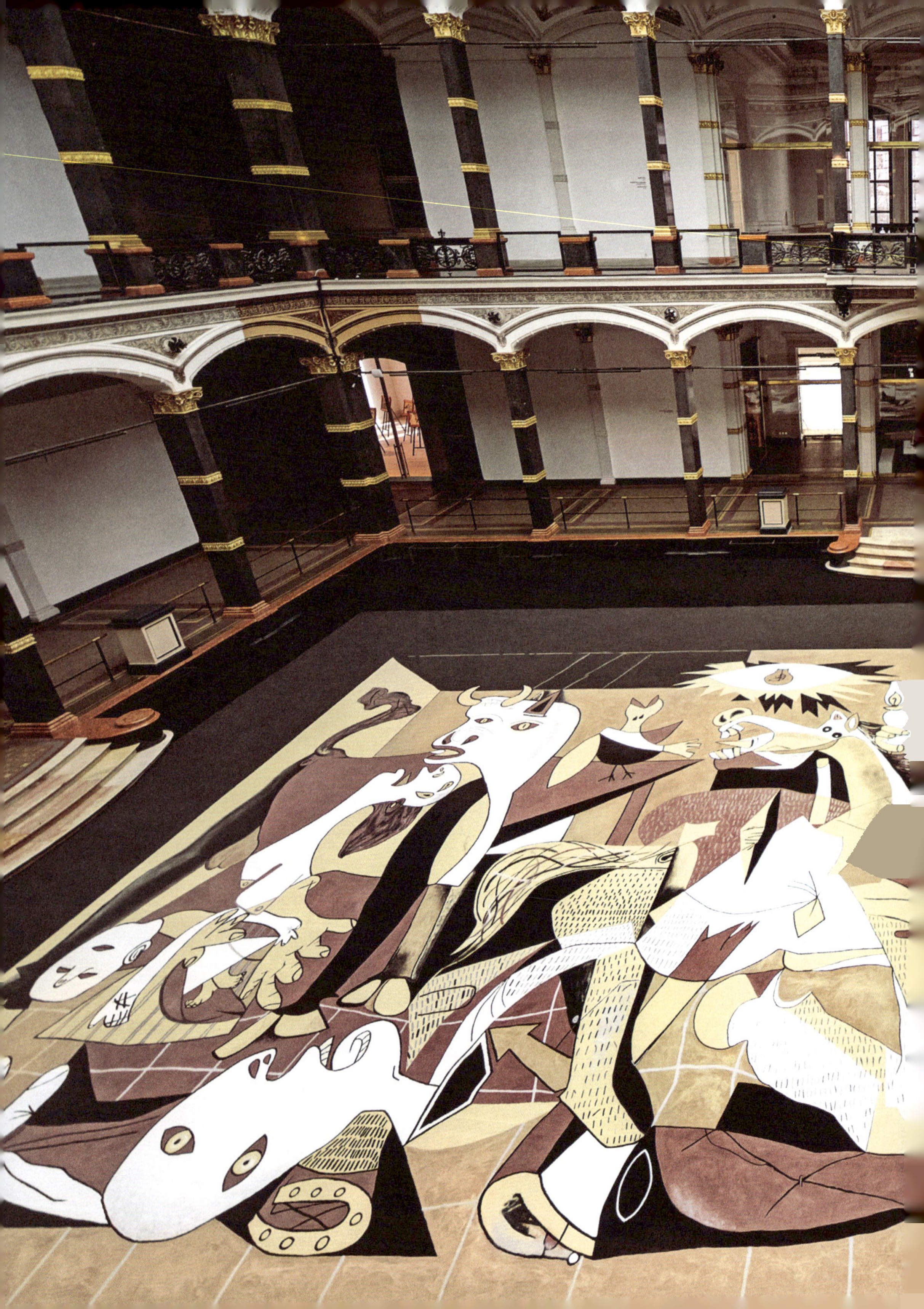